Relocating to the San Francisco Bay Area and the Silicon Valley

Relocating to the San Francisco Bay Area and the Silicon Valley

Everything You Need to Know Before You Move—and Once You Get There!

Cristina Guinot

PRIMA PUBLISHING

PRIMA PUBLISHING and colophon are registered trademarks of Prima Communications, Inc.

Photographs courtesy of PhotoDisc.

LIBRARY OF CONGRESS CATALOGING-IN-PUBLICATION DATA

Guinot, Cristina.
Relocating to the San Francisco Bay Area and the Silicon Valley : everything you need to know before you move—and once you get there / Cristina Guinot.
    p.   cm.
Includes index.
ISBN 0-7615-1624-7
1. San Francisco Bay Area (Calif.)—Guidebooks. 2. Santa Clara County (Calif.)—Guidebooks. 3. Moving, Household—California—San Francisco—Handbooks, manuals, etc. 4. Moving, Household—California—Santa Clara County—Handbooks, manuals, etc.
I. Title.
F869.S33G854   1998
979.4'6053—dc21
                                                    98-50036
                                                    CIP

00 01 02 03 04 05 AA 10 9 8 7 6 5 4 3
Printed in the United States of America

How to Order

Single copies may be ordered from Prima Publishing, 3000 Lava Ridge Court, Roseville, CA 95661; telephone (800) 632-8676 ext. 4444. Quantity discounts are also available. On your letterhead, include information concerning the intended use of the books and the number of books you wish to purchase.

Visit us online at www.primalifestyles.com

CONTENTS

v

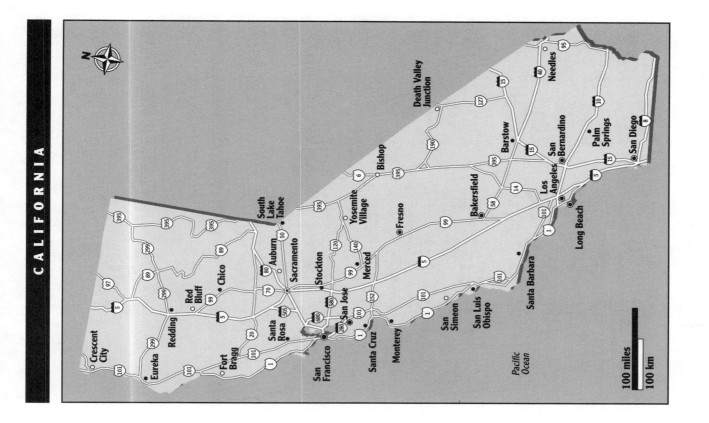

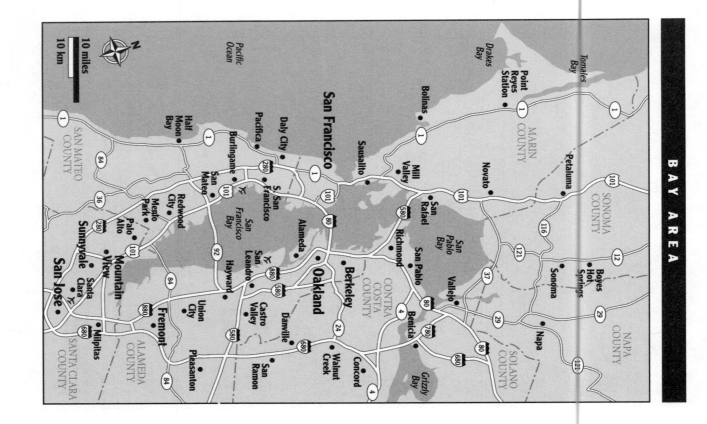

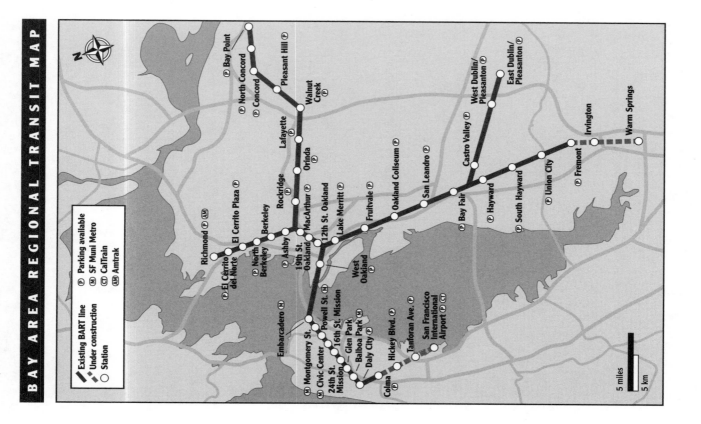

BAY AREA REGIONAL TRANSIT MAP

Legend:
- Existing BART line
- Under construction
- ○ Station
- Ⓟ Parking available
- Ⓜ SF Muni Metro
- ⒸⓉ CalTrain
- ⒶⓂ Amtrak

Bay Point Ⓟ
North Concord Ⓟ
Concord Ⓟ
Pleasant Hill Ⓟ
Walnut Creek Ⓟ
Lafayette Ⓟ
Orinda Ⓟ
Rockridge Ⓟ
El Cerrito Plaza Ⓟ
Berkeley
North Berkeley Ⓟ
Ashby Ⓟ
MacArthur Ⓟ
19th St. Oakland
12th St. Oakland
Lake Merritt Ⓟ
Richmond Ⓟ ⒶⓂ
El Cerrito del Norte Ⓟ
West Oakland Ⓟ
Embarcadero Ⓜ
Montgomery St. Ⓜ
Powell St. Ⓜ
Civic Center Ⓜ
16th St. Mission Ⓜ
24th St. Mission Ⓜ
Glen Park Ⓟ
Balboa Park Ⓜ
Daly City Ⓟ
Colma Ⓟ
Hickey Blvd. Ⓟ
Tanforan Ave. Ⓟ
San Francisco International Airport Ⓟ ⒸⓉ
Fruitvale Ⓟ
Oakland Coliseum Ⓟ
San Leandro Ⓟ
Bay Fair Ⓟ
Hayward Ⓟ
South Hayward Ⓟ
Union City Ⓟ
Castro Valley Ⓟ
West Dublin/Pleasanton Ⓟ
East Dublin/Pleasanton Ⓟ
Fremont Ⓟ
Irvington
Warm Springs

N

5 miles
5 km

PART 1

MAKING THE MOVE

CHAPTER ONE

The Cost of Moving

Moving isn't cheap, but that shouldn't prevent you from looking for adventure, expanding your horizons, seeking your fortune, or whatever is motivating you to make the move. I could lecture you on accumulating six months of savings and having a job lined up before you go, but let's face it—life for most of us doesn't work that way. This chapter will help you take a realistic look at the costs of moving. It is possible to move with $1,000 in your pocket, but that means you will need to start working right away. It also means you are not going to have enough money to get your own apartment. But that's okay. Living with roommates is like having instant friends in a new city. You will also have to put fun things that cost money, like going out to dinner, on the back burner until you can catch up financially. It should be no surprise that the more money you have, the easier your move will be. But don't let a little thing like money prevent you from moving on to greener pastures.

So what are the costs of moving? I've divided them up into three categories: big costs, setup costs, and daily living costs.

BIG COSTS

Big costs are just what they seem—costs that can really deplete your savings. These include the following:

- **Movers.** These are the guys that pull up in the big truck and do all the grunt work. You may be in a financial position to hire professional movers to pack and move your stuff.

- **Moving van rental.** For do-it-yourself movers, moving van rentals aren't cheap, but they do offer a considerable savings over hiring professional movers.

- **Short-term accommodations.** Chapters 4 and 14 discuss short-term accommodations that may seem pricey but cost less than staying at a basic hotel. Many also have kitchenettes or meal service, which can help justify the higher cost.

- **UPS or mail delivery of boxes.** If you don't feel like renting a moving van, you can cram as many of your belongings in your car or suitcase (depending on how you will be traveling) and pack the rest away for UPS delivery. Besides UPS and U.S. Postal Service charges, you may have to buy packing materials like boxes, tape, and bubble wrap.

- **Transportation to your destination.** If you're driving, you'll have to pay for gas, tolls, car inspections, and any unexpected mechanical problems that arise. If you're flying, consider the price of an airplane ticket. If you're taking the train, it will probably cost you as much as flying.

- **Monthly storage fees.** If you need to store your furniture and boxes until you find an apartment, take into account monthly storage fees.

You will have to do your own research on these big costs (except for the estimated costs of short-term accommodations, which are provided in chapter 4), because they will depend on your personal circumstances.

SETUP COSTS

Setup costs are the expenses of setting up your new life. The following are necessary financial considerations when moving:

- **Apartment deposits.** Most landlords or apartment managers will charge an application or credit check fee, the last month's rent, and a security deposit. Review chapters 6 and 13 to get an idea of rental costs in different areas.

- **Apartment broker fees.** If you join an apartment- or roommate-finding agency, a fee will be involved. Review chapters 5 and 14 to get an idea of agency fee amounts.

- **Necessary furniture.** If you have no furniture, you will need to buy a bed and some other necessary pieces.

- **Services deposits.** Once you find your apartment, you will need to set up electric, phone, and gas services, which all require deposits.

- **Auto registration and insurance.** You will have to register your car in the state of California, which involves a safety check and smog inspection. If your car doesn't pass, then getting it up to standards could cost several hundred dollars. Also, when you notify your insurance company of your new address, your rates may change.

- **Memberships.** This could include professional organizations you join to help you find work, a health club membership, or a social organization to get you involved in the city.

DAILY LIVING COSTS

Day-to-day living costs are those costs that make you say, "Where did all my money go?" It's that $2 latte and the $1 diet cola. As you may have experienced, these daily living costs can really add up. If you buy your lunch every day, for example, plan on spending around $6 for a sandwich; multiply that by five days, and that's $30 a week.

- **Food.** This includes trips to the grocery store, your morning coffee at a café, the afternoon snack at McDonald's when you're job hunting, and whatever your eating habits necessitate.

- **Transportation.** Think about your transportation needs. These could include bus fares, monthly bus passes, cab fares, BART (Bay Area Rapid Transit) fares out to the East Bay, ferry service to Marin or Oakland, and car rentals. Remember that San Francisco is a city that you can walk and bike in, and those modes of transportation are free.

- **Laundry.** As much as you would like to overlook laundry, it must be done. Many neighborhood Laundromats and wash-and-fold services are available. If you are looking for a job that requires a professional look, take into account dry cleaning charges.

- **Photocopies and computer rental.** Part of your daily expenses may include services to help you with your job search. You might need to make copies of résumés and letters of recommendation for prospective employers. If you do not have a computer, you may have to visit a Krishna Copy Center or Kinko's to lease a computer by the hour. These charges will pay off in the long run because they are an investment toward getting a good job.

There are many other details that will be specific to your situation. To get a clearer idea of your spending habits, keep an expense diary for a week or two to track where your money goes. This will help you figure out how to save money by making some temporary lifestyle changes. You might find a few surprises, like that the café mocha you drink every morning adds up to $50 a month.

MONEY-MAKING VENTURES/BUDGET PLAN

If the words *savings account* aren't in your vocabulary, the following are some ideas on how to come up with quick cash or save some cash for your move.

Stop dining out. Eating out can eat away your money. Eat at home and shop more conservatively at the supermarket. The sacrifice will pay off.

Cut out entertainment. It's only for a short while, but avoid pricey movies (discount matinees and video rentals can be a replacement treat). Entertainment also includes travel, weekend getaways, expensive sports like skiing and golf, and anything fun that costs money. Instead of being disappointed about this, think of all the fun things that await you in the Bay Area once you get a job and have fewer financial worries. Chapter 10, "Something for Nothing," lists free activities in San Francisco.

Hold a garage or yard sale. The less material possessions you take with you on your move, the easier and cheaper your move will be. Remember, just because you have a dining room (and a dining room set) now doesn't mean you will find an apartment with a dining room in San Francisco. That dining room table could fetch some good money for your move. Other items you could sell are clothes, tapes and CDs, kitchen items, books, barbecue equipment, jewelry you never wear, bikes and sports equipment, and more. This is also a good time to return to your parents' home and clean out your childhood room. If you can bear to part with childhood trinkets and memorabilia, you can sell them to finance your move.

Remember deposits for which you will be reimbursed. Make sure you know what money you are entitled to or what bills you have prepaid for the last month's services. Most services you currently use, such as phone, gas, and cable, required a deposit at the time they were set up. Your landlord probably collected a hefty sum of money from you for the last month's rent and deposits. Make sure you don't double-pay your rent and that you get your deposit back with interest (some states require landlords to pay tenants interest on any deposits they hold). Ask about partial refunds for cancellation of a health club or other club membership.

Get paid for vacation time not taken. Most companies will pay you cash for vacation time not taken.

Collect outstanding debts from friends. If you've been hesitating to ask friends and acquaintances for money they've borrowed in the past, hesitate no longer. Moving is a great excuse for collecting old debts.

Sell big-ticket items. Do you really need your car? San Francisco is a small city with good public transportation and a bad parking situation. Silicon Valley, on the other hand, is more spread out and will require a car. What about that jet ski you hardly ever use? Or the extra television in the bedroom? Do you really need two TVs? Take inventory of your durable goods and sell or pawn them for the money to move.

CHECKLIST OF ITEMS TO BUDGET FOR

√ Apartment deposits

√ Services setup

√ Movers

√ Moving van rental

√ Short-term accommodations

√ Mail delivery of boxes

√ Transportation to your destination

√ Monthly storage fees

WORLD WIDE WEB RESOURCES

The Gate
(www.sfgate.com)
The *San Francisco Chronicle* and *Examiner* newspapers' Web sites have classified listings that include garage/storage and transportation/carpool sections. Browsing these can help you budget for storage, parking, and transportation, if necessary.

Share a Load
(www.synapse.net/~tall/move/sharefrm.htm)
This Web site helps people moving long distances find others who may be able to share costs by sharing trucks and equipment.

The Virtual Mover
(www.mfginfo.com/mover.htm)

Has a mission to create, develop, and maintain a medium on the Internet for the moving and storage industry that will catalog and deliver resource information about and for the industry. Some useful categories are classified bulletin boards, storage, destination information, and move estimates.

Moving Guide
(www.moving-guide.com)

This is a directory of movers and moving services worldwide. Relocation information and move estimates are also available on this site.

Mover Quotes
(www.moverquotes.com)

They advertise as being the largest moving company database in cyberspace. They cover every state, full-service and do-it-yourself moves, and prices.

CHAPTER TWO

PLANNING THE MOVE

AN ORGANIZED MOVE is a successful move. It doesn't take much effort to organize and plan your move, but it does save many possible headaches and frustrations. This chapter is structured as a timeline for your move, with suggestions of things you could be doing from three months prior to your move up until the day you move. These suggestions are intended to be a starting point, so that you are not overwhelmed or unsure of how to proceed. Also, visit the Virtual Relocation Web site (**www.virtualrelocation.com**), a national moving and relocation directory with useful links for moving and storage, property searches, government agencies, and local weather, to name a few.

THREE MONTHS BEFORE THE MOVE

- Get acquainted with the Bay Area and the Silicon Valley by reading the local *San Francisco Chronicle* and *Examiner* and *San Jose Mercury News* newspapers. The Sunday editions will give you an idea of apartment rentals, job opportunities, local activities, and local news. For a subscription to the *Chronicle* and *Examiner*, call (415) 777-5700; if you have access to the World Wide Web, the address is **www.sfgate.com**. For the *San Jose Mercury News*, call (408) 920-5000 or visit **www.sjmercury.com**.

- Start saving some money for the move.

- If possible, visit the area and explore it from a resident's point of view.

- Order and review your credit reports. These will be necessary when you look for an apartment. The three major credit reporting agencies are Equifax (800) 685-1111 (**www.equifax.com**); Experian (formerly TRW) (888) 397-3742 (**www.experian.com**); and Trans Union (800) 888-4213 (**www.tuc.com**). Credit bureaus charge a fee between $8 and $20 unless you have been denied credit within the previous sixty days. In that case, you are legally entitled to a free copy.

ONE MONTH BEFORE THE MOVE

· Make moving van rental reservations or arrangements with a moving company.

· Make the appropriate reservations if you are traveling by means other than a car.

· If you are driving, it is time to get that tune-up you've been putting off.

· Start collecting boxes, tape, and any other packing supplies. Instead of recycling your newspaper, use it to wrap dishes and other breakables.

· Save moving receipts, because many of them are tax deductible.

· Start tying up loose ends at your job. Ask around for job leads in your new town.

· Give your one-month notice to vacate your apartment. Work out how security deposits and other refunds will be handled.

· If you do not have a place to stay when you move, make a reservation at a short-term housing facility (see chapters 4 and 14).

· If you need to store your furniture someplace, start making arrangements with friends, relatives, or a storage facility (see the "Bay Area Storage Companies" section later in this chapter).

· Gather your unwanted belongings for a yard sale.

· If you want to set up a post office box at your new destination ahead of time so you can forward your mail, now is the time. Research the post office location at which you wish to have your P.O. Box. You can call (800) 275-8777 for assistance. Contact that post office to make sure there are boxes available and find out what the fees are. Explain what you are doing in case these procedures vary.

- Visit your local post office and complete a P.O. Box Application Form. Mail the completed form to your destination post office with any payments.

- Cancel memberships to places like your health club or other organizations.

- Cancel, forward, or put on hold magazine and newspaper subscriptions.

TWO WEEKS BEFORE THE MOVE

- Start packing.

- Notify gas, electric, water, cable, and phone companies of your move.

- Arrange to close or move your bank accounts.

- Call temporary employment agencies in San Francisco and the Silicon Valley to make registration appointments.

- Update your résumé and have many copies on hand.

- Contact the California Department of Food and Agriculture at (916) 654-0312 for current information about what types of plants California allows into the state. Find new homes for your plants if they are restricted.

- Hold a yard sale.

- Clean your apartment.

- Give notice at your job.

- Get letters of recommendation from employers and professional acquaintances.

- Pull together a job-finding packet that includes résumés, letters of recommendation, a passport, portfolio of work accomplishments, and nice stationery for cover letters and thank-you notes.

- Pick up clothes from the dry cleaner.

- Return library books.

- Ask a veterinarian for advice about moving with your pet.

ONE DAY BEFORE THE MOVE

- Pick up the rental van.

- Check oil and gas in your car.

- Make sure you have any important or necessary items with you, such as medications or valuables.

- Make your final inspection of your apartment or house.

- Call to confirm housing and any other reservations you made.

- Tell loved ones how they can reach you while you are in transit.

- Review your travel itinerary and plans for when you reach your destination.

- Eat well and rest before the big day.

THINGS TO DO ONCE YOU MOVE

- Start looking for an apartment or living situation.

- Start looking for work, either temporary, permanent, or both.

- Register your car (this will include a car inspection).

- Register to vote.

- Get a new driver's license.

- Get to know the area by taking a walking tour or spending time in different neighborhoods.

PACKING TIPS

The following are some basic packing tips for your move. Moving van companies, such as Ryder and U-Haul, have free moving booklets with more information on how to pack and plan your move. Call your local moving business directly for details.

- Pack small appliances in their original containers if possible or cartons cushioned with wadded newspaper or bubble wrap. Do not use shredded paper, because it can get into the machinery and cause damage.

- If you are moving dressers, you can leave clothing folded in the drawers. Trash bags are good for casual clothes, while suits and more expensive clothes can be folded in suitcases or placed in garment bags.

- Individually wrap each dish first in plastic bags (to save dishwashing later) and then with newspaper. Do not stack flat. Instead, place saucers, plates, and platters on their edge. Cups and bowls may be placed inside each other.

- Wrap glasses separately in bubble wrap and use newspaper for cushioning.

- Pots and pans can be stacked with some paper between them.

- If you are restricted from bringing certain plants into California, either sell them at your garage sale or give them away as gifts.

- Pack a personal suitcase with necessities like toiletries, medicines, toothbrush, a change of clothes, a book, your pillow, and whatever else will keep you comfortable for a day or two if you can't unpack or get settled.

- Label every box with the address of your destination and contents. If you are mailing multiple boxes, number them (1 of 12, 2 of 12, etc.) and keep an inventory list in your possession.

- Do not pack jewels or other valuables. Keep them on your person.

- If you are overwhelmed, pack one room at a time.

- Pack everything that can't walk on its own.

- Pack heavy items, such as books, in small boxes so they will be easier to handle.

- Wrap towels and sheets around fragile items like lamps and ornaments.

MATERIALS NEEDED FOR PACKING

√ Packing paper such as newspaper √ Tape

√ Boxes of assorted sizes   √ Markers

√ Bubble wrap

BAY AREA STORAGE COMPANIES

There are so many storage companies in the Bay Area that choosing the right one is a personal decision. You can pick one by how accessible it is to you or what features it has or how much it costs. The following are some things to ask a storage company that will help you select the right one:

- When are you open? What are your hours?

- Can I drive up to the storage area?

- Who holds on to the key?

- Do you offer short-term and long-term rentals?

- What size storage spaces do you have?

- Do you offer insurance?

- Do you have any discounts or specials?

- What type of security do you have in place?

- Does the storage space have an alarm?

- Does the storage space have a sprinkler system?

- Are storage units at ground level? If not, are elevators available?

- Is a deposit required?

- Do you have a resident manager?

You can find a listing of local storage companies in the Pacific Bell Yellow Pages under storage. Most main branch libraries carry out-of-state phone books to do this research.

The local phone company has a free tips line called Local Talk to give you information on storage companies. The main number is (415) 837-5050, and the choices are

2230 Insurance and self storage units

2235 Leases and contracts

2240 Defining your storage needs

2245 How to ensure maximum security for your stored items

PART 2

RELOCATING TO THE SAN FRANCISCO BAY AREA

CHAPTER THREE

SAN FRANCISCO OVERVIEW

The SAN FRANCISCO Bay Area is a great place to call home, and in 1997 alone it became home for over 71,900 people. What makes the area so attractive is the strong economy, great weather, and overall good quality of life.

According to the State of California Employment Development Department (EDD), the unemployment rate in San Francisco has reached an all-time low of about 3.2 percent. Just six short years ago, in 1993, the figure was more than twice that—7.8 percent. According to projections by the EDD, job growth is expected to continue through the start of the

CITY TIME LINE

1769	San Francisco Bay is discovered by Sergeant Jose Ortega of the Portola–Serra Expedition.
1772	San Francisco Bay shores are explored by land by Captain Pedro Fages and Father Juan Crespi.
1776	Presidio of San Francisco and Mission Dolores are founded.
1833	The Pueblo of San Francisco is duly erected and constituted a municipal corporation.
1834	Elections are held to elect municipal officers.
	Boundaries are assigned to the Pueblo of San Francisco by Governor Figueroa.
1835	First building is erected at 823–37 Grant Avenue.
1840	Monterey becomes the capital of California.
1845	Mary Elizabeth Davis is the first Anglo-Saxon child born in San Francisco.
1846	Entrance to the San Francisco Bay is named Golden Gate.
	First public school is opened.

new millennium. There will be a continuing rise in the service industry, with business services leading the growth by 60 percent. This includes computer services, employment agencies, protective services, building maintenance, advertising, and credit reporting. These industries combined are expected to employ some 56,900 workers by the year 2001.

Though job prospects are very favorable in the San Francisco Bay Area, the same can't be said for housing. According to the 1997 Housing Inventory published by the San Francisco Planning Department, 65 percent of San Francisco residents are renters, while only 35 percent are homeowners. The vacancy rate is currently estimated at an all-time low of 1 percent, and the demand for apartments has caused rent prices to climb well above the national average. It is truly a tough housing market when 99 percent of the 182,000 existing rental units remain occupied. And there is little consolation for those seeking to buy a home. The sale price for a home in San Francisco averaged $329,000 in 1998, almost a 17 percent rise from the previous year.

If you can land that high-paying job and find a decent place to live, San Francisco can offer a pretty good quality of life. The city has it all—good weather, great views, world-class cultural activities, top restaurants, friendly neighborhoods, and diverse people. Residents have much pride in their city, and improvement projects always seem to be in the works. A good example is the change that occurred after the 1989 Loma Prieta earth-

---

1847   San Francisco's first newspaper, the *California Star*, publishes its first issue.
San Francisco is renamed from Yerba Buena.

1848   First commercial bank is established in San Francisco.
Gold is discovered in Coloma, California.
First shipload of Chinese immigrants arrives in San Francisco.
First post office opens at Clay and Pike Streets.

1850   California Exchange opens.
Legislature creates bay region counties: San Francisco, Contra Costa, Marin, Santa Clara, Sonoma, Solano, and Napa.
San Francisco County government established.
City of San Francisco charter goes into effect.
First San Francisco city directory is published.

quake. The city went through a renaissance that included the development of the South of Market area and Embarcadero waterfront, conversion of the Presidio military base into a national park, and improvements of neighborhoods and historic buildings that were near collapse.

South of Market has experienced tremendous positive growth with the opening of the new San Francisco Museum of Modern Art as well as the Yerba Buena Gardens. Along the Embarcadero waterfront, where the freeway used to block magnificent views of the bay, now stands a double row of sixty-five Canary Island date palms running from the Ferry Building down to China Basin. This section also has under construction a streetcar system that will travel two and a half miles along the bay from the CalTrain Station in China Basin to Fisherman's Wharf.

The 200-year-old Presidio military base has turned over its 1,480 acres to the management of the National Park System. Now this open space is enjoyed by residents and tourists alike. Besides outdoor recreation such as hiking and biking, one can visit more than five hundred historically significant buildings that represent every major period of U.S. military history since 1853.

The Civic Center neighborhood is getting back some of its luster with the opening of the new Main Library, a $137.4 million project that was completed in 1996, and the recent $84.5 million renovation of the San Francisco Opera House.

1851	Fire destroys entire city except for submerged hulk of ship.
	Chamber of Commerce organized.
	State capital moves from Monterey to Vallejo.
1852	First legal execution, a hanging, takes place on Russian Hill.
1853	California Academy of Science is organized.
	The first city street signs go up.
	State capital moves from Vallejo to Benicia.
1854	Principal streets are lighted with coal gas for the first time.
	First U.S. Mint opens.
	Lighthouse on Alcatraz is established.
	Old St. Mary's Church is dedicated.
	State capital moves from Benicia to its current home of Sacramento.
1856	San Francisco city and county are consolidated.

There are also many new projects in the pipeline that will be completed in the near future:

- The Children's Center at Yerba Buena Gardens will have a full-size ice rink, twelve-lane bowling alley, old-fashioned carousel, and a hands-on high-tech center.

- Metreon, a Sony Entertainment Complex, will feature a 600-seat IMAX theater, fifteen movie theaters, restaurants, and shops.

- Pacific Bell Park is being built for the pennant-winning San Francisco Giants baseball team.

- A new International Terminal will open at San Francisco International Airport, adding twenty-six new gates to accommodate wide-body jets.

- The Jewish Museum of San Francisco will expand into the historic Jesse Street Substation building across from Yerba Buena Gardens.

- The Mexican Museum is also planning a move to Yerba Buena Gardens at a building being constructed between Third and Mission Streets.

- Another museum making a move is the Asian Art Museum, which will be taking over the old San Francisco Library location at Civic Center.

- Bloomingdale's is planning on opening a store in the old Emporium-Capwell building next to the San Francisco Center.

1858	San Francisco Water Works Company begins operation.
1859	Present seal of the City of San Francisco is adopted.
1860	First Pony Express rider arrives in San Francisco from St. Joseph, Missouri. Service begins on the city's first street railway from the foot of Market Street to Mission.
1863	The famous Cliff House opens.
1866	Equal rights to all men without distinction as to color is adopted as a resolution.
1868	SPCA is formed.
1869	Free postal delivery is formally inaugurated.
1870	Legislation to create Golden Gate Park is approved.
1873	Postcards are sold for the first time in San Francisco. Ground is broken for world's first cable street railroad.

As far as cultural and leisure activities, San Francisco truly offers something for everyone, both residents and visitors alike. There are the world-renowned and respected opera, symphony, and ballet companies, the Mario Botta–designed San Francisco Museum of Modern Art, the nationally recognized American Conservatory Theater, and Golden Gate Park, the largest constructed park in the world, encompassing 1,017 acres. It is no wonder that San Francisco keeps topping the travel polls of nationally respected magazines like *Condé Nast Traveler* and *Travel & Leisure*.

For all its magnificence, San Francisco had a humble beginning. It was discovered by accident in 1769 by an overland expedition of Spanish soldiers from Mexico who were trying to reach Monterey. This discovery occurred more than two hundred years after the founding of California. It is believed the thick fog obscured the narrow entrance to the bay, making its appearance invisible. At first San Francisco was mostly inhabited by Christian missionaries, until 1846, when the Gold Rush brought some forty thousand people from all backgrounds and walks of life to the city. Most of these people stayed on, and even today the city has a strong multicultural population.

The greatest feature about living in San Francisco is the sense of community one feels, a feature almost unheard of in big-city living. This sense of community is evident in the over thirty neighborhoods that make up the city, many of them with their own neighborhood newspapers and neighborhood groups. There is also a very active nonprofit and volunteer

1875	Pacific Stock Exchange formally opens.
	Native Sons of the Golden West is organized.
	Palace Hotel opens.
1878	Hastings Law School is founded.
	San Francisco's first telephone book is issued.
1879	Public library opens in rented quarters.
1880	The New State Constitution of California goes into full effect.
1887	Snow covers San Francisco.
1891	Stanford University is chartered.
1892	John Muir establishes Sierra Club and becomes lifetime president.
	First buffalo is born in Golden Gate Park.
1896	Sutro Baths open.
1897	Ferry Building opens.

network that helps the poor, homeless, and disenfranchised in the city. If there is a need in the city, there is most likely an organization to fill it. San Francisco is an easy city to move to because of all the support networks that are already in place. This support includes many apartment- and job-finding agencies as well as countless social and professional organizations. Even if you don't know a soul, there are numerous resources to help you get settled and start your new life.

The San Francisco Bay Area refers to nine counties: Alameda, Contra Costa, Marin, Napa, San Francisco, San Mateo, Santa Clara, Solano, and Sonoma. San Francisco County is the smallest county not only in the Bay Area, but also in California, measuring 128.76 square miles. San Francisco City is 46.4 square miles laid out over forty hills reaching heights of almost one thousand feet, lending itself to some amazing views. It also has some very comfortable and consistent weather, with temperatures averaging about 60°F. Of course, the type of weather conditions you experience depends on where you are in the city. The hilly terrain is the reason for the different microclimates one will find. When it's sunny and warm in the Mission neighborhood, it could be cold and foggy in the Sunset district.

The San Francisco Bay Area section of this book is divided into three parts that will ease your transition to the Bay Area. The first part provides detailed information on apartment-searching techniques, neighborhoods, and services. The second part gears you up for the job search with information about job lines, temp services, and more. Once you've settled in,

1898	New city charter is approved, authorizing municipal acquisition and ownership of public utilities.
1899	New city hall opens after twenty-nine years of construction.
1900	Bubonic plague hits San Francisco.
1904	Bubonic plague epidemic ends.
1906	Great earthquake of 1906 occurs. Fire destroys large part of city.
1907	First prisoners are moved from city jail to Alcatraz.
1910	A. P. Giannini, Bank of America founder, introduces branch banking.
1911	Angel Island opens West Coast immigration station.
1912	San Francisco Symphony Orchestra is formed.
1914	Women vote for the first time in San Francisco. Stockton Street Tunnel is completed.

the third part lists a wide variety of activities and organizations that will get you involved in your new city.

As you read more about San Francisco and the Bay Area, you will soon agree that it is a wonderful place to live. Enjoy!

WORLD WIDE WEB RESOURCES

CitySearch.Com
(**www.citysearch7.com**)
ABC news affiliate Web site of local arts, entertainment, community happenings, and more.

BayInsider.Com
(**www.bayinsider.com**)
Coverage on what's going on throughout San Francisco and the greater Bay Area. Information is continuously updated with local news and sports as well as entertainment, weather, traffic, and local politics.

The Gate
(**www.sfgate.com**)
This is the homepage for the local city newspapers, *San Francisco Chronicle* and *San Francisco Examiner*, as well as local NBC affiliate KRON-TV.

SF Bay Area
(**www.sfbayarea.com**)
The source for Bay Area classifieds, government, events, shopping, dining, and more.

1915	Civic Auditorium is dedicated.
	Alexander Graham Bell speaks from New York to Thomas Watson in San Francisco, making the first transcontinental conversation by phone.
1917	Nonstop distance flight record is set by Katherine Stinson, who flew 610 miles from San Diego to San Francisco in 9 hours and 10 minutes.
1918	Ferry Building siren sounded for the first time.
1921	The de Young Museum in Golden Gate Park opens.
1923	President Warren Harding dies at Palace Hotel.
	Steinhart Aquarium in Golden Gate Park opens.
1924	Palace of the Legion of Honor is dedicated.
1925	Kezar Stadium in Golden Gate Park opens.
	Embarcadero subway opens.
	Harding Memorial Park opens.

SF Bay Interactive
(www.sftoday.com)

This Web site has information on San Francisco as well as the East Bay, Peninsula, and Marin.

The San Francisco Insider
(www.theinsider.com/sf)

Its mission is to provide insider tips that will help you navigate through San Francisco and take full advantage of the many fantastic things the Bay Area offers, without going broke in the process.

Z San Francisco
(www.zpub.com/sf/)

This is the eclectic guide to an eclectic city. It lists many San Francisco resources and information about neighborhoods, jobs, history, weather, and more.

1929	New pedestrian traffic signal system is inaugurated.
1932	Stern Grove is dedicated.
1933	Opera House is dedicated with performance of LaTosca.
	Coit Tower is dedicated.
	San Francisco Ballet debuts.
1936	Alcatraz Island becomes a federal prison.
1937	Bay Bridge opens to traffic.
	Golden Gate Bridge is dedicated.
1939	San Francisco Chronicle newspaper begins publishing Herb Caen column.
1941	Aquatic Park is dedicated.
1954	Cow Palace opens.
	Joe DiMaggio and Marilyn Monroe marry at city hall.
	San Francisco International Airport opens.
1964	Cable cars are declared a national landmark.
1967	Summer of Love in Haight-Ashbury.
1971	McDonald's opens first restaurant in city.
1974	Muni's "Fast Pass" is initiated.
1978	Mayor George Moscone and Supervisor Harvey Milk are assassinated. Dianne Feinstein is elected as the first female mayor of San Francisco.

INTERESTING STATISTICS

Following are some interesting statistics about San Francisco:

Size	46.4 square miles
Population	789,600
Tallest building	Transamerica Pyramid (853 feet, 48 stories)
Oldest building	Mission Dolores (dedicated on August 2, 1791)
Number of Victorian houses	14,000
Number of restaurants	3,300 (more per capita than any other U.S. city)
Oldest street	Grant Avenue
Steepest street	Filbert Street between Hyde and Leavenworth Streets (31.5 percent grade)
Longest street	Mission Street (7.29 miles)
Widest street	Sloat Boulevard (135 feet)
Narrowest street	DeForest Way (4.5 feet)
Crookedest street	Lombard Street, between Hyde and Leavenworth Streets (eight turns)
Geographical center	East side of Grandview Avenue, between Alvarado and 23rd Streets
Highest hill	Mount Davidson (938 feet)
Number of cable cars	39
Cable car speed	9 mph
City colors	Black and gold
City flower	Dahlia
City tree	Monterey cypress, located in front of McLaren Lodge at Kennedy Drive near Fell Street in Golden Gate Park
Patron Saint	Saint Francis
Motto	Oro en Paz, Fierro en Guerra (Gold in Peace, Iron in War)
Most common fear	Gephydrophobia (fear of crossing bridges)

1980	Last day milk is delivered at home in San Francisco.
	Davies Symphony Hall opens.
1989	7.1 earthquake hits Bay Area.
1991	Oakland Hills fire is the largest urban wildland fire in U.S. history.
	Former Police Chief Frank Jordan is elected mayor.
1992	Rodney King verdict riots occur in downtown San Francisco.
1996	Willie Brown, San Francisco's first black mayor, is elected.

CHAPTER FOUR

WHERE TO STAY
WHEN YOU ARRIVE

C HANCES ARE WHEN you move to San Francisco you won't have an apartment already rented. How could you? How would you check out the different places there are to rent? How do you know if you'll like the neighborhood? What about meeting the landlord or completing application paperwork? You can't really find a place to live until you move, but when you move, you will need a place to live.

Short-term housing is an ideal solution to this apparently no-win situation. Whether it's a furnished apartment or shared room, temporary housing offers a home base for newcomers to the city. It serves not only as a place to stay but as an address for mail and as a point of contact for job and apartment leads. There is no need to rush into a less-than-ideal living situation when you have short-term housing to fall back on. It gives you the chance to determine your housing needs and get acquainted with the city. Reservations for temporary housing can usually be made in advance, so a place to stay will be available upon your arrival to the city.

San Francisco has several types of short-term housing available. In this chapter, I discuss furnished apartments, residence hotels, and budget-minded options such as youth hostels and the YMCA. Using the Internet is included in the budget section, since it is a way to arrange for an inexpensive apartment sublease or house-sitting situation. (Please note that the prices and amenities of housing listed in this chapter are subject to change.) Many of the apartments and residence hotels discussed in this chapter can provide you with brochures and additional information. Simply write or call them to make your request.

FURNISHED APARTMENTS

Furnished apartments try to make you feel at home by including everything a typical household would have. Items such as sheets, towels, kitchen utensils, microwave, television, and VCR are provided to make you feel like you are living at home until you find a place of your own. The goal of furnished apartments is to provide all the necessary amenities, so a tenant can move in with only a suitcase of clothes. Short-term leases normally require a minimum one-week stay. The following are some short-term furnished apartment options:

American Property Exchange

2800 Van Ness Avenue
San Francisco, CA 94109
(415) 447-2000 or 800-747-7784
www.we-rent-sanfran.com

The American Property Exchange is a real estate brokerage company that offers a wide range of real estate services like short-term accommodations, unfurnished residential rentals, executive relocation and home-finding services, vacation rentals, and property management. They feature over 400 furnished short-term rental units all over the city. Competitive rates start at $95 nightly, $600 weekly, and $1,200 monthly. The company can locate available units to meet individual needs, handle all paperwork, and arrange cleaning, parking, phones, and other requested services. An $800 deposit will hold advance reservations for monthly rentals; a $300 deposit is required for daily or weekly rentals. There is also a departure service fee that ranges between $125 and $200 and a maid service fee between $60 and $80. Note that there are no refunds for early checkout. Personal checks and Visa, MasterCard, and American Express are accepted.

TYPES OF APARTMENTS

Studio: Starting at $1,200 per month

One-bedroom: Starting at $1,700 per month

Two-bedroom: Starting at $2,500 per month

PARKING

If requested, only apartments with parking will be searched and compiled. Depending on the property, the cost of parking may be included in the rent or as an extra charge.

HOUSEWARES AND LINENS

All linens and housewares are included.

TV/CABLE

Available if requested.

TELEPHONE

Telephones are installed in all units. Local phone service is provided free of charge. Calling cards should be used for long-distance calls. There is a 25 percent surcharge on any toll or long-distance calls.

KITCHEN

All units have kitchens; select units have gourmet kitchens.

HOUSEKEEPING

Maid service is available daily, weekly, or monthly for an extra charge. In some complexes it is included in the rental charge.

LAUNDRY

Laundry facilities are available, depending on the building and apartment.

Ashlee Suites

1029 Geary Street
San Francisco, CA 94109
(415) 771-7396

The Ashlee Suites are located in a culturally diverse neighborhood near movie theaters, shops, and many ethnic restaurants. Several bus lines in the area go to places such as Fisherman's Wharf, the Financial District, Union Square, and South

of Market. The building is clean but could use new paint and carpeting. The apartments are cute, clean, and tidy, and a manager lives on the premises. An application needs to be completed, and a credit check is processed. Reservations are suggested three weeks to one month in advance. A $300 deposit and $25 key deposit are required, both of which are refundable. A thirty-day minimum stay and thirty-day written notice to vacate is required. Visa, MasterCard, American Express, and Diner's Club are accepted.

TYPES OF APARTMENTS

Studio: $1,000 per month (they have a high occupancy rate and are usually not available)

One-bedroom: $1,250 per month

Two-bedroom: $1,750 per month

Apartment rental costs include utilities.

PARKING

There is no parking on the premises. Local lots cost about $150 per month. The Ashlee can provide you with names of local lots, but you make your own arrangements.

HOUSEWARES AND LINENS

Towels, dishes, and kitchen items are provided and are included in monthly rent.

TV/CABLE

A color television and basic cable are included in the rent.

TELEPHONE

A phone is provided, but tenants are responsible for setting up and paying for service. The front office has a fax machine.

KITCHEN

Each unit has a fully stocked electric kitchen with microwave.

HOUSEKEEPING

An additional $100 per month will provide you with once-a-week maid service, which includes vacuuming and changing the linens.

LAUNDRY

Coin-operated machines are located in the building.

Mayflower Hotel

975 Bush Street
San Francisco, CA 94109
(415) 673-7010

The Mayflower Hotel is located in the downtown area known as lower Nob Hill. The hotel is actually 104 studio rooms with Pullman kitchenettes (these usually consist of a counter with a small sink and a couple of hot plates). The bad news is you can't reserve rooms in advance. The good news is, according to management, there is usually something available. You are required to complete an in-person application that takes a day to process. Rent needs to be paid up-front along with a refundable $100 security deposit and $50 phone deposit. Be careful when estimating your length of stay, because if you move out early, you are not refunded for unused days. One week's notice is required to vacate the premises, and the minimum length of stay is three days. Cash and traveler's checks are accepted. After your first month, personal checks are accepted. Credit cards are not accepted. Buses and cable cars run nearby.

TYPES OF APARTMENTS

Studio: $350 per week with tax or $775 per month with no tax

PARKING

A garage is located in the building. The cost is $15 per day or $170 per month when available.

HOUSEWARES AND LINENS

Towels, sheets, and dishes are provided and are included in monthly rent. Residents need to bring their own kitchen items.

TV/CABLE

Each unit has a color television.

TELEPHONE

The Mayflower will supply the telephones, but phone service is extra. Local calls are 75¢; direct-dial long-distance has a $1 usage fee plus any phone company charges.

KITCHEN

Each unit has a Pullman kitchenette with a hot plate and dishes.

HOUSEKEEPING

Daily maid service for weekly rentals and weekly maid service for monthly rentals are included in the rent.

LAUNDRY

There are no laundry facilities on the premises, but you will find a Laundromat next door.

Nob Hill Place

1155 Jones Street
San Francisco, CA 94108
(415) 928-2051

Nob Hill Place is located at the top of Nob Hill overlooking historic Grace Cathedral, an ominous, Gothic-style stone church. The building has a very elegant and formal look that fits in nicely with the character of the neighborhood. Nob Hill Place is situated in a predominantly residential area; a few upscale hotels, like the Fairmont

and Mark Hopkins, are located nearby. Nob Hill Place is conveniently located near the Financial District and the Union Square shopping district. The California Street cable car and #1 California buses are the closest transportation lines. Since only a seven-day notice is required to vacate a unit, upcoming rentals are not known in advance. Contact the building manager to be placed on a waiting list for one of the forty short-term rental units. An application needs to be completed and a deposit is required. Deposit amount is one-half of the rent of the unit, and first month's rent is required up front. Credit cards are accepted.

TYPES OF APARTMENTS

Efficiency studio, kitchen not separate: $1,150 to $1,250 per month

Studio, separate kitchen: $1,350 to $1,550 per month

Junior one-bedroom: $1,680 to $1,900 per month

One-bedroom: $2,000 to $2,070 per month

Two-bedroom, fireplace: $3,500 to $3,700 per month including parking

PARKING

The building has very limited parking (eighteen spaces). You will find three garages in the neighborhood: Fairmont Hotel, Crocker, and Masonic Temple. Neighborhood street parking is scarce and by city permits only (see Appendix B, "Bay Area Numbers to Know" for parking information). Nob Hill Place and local garage parking costs around $150 to $250 per month.

HOUSEWARES AND LINENS

Towels, dishes, and kitchen items are provided and are included in monthly rent.

TV/CABLE

Basic cable and a color television are provided and are included in monthly rent.

TELEPHONE

The management furnishes telephones, but tenants are responsible for hooking them up and paying for service.

KITCHEN

The kitchen has all gas appliances and a microwave.

HOUSEKEEPING

There is maid service twice a month, including changing beds, cleaning the bathroom, and mopping the kitchen. This service is included in the price of the rent.

LAUNDRY

Coin-operated laundry machines are in the building. Two-bedroom units have their own washer and dryer.

RESIDENCE HOTELS

Residence hotels have a more temporary and less private feel than furnished apartments. There is a definite social atmosphere in many of these places because of shared rooms, group dining, and recreation areas. Residence hotels rent single and shared rooms with or without a bathroom. Rates are reasonable and may include meals and maid service as part of the package. The more private the accommodations (for example, a single room with private bath), the higher the cost. Sharing a room and bath can save considerable money. The length of stay can be one week to indefinite.

Abigail

246 McAllister Street
San Francisco, CA 94102
(415) 861-9728

This is a beautiful, Art Deco-style hotel located in the Civic Center neighborhood, where city government is centered and many poor and homeless reside. The hotel lobby has a marble checkerboard-patterned floor and stained glass detailing on the windows that look out onto the domed city hall. The rooms are furnished in antiques and are very clean and well kept. Millennium, an organic restaurant, is featured on the premises. But if you want to save some money, a microwave and small refrigerator can be requested for your room, and TVs are available. If your stay is longer than one week, an application must be completed for a credit check, and a $250 deposit is required. Visa, MasterCard, American Express, Discover, Diner's Club, and traveler's checks are accepted.

TELEPHONE
The rooms have phones. Incoming calls are free, and outgoing calls are billed directly to the room.

MEALS
Continental breakfast is served. No kitchens are available, but microwaves and refrigerators can be rented for $10.

HOUSEKEEPING
Maid service three times a week is included in the price of the room.

LAUNDRY
No laundry facilities are located in the building, but management will send out your laundry.

TYPES OF ROOMS
Single: $94 a night, $375 per week, or $750 per month (requires a $250 deposit and credit application)

BATHROOM
All rooms have private baths.

PARKING
Parking arrangement with a garage a block away is available for about $12 per day.

HOUSEWARES AND LINENS
Towels and sheets are provided.

TV/CABLE
Each room has a color TV with cable.

Ansonia Hotel
711 Post Street
San Francisco, CA 94109
(415) 673-2670

The Ansonia Hotel has an old-fashioned feel with its decor of floral wallpaper, lace curtains, and red velvet-covered furniture in the lobby area. The facilities are clean but a little worn. The stairs give a tired creak under step, and the carpet is balding in spots. The hotel is well located near Union Square and can serve as a quiet, peaceful, and affordable respite after a day of apartment and job hunting. Make reservations three to four weeks before your

Brady Acres

649 Jones Street
San Francisco, CA 94102
(415) 929-8033
www.bradyacres.com

Brady Acres is located downtown near the Union Square shopping district. It is a small, comfortable hotel that has twenty-five clean studio rooms with newly tiled bathrooms. Rooms also have fully accessorized wet bars with a refrigerator, microwave, coffeemaker, and toaster. The management is very friendly and helpful and provides residents with cleaning supplies and even laundry detergent. Brady Acres is near three bus stops that service multiple bus lines. Several convenience stores are located in the neighborhood.

Brady Acres will hold a reservation with a $100 deposit. An application must be completed, and the length of stay (a check-in and checkout date) must be given when arrival and guarantee it with a credit card. Visa, MasterCard, and American Express are accepted. There is no application, credit check, or deposit.

TYPES OF ROOMS

Single with hall bath: $235 per week

Single with private bath: $310 per week

Shared room with semiprivate bath: $180 per week

BATHROOM

Private and shared baths are available, depending on the room rate.

PARKING

No parking is available on the premises. Neighborhood garages cost about $200 per month.

HOUSEWARES AND LINENS

Towels and sheets are provided.

TV/CABLE

Each room has a TV without cable.

TELEPHONE

The rooms have phones. Incoming calls are free, and outgoing calls are billed directly to the room.

MEALS

Breakfast and dinner are served daily (except no dinner on Sunday (except no dinner on Sun-

days). Meals are included in the price of the room.

HOUSEKEEPING

Daily maid service is included in the price of the room.

LAUNDRY

Laundry facilities are located in the building.

the price of the room. Either calling cards or pay phones must be used for long-distance calls. A fax machine is on the premises, and incoming faxes are free (outgoing faxes are $1 per page).

making a reservation. The minimum one-week stay can be extended if a room is available. If you shorten your stay, your money will be refunded for unused days. MasterCard and Visa are accepted.

MEALS

The rooms have a wet bar with a microwave, toaster oven, refrigerator, coffeemaker, dishes, and silverware.

TYPES OF ROOMS

Single: $390 to $500 per week for the first four weeks; after four weeks, you are eligible for monthly rates of $650 to $750. Monthly stays require an approved credit application and $325 security deposit.

HOUSEKEEPING

Guests who use Brady Acres as a hotel and do not take advantage of the weekly specials receive daily maid service. Long-term guests can use the cleaning equipment available or pay an additional $25 per week for daily maid service.

BATHROOM

All rooms have newly tiled private baths and hair dryers.

PARKING

No parking is available on the premises. Universal Parking at 644 Geary Street has $15 to $17 daily rates.

LAUNDRY

Coin-operated machines are located in the building, and laundry soap is free.

HOUSEWARES AND LINENS

Towels and sheets are provided.

TV/CABLE

Each room has a color television without cable and a radio/cassette player.

TELEPHONE

Each room has a telephone with a private number and answering machine. Local calls are included in

Cornell Club

715 Bush Street
San Francisco, CA 94108
(415) 421-3154

The Cornell Club is a charming European-style hotel located between Nob Hill and Union Square. This is a nonsmoking facility with sixty clean, individually decorated rooms with private and shared baths. Weekly rentals include breakfast and dinner. Dinner is prepared by a French chef and served in the Cornell Club restaurant, Jeanne d'Arc. Stays are limited to twenty-eight days. Visa, MasterCard, American Express, Diners Club, traveler's checks, and cash are accepted. There is no application process or credit check.

The Harcourt

1105 Larkin Street
San Francisco, CA 94109
(415) 673-7720

The Harcourt is a residence club that offers room and board to its short-term and long-term guests. It is located near the downtown San Francisco business and shopping districts and is convenient to several citywide bus lines. The Harcourt is clean, decorated with functional furniture of the '70s and is serviced by a helpful staff that includes a switchboard operator and manager. Guests can enjoy a television lounge as well as a sun deck. The clientele is

TYPES OF ROOMS

Single with private bath: $595 per week

Single with shared bath: $525 per week

BATHROOM

Private and shared baths are available, depending on the room rate.

PARKING

You can make arrangements with the garage across the street for $12 per day.

HOUSEWARES AND LINENS

Towels and sheets are provided.

TV/CABLE

Each room has a color TV with cable.

TELEPHONE

The rooms have phones with private voicemail. Incoming calls are free, and outgoing calls are billed directly to the room.

MEALS

Breakfast is served seven days a week, and dinner is served Monday through Friday. Meals are included in the price of the room.

HOUSEKEEPING

Daily maid service is included in the price of the room.

LAUNDRY

No laundry facilities are located in the building. There are Laundromats down the street.

screened by the management and includes foreign students and newcomers to the city.

Making reservations two weeks in advance is recommended. Rent can be paid either weekly, biweekly, or monthly. There is a $20 key deposit. No application paperwork is required, and MasterCard, Visa, and American Express are accepted.

TYPES OF ROOMS

Private room with private bath: $980 per month or $250 per week

Private room with hall bath: $860 per month or $220 per week

Shared room with private bath: $680 per month or $175 per week

Shared room with hall bath: $550 per month or $150 per week

BATHROOM
Rooms are available with either private or shared baths.

PARKING
No parking is available on the premises. Neighborhood parking lots cost around $150 per month. You can park on the street with a permit.

HOUSEWARES AND LINENS
Towels and sheets are supplied.

TV/CABLE
A giant-screen TV is located in the community room, and there are movies shown nightly.

TELEPHONE
You can use phones in the rooms to make outgoing calls. All incoming messages are routed through the switchboard.

MEALS
Breakfast and dinner are included in the price of the room.

HOUSEKEEPING
Twice-a-week maid service is included in the price of the room.

LAUNDRY
Coin-operated machines are located in the building.

The Kenmore
1570 Sutter Street
San Francisco, CA 94109
(415) 776-5815

The Kenmore Residence Club is located on a quiet, tree-lined street two blocks from bustling Van Ness Avenue and several citywide bus lines. It offers its guests decent meals, clean and comfortable rooms, housekeeping, and a twenty-four-hour message service. Guests can also enjoy a TV room, game room, small library, and reading room.

Reservations can be made two weeks in advance. A $50 deposit holds a room and can be applied toward rent. A refundable $20 key deposit is also required. No application paperwork is necessary, and the minimum stay is one week. MasterCard, Visa, local checks, and traveler's checks are accepted.

PARKING

No parking is available on the premises. You can park on the street with a permit.

HOUSEWARES AND LINENS

Towels and sheets are supplied.

TV/CABLE

The community room has a television. Some deluxe private rooms have color TVs.

TELEPHONE

All rooms have direct-dial phones. Local calls cost 30¢; long-distance calls are a $1 flat fee plus toll (with a $20 limit on long-distance calls). Incoming calls are routed through the switchboard. A twenty-four-hour message service is available free of charge.

MEALS

Breakfast and dinner are served Monday through Saturday. Continental breakfast and brunch are served on Sunday. Meals are included in room rental. (When I stopped by, the menu featured turkey with all the fixings.)

TYPES OF ROOMS

Deluxe private room with bath, color TV, and refrigerator: $1,080 per month or $275 per week

Private room with private bath: $980 per month or $250 per week

Private room with hall bath: $840 per month or $215 per week

Deluxe double suite with private bath, color TV, and room refrigerator: $880 per month or $225 per week

Double room with private bath: $740 per month or $190 per week

Double room with shared bath: $680 per month or $175 per week

Double room with hall bath: $640 per month or $165 per week

HOUSEKEEPING

Daily maid service is included in the room rental.

BATHROOM

Rooms have a sink and either a private bath or shared hall baths.

LAUNDRY

Coin-operated machines are located in the building.

The Monroe

1870 Sacramento Street
San Francisco, CA 94109
(415) 474-6200

Built before the 1906 earthquake, the Monroe survived without a scratch and began its career as a residence club. It started housing U.S. military personnel aiding earthquake victims and then the earthquake victims themselves. Today, this busy residence hotel serves foreign students and others moving to San Francisco.

The Monroe's elegant interior is decorated with warm mahogany paneling, hardwood-beamed ceilings, and a massive carved wood fireplace. This clean, quiet, softly lit interior could be mistaken for a private business club but is as unstuffy as a college dorm. Guests enjoy plenty of activities, such as billiards, table tennis, chess, and television watching in the lounge. A block away from the Monroe is the Hard Rock Cafe as well as several bus and cable car lines.

Besides clean and comfortable facilities, the Monroe has a desk clerk on duty twenty-four hours a day as well as a twenty-four-hour switchboard that takes messages and provides wake-up calls. Rooms can be reserved with a $50 deposit that will be applied toward the rent. The minimum stay at the Monroe is one week. Visa, MasterCard, local checks, and traveler's checks are accepted.

TYPES OF ROOMS

Private room with shared bath: $920 per month or $235 per week

Private room with hall bath: $840 per month or $215 per week

Shared room with private bath: $740 per month or $190 per week

Shared room with shared bath: $680 per month or $175 per week

Shared room with hall bath: $640 per month or $165 per week

BATHROOM

Rooms have either private, shared, or hall baths, depending on the cost.

PARKING

No parking is available on the premises. Neighborhood parking lots cost around $110 to $115 per month. You can park on the street with a permit.

HOUSEWARES AND LINENS

Towels and sheets are supplied.

deposits or application fees except for a $10 key deposit. Maximum stay is three weeks.

TYPES OF ROOMS

Single with private bath: $166 per week

Single with shared bath: $156 per week

BATHROOM

Private and shared baths are available, depending on the room rate.

PARKING

No parking is available on the premises. Pricey garages are located nearby.

HOUSEWARES AND LINENS

Towels and sheets are provided.

TV/CABLE

The community room has a giant-screen TV without cable.

TELEPHONE

The rooms have phones to make outgoing calls. All incoming messages are routed through the front desk.

MEALS

Breakfast and dinner are included in the price of the room.

HOUSEKEEPING

Daily maid service is included in the price of the room.

LAUNDRY

There are coin-operated laundry machines in the building.

Post Hotel

589 Post Street

San Francisco, CA 94102

(415) 441-9378

This no-frills hotel is no match for the swanky Olympic Club and five-star Pan Pacific hotel across the street. The lobby has 1970s-style carpeting and plastic wood furnishings, and iron bars separate the guests from the hotel clerk. The location is good and somewhat safe, and the price is reasonable. Credit cards are not accepted, but cash and traveler's checks are. There are no

TV/CABLE

Each room has a color TV without cable.

TELEPHONE

The rooms have no phones. The hotel receives incoming calls for residents; calls can be returned on the pay phones located on each floor.

MEALS

The hotel provides no meals and no kitchen access. No cooking is deposit confirms the reservation, and credit cards are not accepted.

TYPES OF ROOMS

Single with a private or shared bath: $925 to $2,100 per month

BATHROOM

All rooms have a sink. Most rooms share a bath.

PARKING

There is no parking on the premises. Limited street parking available by permit. Stanford Court parking is about $25 per day, and other local lots are about $200 to $250 per month.

HOUSEWARES AND LINENS

Towels and sheets are provided.

TV/CABLE

No televisions are in the rooms, although guests can bring their own. There is a TV lounge.

TELEPHONE

The rooms are wired for telephones, so guests can bring their own and hook them up. The front office has a message service and fax machine.

MEALS

Breakfast and dinner are served Monday through Saturday and are included in the price of the room.

allowed in the rooms, but the rooms have refrigerators.

HOUSEKEEPING

Weekly maid service is included in the price of the room.

LAUNDRY

No laundry facilities are located in the building.

San Francisco Residence Club

851 California Street
San Francisco, CA 94108
(415) 421-2220

It advertises itself as a European pension atop of Nob Hill, and it doesn't lie. The charm of this old building is the creaky hardwood floors, worn rug runners, and threadbare velvet parlor furniture. The rooms are on the small side, but if you go stir-crazy, you can visit the TV room. A cable car ride away you will find movie theaters, shopping, and restaurants. Meals are included in the price of the room and are served in a dining room that opens to a courtyard garden with outdoor seating.

The residence club is located adjacent to the Fairmont Hotel and two blocks from the heart of the Financial District. Reservations are recommended at least two weeks in advance; a two-week notice to vacate is required. There is no application, just hotel registration. A $100

BATHROOM

Private and shared baths are available depending on the room rate.

HOUSEKEEPING

Daily maid service is included in the price of the room.

HOUSEWARES AND LINENS

Towels and sheets are provided and are changed weekly.

LAUNDRY

Coin-operated machines are located in the building.

PARKING

No parking is available in the building. There are neighborhood garages, and street parking is very limited.

TELEPHONE

The rooms do not have phones, but you will find pay phones on every floor. The front desk takes incoming messages.

TV/CABLE

Each room has a color TV without cable.

Spalding Hotel

240 O'Farrell Street
San Francisco, CA 94102
(415) 788-9419

The lobby is stark, with a couple of folding chairs and fluorescent lighting. The rooms are worn-looking but clean. Each room has a refrigerator and color TV, and in-house movies are shown. MasterCard, Visa, and American Express are accepted, but checks are not. A credit check and background check are run on guests who want to stay longer term. The maximum stay is usually twenty-eight days but can "depend on the person"—whatever that means. There is no application fee, but a $10 key deposit is required. Reservations are not accepted, but you can call a day ahead to see if a room can be saved for you.

HOUSEKEEPING

Weekly maid service is included in the price of the room.

LAUNDRY

Laundry facilities are not available on the premises, but there are Laundromats nearby.

MEALS

The hotel has no meals and no kitchen facilities except for a small refrigerator in each room.

TYPES OF ROOMS

Single with private bath: $198 per week

Single with shared bath: $147 per week

BUDGET-MINDED OPTIONS

Budget-minded options are creative ways to solve your short-term housing crisis without abusing your credit card limits. Places such as youth hostels and the YMCA may not be homey and quaint, but they can be extremely affordable. Expect to room with other people, sometimes ten or more to a room. But don't worry; everyone will have his or her own bed. Whether or not you are a people person, bring your patience, tolerance, and sense of humor—and think about all the money you will be saving.

The following is a review of some San Francisco hostels and YMCA housing.

American Youth Hostel (AYH) at Fort Mason

Franklin and Bay Streets,
Building 240
San Francisco, CA 94123
(415) 771-7277

American Youth Hostel at Fort Mason is located on the waterfront in the very yuppie Marina neighborhood. Rooms are dorm-style with bunk beds, coed or single-sex, and fit ten to twelve people in one room. The hostel has smaller four-person rooms, but they require advance reservations.

The Fort Mason hostel has a communal kitchen with a stove, a TV room that shows nightly movies, a reading room, and a common area. Smoking is not permitted indoors. Laundry machines are on the premises, as is free parking. This location requires guests to do some chores, such as making beds, vacuuming, and taking out the trash

(but don't worry, there is no bathroom duty). No curfew is in place.

Reservations can be made a minimum of forty-eight hours in advance and require a credit card number. During the summer months, the hostel keeps busy, so reservations should be made a couple of weeks in advance. No application paperwork is necessary, and the maximum stay is two weeks due to local residency laws. MasterCard, Visa, cash, and traveler's checks are accepted.

TYPES OF ROOMS
Dormitory-style rooms: $17 per night for AYH members and non-members

BATHROOM
Each floor has three male and three female bathrooms.

PARKING
Free parking is available on the premises.

HOUSEWARES AND LINENS

Sheets and towels are supplied.

TV/CABLE

The community room has a television that does not have cable but shows movies nightly.

TELEPHONE

The hostel has pay phones in the hallways and a phone-card machine.

MEALS

Breakfast is served daily in a communal kitchen that also has a refrigerator, stove, microwave, toaster, sink, pots, pans, dishes, and silverware. Residents must clean up after themselves and put dishes away.

HOUSEKEEPING

Daily housekeeping at the facility handles the messier jobs. Residents are required to do some chores. They are also permitted to change their own sheets and towels daily if they wish.

LAUNDRY

Laundry facilities are on the premises.

American Youth Hostel (AYH) at Union Square

312 Mason Street
San Francisco, CA 94102
(415) 788-5604

American Youth Hostel at Union Square is centered in San Francisco's most famous shopping district. It is conveniently located near many bus, subway, and cable car lines, not to mention some of the greatest stores around. The hostel has dormitory-style, single-sex rooms that sleep two to six people. Most rooms share common bathrooms, but a few come with private baths and should be requested ahead of time. Daily housekeeping keeps the place ship-shape. Guests are welcome to use the communal kitchen, which has a refrigerator and microwave. The hostel also has a reading room and TV room that shows nightly movies. The good news is that there are no curfews or chores.

Reservations can be made a minimum of forty-eight hours in advance using a credit card. During the summer months, the hostel keeps busy, so reservations should be made a month or two in advance. No application paperwork is necessary; the maximum stay is two weeks due to local residency laws. Visa and MasterCard are accepted.

To become a member of American Youth Hostel, you can register when you arrive at the hostel. The annual dues are $25 and provide discounts at hostels around the country. Visit their homepage at **www.hiayh.org** for more information.

Central YMCA

220 Golden Gate Avenue
San Francisco, CA 94102
(415) 885-0460

The Central YMCA of San Francisco is located in the neighborhood known as Civic Center. This area is the center of city government and culture; it also contains a large homeless population. City Hall is across the street from the famous Opera House. A new main library has been built next door to its old granite, non-retrofitted home. Fast-food chains keep busy throughout the night. This is San Francisco's center of urban life.

The Central Y is an affordable, temporary place to stay in this eclectic neighborhood. Reservations are not accepted, and rooms fill up on a first-come first-serve basis. Room cost includes access to the gym and swimming pool and a continental breakfast. Visa, MasterCard, traveler's checks, and cash are accepted.

TYPES OF ROOMS

Single: $40 per night, $234 per week, or $700 per month

Double: $50 per night, $304 per week, or $710 per month

LAUNDRY

A Laundromat is located two blocks away.

TYPES OF ROOMS

Dormitory-style rooms: $18 per night for AYH members, $21 per night for nonmembers

BATHROOM

Mostly shared baths are available. Each room has a sink.

PARKING

No parking is available on the premises. Garages in the area cost around $12 per day.

HOUSEWARES AND LINENS

Sheets are supplied. Bring your own towels.

TV/CABLE

The community room has a television that does not have cable but shows movies nightly.

TELEPHONE

You will find pay phones in the hallways and a phone-card machine.

MEALS

No meals are served. A communal kitchen offers a refrigerator, microwave, toaster, sink, pots, pans, and dishes, but no stove.

HOUSEKEEPING

Daily housekeeping is provided at the facility, but it does not include bed changes.

Green Tortoise

494 Broadway Street
San Francisco, CA 94108
(415) 834-1000

This is a hostel that operates as part of the Green Tortoise Adventure Travel Company. The travel company offers self-service, no-frills vacations oriented toward hiking and swimming in remote natural spots. The hostel is an active, bustling guest house in San Francisco's North Beach neighborhood. You get what you pay for, such as partially carpeted hallways, noisy lounges, a messy-looking communal kitchen and eating area, and the company of a variety of guests that range from grunge rockers and hippies to Eurotravelers with their kids. Cash and traveler's checks are accepted, and stays are limited to twenty-one days. After twenty-one days, you are required to check out for a day, and then you can check back in and stay another twenty-one days. There is no application, deposit, or credit check. There is a $20 refundable key deposit. Only cash or traveler's checks are accepted.

TYPES OF ROOMS
Dormitory-style (usually single-sex unless there is a spillover): $39 per day

BATHROOM
The Y offers shared single-sex bath and showers. Each room has a sink. Rooms with private baths can be requested for an extra $10 only if available.

PARKING
Parking is available for $12 per day.

HOUSEWARES AND LINENS
Sheets and towels are supplied.

TV/CABLE
There is a TV lounge without cable.

TELEPHONE
No phones are in the rooms, but you'll find public phones in the building.

MEALS
Continental breakfast is included in the price of the room. A cafeteria on the premises has a reasonably priced fare. There is no kitchen for residents, and no cooking is allowed in the rooms.

HOUSEKEEPING
Daily housekeeping is provided. Sheets are changed every other day, and towels are replaced every day.

LAUNDRY
Laundry machines are on the premises.

BATHROOM

There are no private baths. Most rooms have a sink.

PARKING

No parking is available on the premises. Neighborhood parking is difficult and by permit only.

HOUSEWARES AND LINENS

Towels and sheets can be rented for $4 and $1 respectively. There is a $12 refundable deposit involved.

TV/CABLE

There is a television in the community room.

TELEPHONE

The hotel will take messages, but guests must use pay phones for outgoing calls.

MEALS

Free daily breakfast is served. You can prepare your own meals in a communal kitchen.

HOUSEKEEPING

Daily cleaning service cleans the rooms and building.

LAUNDRY

Coin-operated machines are located in the building.

WORLD WIDE WEB RESOURCES

Rentals Online
(www.rentalguide.com)

This is a Web site produced by *Bay Area Rental Guide* magazine. It has a comprehensive list of San Francisco short-term rentals including hotels and apartments. This is an excellent resource.

The San Francisco Chronicle *and* Examiner Newspapers
(www.sfgate.com)

They list their classified sections online, including short-term rentals.

National Temporary Housing Network
(www.csn.net/ih)

This is a national short-term housing consortium with a directory that lists temporary accommodations. You e-mail them your requirements, and they will e-mail back what is available.

Rent Net
(www.rent.net)

They list temporary furnished apartments located in San Francisco and the Bay area.

List Foundation
(www.listfoundation.org)

Focuses on the arts and technology community with listings of apartment sublets, jobs, and events. This site is a good place to search for rooms and apartments for rent as well as post your housing needs.

UCSF Housing Options
(stu-housing-mac17.ucsf.edu/cho)

This is the student housing Web site for the University of California-San Francisco. It includes a list of short-term housing options.

OVERVIEW OF SHORT-TERM HOUSING OPTIONS

	PRICE RANGE	PARKING ON PREMISES	TV IN ROOM	SHEETS & TOWELS	KITCHEN SUPPLIES	MAID SERVICE	LAUNDRY IN BUILDING AVAILABLE	MEALS	CHECKOUT NOTICE
FURNISHED APARTMENTS									
AMERICAN PROPERTY EXCHANGE	$1,200–$2,500/mo.	yes	yes	yes	yes	yes	yes	n/a	given at registration
ASHLEE SUITES	$1,000–$1,750/mo.	no	yes	yes	yes	yes	yes	n/a	30 days
MAYFLOWER HOTEL	$775/mo.	yes	yes	yes	yes	yes	no	n/a	7 days
NOB HILL PLACE	$1,150–$3,700/mo.	yes	yes	yes	yes	yes	yes	n/a	none
RESIDENCE HOTELS									
ABIGAIL	$375/week	no	yes	yes	n/a	yes	no	yes	none
ANSONIA	$180–$310/week	no	yes	yes	n/a	yes	yes	yes	none
BRADY ACRES	$650–750/mo.	no	yes	yes	n/a	yes	yes	no	given at registration
CORNELL CLUB	$525–$595/week	no	yes	yes	n/a	yes	no	yes	none
THE HARCOURT	$550–$980/mo.	no	no	yes	n/a	yes	yes	yes	none
THE KENMORE	$640–1,080/mo.	no	no	yes	n/a	yes	yes	yes	none
THE MONROE	$640–$920/mo.	no	yes	yes	n/a	yes	yes	yes	none
POST HOTEL	$156–$166/week	no	yes	yes	n/a	yes	no	no	none
S.F. RESIDENCE CLUB	$925–$2,100/mo.	no	no	yes	n/a	yes	yes	yes	2 weeks
SPAULDING HOTEL	$147–$198/week	no	yes	yes	n/a	yes	no	no	none
BUDGET-MINDED OPTIONS									
ATH (FORT MASON)	$17/day	yes	no	yes	yes	yes	yes	no	none
ATH (UNION SQUARE)	$18–$21/day	no	no	yes	yes	yes	no	no	none
CENTRAL YMCA	$700–$710/mo.	yes	no	yes	no	yes	yes	yes	none
GREEN TORTOISE	$39/day	no	no	yes	n/a	yes	yes	yes	none

CHAPTER FIVE

How To Find
A Place to Live

F INDING A PLACE to live is a time-consuming, expensive, and somewhat stressful process, so it's good to get it right the first time. It is time consuming in that a lot of research goes into finding a place you will call home. It is expensive because the first and last month's rent and a security deposit add up. It is stressful because you are not the only one out there looking for an apartment. San Francisco has become a very desirable place to live. The apartment vacancy rate is at an all-time low of 1 percent. A mediocre apartment in any neighborhood that is available for rent will attract many interested people. But this kind of talk isn't meant to discourage you. Research and planning will help you be the boss when it comes to finding housing that meets your needs.

First, you have to figure out what those needs are, and then you have to be willing to compromise. In this difficult rental market, it is best to be flexible and patient in your search for decent housing.

Ask yourself the following questions to help clarify the living situation you are looking for:

- What can I afford?

- Do I want to live with roommates or alone?

- How many roommates could I live with?

- Do I want roommates of the same sex or of either sex?

- Do I object to smoking?

- Am I a morning person or a night person?

- Do I want a roommate who is a homebody or someone who is away most of the time?

- Can I live with a roommate who is a party animal?

- Can I live with a roommate whose boyfriend or girlfriend stays over all the time?

- Can I live with a roommate who is a neat freak?

- Can I live with a roommate who is untidy?

- If I choose to live alone, do I want a studio or a one-bedroom apartment?

- Do I want a front or rear unit?

- Do I prefer a top- or bottom-floor apartment?

- Is parking an issue with me?

- What neighborhood would I prefer to live in?

- Do I have pets to consider?

- Do I want pets to consider?

- Do I want my bedroom facing the street?

- Is street noise an issue?

- Do I want a quiet, residential neighborhood or do I like to be where the action is?

- Am I willing to sign a lease or do I want the freedom of a month-to-month rental?

- Do I want laundry facilities in the building?

  Once you have figured out what you want—say, a studio apartment in Russian Hill or North Beach for $900 a month that will allow pets and isn't on any bus or cable car lines because you can't deal with the noise—then you are ready to start looking. There are different ways to approach an apartment or roommate search:

- Visit the neighborhoods where you think you would like to live and look for rental signs. In the next chapter, I review the different neighborhoods in San Francisco.

- Read local newspaper classified ads. Local papers include the *San Francisco Chronicle, San Francisco Examiner, Marin Independent,* and *Oakland Tribune.*

- Read the *Bay Area Rental Guide.* I mentioned this as a great resource for finding temporary housing in chapter 4, "Where to Stay When You Arrive," but the guide also lists many rentals. Another resource for apartment listings outside of San Francisco is *Apartments for Rent* (**www.aptsforrent.com**), which is free and available by calling (800) 452-0845. It covers Santa Clara, San Mateo, and Alameda counties.

- Visit real estate agencies in the neighborhood and ask if they have apartment listings. Many real estate agencies will have apartment rental listings in the neighborhood where they do business.

- Call property managers and find out what they have available. They can be found under "Real Estate Management" in the Yellow Pages.

- Let an apartment- or roommate-finding agency do the work for you. Even though a fee is involved, it is usually reasonable and worth the price for all the time and effort you will save.

The following resources will help you in your apartment search. There is not enough room to list everything available, so I have listed the most well-known. If you do some research on your own, you are sure to come up with many more options. Note that prices and services are subject to change.

APARTMENT/ROOMMATE FINDING AGENCIES

American Property Exchange

170 Page Street
San Francisco, CA 94102
(415) 447-2000 or (800) 747-7784
www.we-rent-sanfran.com

Services

This company was mentioned in chapter 4 ("Where to Stay When You Arrive") as a great resource for find-

ing short-term rentals. They also have a department that deals with long-term housing. After a personal consultation, a licensed real estate agent will prepare a property list according to your criteria, find your property, and negotiate the lease.

Fees

Depends on the property.

Apartments Unlimited

2285 Jackson Street
San Francisco, CA 94115
(415) 771-0447
www.find-a-place.com

Services

They have apartment listings citywide including the Peninsula and North Bay.

New listings are published twice a week.

Listings can be mailed, faxed, or e-mailed to you, or you can pick them up at their office.

Fees

$65 fee for total access of listings for forty days.

Fax and e-mail service is an additional $10 charge.

Note

They will do a personally tailored sample search for you to preview their service before you register.

Quick Credit Check service for $25 will run a credit report and deliver it to as many landlords as you wish.

Other services provided are local voicemail, cell phones, and prepaid phone cards.

Check out their roommate matching service under Roommate Resource.

Berkeley Connection

2840 College Avenue
Berkeley, CA 94705
(510) 845-7821
www.berkeleyconnection.com

Services

Listings for rentals in Berkeley, Richmond, Oakland, Alameda, El Cerrito, Claremont, and Rockridge areas.

Office receives ten to twenty new listings a day.

Get listings by fax, phone, e-mail, or in-person.

Roommate searching also available.

Second month free if you do not find the shared housing you are looking for.

$35 refund or second month free if you do not find the apartment rental you are looking for.

Fees

$60 per month for apartment rental listings on a walk-in basis.

$25 per month for shared housing listings on a walk-in basis.

$70 per month for combined rental and shared housing listings on a walk-in basis.

Convenient phone, fax, and e-mail service is an extra $10 fee each.

Community Rentals
470 Castro Street
San Francisco, CA 94114
(415) 552-9595
www.communityrentals.com

Services

Around 300–400 listings citywide at any given time.

Office receives thirty-five to forty listings a day.

Fees

$65 for two months with roommate matching included.

$40 refund if your search is unsuccessful.

Phone, fax, and e-mail service is an additional $25 fee.

Roommate matching separately is $25 for two months.

Homefinders
2158 University Avenue
Berkeley, CA 94704
(510) 549-6450
www.homefindersbulletin.com

Services

Listings in Berkeley, Albany, El Cerrito, and Oakland areas including as far north as Crockett and as far south as Fremont. Also included are Walnut Creek, Concord, Orinda, and Moraga areas.

Get listings by phone, fax, e-mail, or in person.

Phone service of listings is included in the cost of the membership.

Roommate searching is also available.

Preview their listings in person at their location.

Fees

$65 for two months of apartment rental listings. A refund of $40 after the first month if dissatisfied or unsuccessful.

$25 for one month of shared housing listings with a second month for $20.

$77 for both apartment and roommate listings.

$20 monthly charge for fax or e-mail service, Monday through Friday.

Marin Rentals and Roommates
305 Miller Avenue
Mill Valley, CA 94941
(415) 383-1161

Services

Listings throughout Marin County, from Sausalito to Novato.

Listings updated every four days.

Complete a form with information about who you are and what you are looking for. This information is entered into a computer and a list of rentals is generated.

Searches available via fax, e-mail, or Internet as soon as they are entered in the database.

Join by using their Web site.

Credit reporting service and cell phone rental service are available.

Free phone access on the premises to call for appointments.

Fees

$65 for two months for either apartment or roommate listings.

$75 for two months for both the apartment and roommate listings.

No extra charge to get listings by phone, fax, or mail.

San Francisco search: $95 for forty days with a $40 money-back guarantee.

Peninsula search: $85 for forty days with an $85 money-back guarantee.

South Bay search: $95 for sixty days with a $40 money-back guarantee.

In-Office search: $60 for forty days with a $40 money-back guarantee.

$25 credit reporting service.

Metro Rent

2021 Fillmore Street
San Francisco, CA 94115
(415) 563-7368
www.metro-rent.com

Services

Apartment listings in San Francisco, the Peninsula, and South Bay.

New vacancies are listed every day, and all information is kept current.

Descriptions of vacancies are matched to your personal search, complete with contact information.

Original San Francisco Roommate Referral Service

610A Cole Street
San Francisco, CA 94117
(415) 626-0606 information recording
(415) 626-7056 Roommates Now call-in service
(415) 558-9191 office
www.roommatelink.com

Services

Call-in service and walk-in service available.

Over 100 new vacancies each week for gay, straight, and coed households.

Rents range from $300 to $1,000 a month.

Temporary and permanent rental situations available.

Phone access with computer matching twenty-four hours a day.

Complete information about prospective roommates, including a recorded message from the roommate.

Add your profile to the rental database so people can call you.

Fees

$34 for four months of walk-in service plus three months of call-in service.

Notes

Sign up by phone with a credit card twenty-four hours a day.

In business for twenty years.

Rental Reconnaissance
2100 Larkin Street
San Francisco, CA 94109
(415) 929-4000
www.rentalrecon.com

Services

Custom database searches for apartments based on your rental specifications.

Computerized daily printed updates.

Use of office phones to set up viewing appointments.

Credit reporting service that can forward reports to prospective landlords.

$35 refund on your membership if you can't find an apartment.

Fees

$90 for thirty days of daily phone or fax listing updates.

$60 for thirty days of walk-in membership.

Rental Solutions
San Francisco: 369 Hayes
San Francisco, CA 94109
(415) 522-5600
Marin: 1038 Redwood Highway
Mill Valley, CA 94941
(415) 380-4080
East Bay: 2180 Dwight Way,
Suite A
Berkeley, CA 94704
(510) 644-2522
www.bayrentals.com

Services

Full-service rental search company.

Agent works with you to meet your needs (for example, if you want a one-bedroom in Potrero Hill, that's where the agent will look).

Computer searches based on your personal profile.

Maps for each property and of San Francisco.

Use of office phones to call about listings.

When you find a place you like, the agent will negotiate with the landlord.

You can transfer your paperwork to their other offices at no charge if you decide to look in a different area.

Fees

$85 for ninety days of unlimited listings by e-mail, fax, or pager.

$65 for ninety days of unlimited walk-in service.

Other services like credit checks and cellular phone rental for an extra fee.

5 percent of first-year rent or 60 percent of first-month rent.

Additional charge if you are a pet owner.

$30 for interview and prescreening.

Note

Over 40 percent of their listings are pet-friendly.

$40 refund if you do not rent through them.

Rent Tech

4054 18th Street
San Francisco, CA 94114
(415) 863-7368
www.renttech.com

Services

Rental and roommate searches.

Membership includes up to ninety days of unlimited listings.

E-mail, fax, or pager service available to receive new listings.

Roommate and Apartment Network

3129 Fillmore Street
San Francisco, CA 94123
(415) 441-2309 information message
(415) 441-6334 main office

Services

Lists hundreds of share rentals and vacant rental units in San Francisco.

Listings are updated daily.

Will assess the number of listings that meet your criteria before you sign up so you will know if the service is worth your while.

Sign up and get immediate results by fax, phone, or in person.

Unlimited fax, phone, and mail updates for your search.

Additional services include eviction and credit check reports, comprehensive tenant applications, and neighborhood maps.

Fees

$75 for share rental service only.

$65 for apartment rental service only.

$110 for apartment search and share rental service combined.

Satisfaction guaranteed or money back.

Note

The only agency that offers no time limit on active membership.

70 percent of clientele is repeat business.

Roommate Resource
2285 Jackson Street
San Francisco, CA 94115
(415) 771-0223
www.fnd-a-place.com

Services

Offers walk-in binder service and computer matching service.

Computer matching service results are delivered by mail, fax, or e-mail.

Register by phone during business hours.

Listings are updated daily in binders and three times a week in the computer database.

Stop in and preview listings before you sign up.

Fees

$45 in-office binder service for three months.

$55 computer database service with information faxed or e-mailed to you for three months.

REAL ESTATE AND PROPERTY MANAGEMENT COMPANIES

Founders Realty Rental Department
585 8th Avenue
San Francisco, CA 94118
(415) 668-5822

They have listings on voicemail including address, brief description, rental price, and contact.

McGuire Real Estate

2001 Lombard Street
San Francisco, CA 94123
(415) 929-1500

Listings are mostly in Pacific Heights, Marina, Russian Hill, and Nob Hill neighborhoods. These are usually pricey properties.

Paragon Management

185 Berry Street, Suite 4601
San Francisco, CA 94107
(415) 777-5200

This is a property management company that has rental listings in the South of Market and Potrero Hill neighborhoods. Call them and they will tell you what is available and let you visit. If you are interested, complete an application and pay the processing fee for a credit check.

PLS (Property and Loan Services)

599 8th Avenue
San Francisco, CA 94118
(415) 751-0599

You will become familiar with these initials if you scan the rental ads in the Sunday paper regularly. This is a no-fee property management company. Call them and ask about their current listings that are all over the city. A representative will set up an appointment and show you the places that interest you.

SAXE

1360 Franklin Street
San Francisco, CA 94109
(415) 474-2435 or
(415) 661-8110

An agent will take down your information over the phone or in person and call when there is something that matches your criteria. This is a no-fee agency that lists in the Bay Area Rental Guide.

Skyline Realty Rental Department

2101 Market Street
San Francisco, CA 94114
(415) 861-2284

This agency lists studios, one- and two-bedroom apartments, flats, and hotel rooms. It is a no-fee agency. Visit their office for current listings.

Taisch Property

301 Jersey Street
San Francisco, CA 94114
(415) 821-9895

This no-fee agency has apartment rentals throughout the city. There is a $30 credit-check charge.

TCO

1740 Market Street
San Francisco, CA 94102
(415) 621-1100

This is a Haight Street establishment, and most of their rental properties are in the neighborhood. Visit their offices to review binders of listings. If there is a property you like, you can check out a key and visit on your own. An application needs to be completed along with a credit check.

The Union Group (TUG)

1700A Union Street
San Francisco, CA 94123
(415) 202-7444

This no-fee agency will tell you what properties they have available and give you the address so you can drive by. If you like it on the outside, then they can show you the inside. If you want to rent it, then complete an application and they will run a credit check

for a fee. They have listings all over the city.

Trinity Properties

333 Bay Street
San Francisco, CA 94133
(415) 433-3333

They own and manage all the buildings they rent. There is no fee for their service. Simply call and tell them what you are looking for as well as your price range, and they will tell you what they have available. They have buildings all over the city except in the Marina and Cow Hollow neighborhoods. The buildings are modern with wall-to-wall carpeting. No pets are allowed. Parking is available in all buildings for an extra charge.

GETTING YOUR APARTMENT

Now that you have found some listings that sound appealing and have made your calls, be ready for the meetings with landlords or property managers. As in any city, good apartments, especially affordable ones, are hard to find. Some neighborhoods, such as Pacific Heights, are considered more prime than others. Chances are you will be competing with other people for the same places. Here are some tips to gain the advantage:

Try to be the first appointment of the day. This way, if you like the place, you can let the landlord or manager know right away. Many times managers are just interested in getting a new tenant in a vacant apartment as soon as possible because they are losing money.

Come prepared and be prepared to make a decision on the spot. Good apartments do not stay vacant for long. Bring your checkbook with enough money for down payments and security deposits. Also, bring a completed rental application, which can be found in most office supply stores or online at **www.landlording.com**, and a copy of your credit report. The three major credit reporting agencies are Equifax (800) 685-1111; Experian (formerly TRW) (888) 397-3742; and Trans Union (800) 888-4213. You will need the following information for your rental application:

- Names, addresses, and telephone numbers of your current and past employers

- Names, addresses, and telephone numbers of your current and past landlords

- Names, addresses, and telephone numbers of references

- Social Security number

- Driver's license number

- Bank account numbers

- Credit card numbers for credit reference

Look presentable. First impressions do count. Someone who shows up in business clothes or nice casual clothes will look more responsible, professional, and mature than someone who just came off the beach. Landlords want to make sure they are renting to responsible people who can pay their rent on time and take care of the property.

GETTING WHAT YOU WANT

Asking the right questions to a landlord or apartment manager before you move in can prevent unpleasant situations. The following are some key questions to ask:

- If there is a plumbing problem or some other emergency, how would I handle it with you?

- How long does it take for things to get fixed?

- What bills am I responsible for? What are you responsible for (e.g., trash, water)?

- Who else will have keys to my apartment?

- Who are the tenants upstairs and downstairs? (You don't want to be stuck with an aspiring tap dancer upstairs.)

- When is the rent due?

- When will I be receiving interest payments for my deposits? (California law states that landlords must pay interest on deposits they hold.)

- If you or someone you supervise, like a repair person, needs to enter my apartment, how much notice will you give me? (California law states a minimum of twenty-four hours.)

- Are pets allowed?

Try to get a written rental agreement for your records. Even though an oral rental agreement is binding, there is no proof of the terms if you should have a disagreement with your landlord. For more information on tenant rights, the State of California Department of Consumer Affairs publishes a booklet called *California Tenants: A Guide to Residential Tenants and Landlords Rights and Responsibilities*. To purchase, send $2 to:

California Tenants
c/o Department of Consumer Affairs
P.O. Box 989004
Sacramento, CA 95798
www.dca.ca.gov/legal/landlordbook/howorder.htm

Nobody said apartment hunting was easy. Depending on the circumstances, it could take six days or six months to find a decent place to live. If you have to settle for a quick fix, make sure no lease is involved. Good luck!

WORLD WIDE WEB RESOURCES

The Gate
(www.sfgate.com)

This is the Web site for San Francisco's two major newspapers, the *San Francisco Chronicle* and *Examiner*. Select "classifieds" and you will find a breakdown of apartment rentals in San Francisco, East Bay, Peninsula, and Marin, both furnished and unfurnished. There are also classified listings for rooms for rent, residential hotels, and shared rentals.

Rent Net
(www.rent.net)

This is an online service that will help you find an apartment anywhere in the San Francisco Bay Area according to your specifications. It also includes other resources like temporary housing and self-storage information.

Apartments.Com
(www.apartments.com)

This is a leading provider of visual, interactive apartment rental listings nationwide. They also offer valuable moving and relocation information.

All Apartments.Com
(www.allapartments.com)

This is an Internet-based nationwide apartment search service. You can search San Francisco or other Bay Area cities by type of apartment, rent, and amenities.

Rentals Online
(www.rentalguide.com)

This is a Web site produced by the *Bay Area Rental Guide* magazine. It lists property management and real estate companies with multiple listings as well as individual listings.

Landlording Homepage
(www.landlording.com)

This is a downloadable rental application and tenancy reference form that may give you the advantage when vying for an apartment.

UCSF Housing Options
(stu-housing-mac17.ucsf.edu/cho)

This is the housing Web site for the University of California–San Francisco. It has information about off-campus housing including a database that will search for listings based on the rent you can afford. The Off-Campus Living Guide is also a great resource.

CHAPTER SIX

WHERE TO FIND A PLACE TO LIVE

SAN FRANCISCO is comprised of more than thirty different neighborhoods, each with a flavor of its own. North Beach, with its abundance of Italian eateries and European-style cafés, is considered the Little Italy of the city. The Mission is a mostly Hispanic neighborhood where many artists are taking advantage of lower rents and enjoying the cafés, used book stores, and art house theaters. The Marina is for yuppies who enjoy bayfront recreation and a pristine shopping district full of chain stores such as Starbucks and Pottery Barn. Whatever your lifestyle, there is sure to be a neighborhood that will suit your personality or satisfy your alter ego.

This chapter will describe some of the many different neighborhoods in San Francisco. The neighborhoods I will not detail are those that are suburban, family-style communities, because they do not offer many opportunities for renters. I will, however, venture outside of San Francisco city limits to mention some Bay Area communities that provide an alternative to city living.

The resources I list for each San Francisco neighborhood have not been rated and do not represent the best of their type. The reason some businesses are listed over others is because they are more well known or convenient to that neighborhood. For example, in a neighborhood that has many dry cleaners, I may name only one on the main business strip that is, therefore, easy to find. The purpose of the resource list is to assist new community residents to locate basic services in their neighborhood, such as a post office, grocery store, or Laundromat. As you familiarize yourself with your community, you will find many fine businesses and services

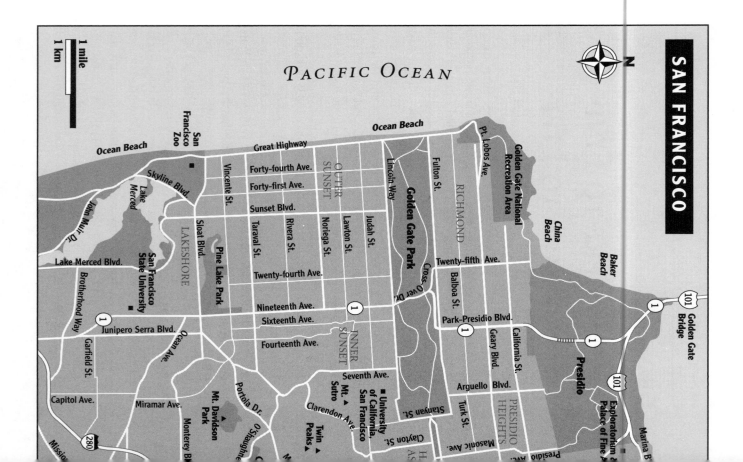

PACIFIC OCEAN

SAN FRANCISCO

N

1 mile
1 km

Ocean Beach

Ocean Beach

Great Highway

Forty-fourth Ave.

Forty-first Ave.

Sunset Blvd.

OUTER SUNSET

Vincente St.

San Francisco Zoo

Skyline Blvd.

John Muir Dr.

Lake Merced

Lake Merced Blvd.

LAKESHORE

Sloat Blvd.

Pine Lake Park

San Francisco State University

Brotherhood Way

Juniper Serra Blvd.

Garfield St.

Capitol Ave.

Miramar Ave.

Mt. Davidson Park

Portola Dr.

Monterey Blvd.

O'Shaughnessy

Mt. Sutro

Twin Peaks

Clarendon Ave.

University of California, San Francisco

Seventh Ave.

Fourteenth Ave.

Sixteenth Ave.

Nineteenth Ave.

Twenty-fourth Ave.

Taraval St.

Rivera St.

Noriega St.

Lawton St.

Judah St.

INNER SUNSET

Clayton St.

Lincoln Way

Golden Gate Park

Cross Over Dr.

Fulton St.

Pt. Lobos Ave.

Golden Gate National Recreation Area

RICHMOND

Twenty-fifth Ave.

Balboa St.

Park-Presidio Blvd.

Geary Blvd.

Arguello Blvd.

Turk St.

Stanyan St.

Masonic Ave.

California St.

PRESIDIO HEIGHTS

Presidio

China Beach

Baker Beach

Golden Gate Bridge

Exploratorium Palace of Fine A

Marina B

Presidio Ave.

101

1

1

1

280

Mission

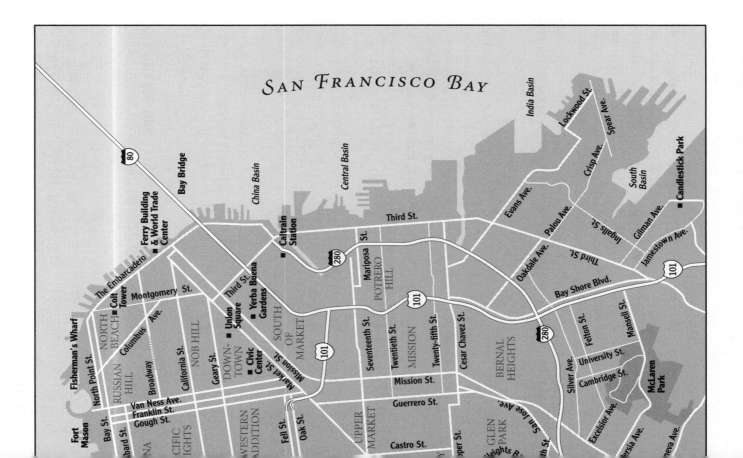

SAN FRANCISCO BAY

India Basin

Lockwood St.

Central Basin

China Basin

Candlestick Park

South Basin

Crisp Ave.

Spear Ave.

Bay Bridge

Gilman Ave.

Evans Ave.

Palou Ave.

Jamestown Ave.

Ferry Building & World Trade Center

Caltrain Station

Third St.

Ingalls St.

Oakdale Ave.

Third St.

Mariposa St.

Bay Shore Blvd.

The Embarcadero

Third St.

POTRERO HILL

Fisherman's Wharf

Colt Tower

Montgomery St.

Yerba Buena Gardens

Union Square

South of Market

Seventeenth St.

Twentieth St.

Twenty-fifth St.

Mansell St.

Felton St.

NORTH BEACH

Columbus Ave.

NOB HILL

DOWN-TOWN

MISSION

Cesar Chavez St.

BERNAL HEIGHTS

RUSSIAN HILL

Broadway

California St.

Geary St.

Civic Center

Market St.

Mission St.

Silver Ave.

University St.

Cambridge St.

McLaren Park

Fort Mason

North Point St.

Van Ness Ave.

Franklin St.

Gough St.

Mission St.

Guerrero St.

San Jose Ave.

Excelsior Ave.

Bay St.

Hubbard St.

PACIFIC HEIGHTS

WESTERN ADDITION

Fell St.

Oak St.

UPPER MARKET

Castro St.

Upper St.

GLEN PARK

Heights B...

Geneva Ave.

that better suit your needs. Pacific Bell, the local phone company, has a Web site called SmartPages (**www.smartpages.com**) that is an online directory of business and community listings like churches, cleaners, plumbers, hospitals, and schools, to name a few. It is designed to help consumers shop, research products and services, and locate merchants throughout San Francisco and the Bay Area.

THE BIG PICTURE

The northern section of San Francisco has many opportunities for renters. This is a desirable section of the city, with many great outdoor spaces for sports and recreation. Along the waterfront is a running and biking path. Park Presidio is located in the northwest corner of the city and is another recreation area for hikers, bikers, runners, and golfers. The north side of Golden Gate Park runs along the Richmond District neighborhood. This side of the park has museums, tennis courts, the Japanese gardens, and a golf course. Neighborhoods in the northern part of San Francisco include North Beach, Russian Hill, Nob Hill, Pacific Heights/Lower Pacific Heights, Marina, Presidio Heights/Laurel Heights, and Richmond District.

The central part of the city includes those neighborhoods right below the northern neighborhoods. Though there is no waterfront access, some areas still have great views of the bay, and others are located near Golden Gate Park. This section of the city is more diverse and gentrified than its northern neighbors. For example, the funky Haight-Ashbury neighborhood borders the gay Upper Market neighborhood, which borders a homey Noe Valley community. As you head out toward the ocean, neighborhoods tend to get more suburban and family-oriented. For example, if you choose to live in the Sunset District, Inner Sunset is a young, vibrant neighborhood located near the University of California, San Francisco, campus, with a main street full of coffee shops and local bars for people to meet and hang out. If you go to Outer Sunset, which is near the ocean, you will find mostly single-family homes with few social areas but lots of parking. Neighborhoods in the central part of the city include Western Addition, South of Market, Upper Market, Civic Center, Haight-Ashbury, Potrero Hill, Mission, Bernal Heights, Twin Peaks, Noe Valley, Glen Park, and Sunset District.

The southern section of the city is a combination of unsafe neighborhoods to the east and residential family neighborhoods to the west. Bayview has many housing projects and high crime. Excelsior, Visitation Valley, Crocker Amazon, and Outer Mission are lower-middle- to middle-class areas with diverse ethnic populations, mostly families. Ocean View, Lakeshore, Parkside, and Mount Davidson/Diamond Heights are located closer to the ocean and are more solid, middle-class, family neighborhoods. In the Lakeshore district, San Francisco State University has the largest college student attendance in the city. This part of town also has public golf courses such as Harding Park and private clubs such as the tony Olympic Club. Lake Merced is a recreational park with a constructed lake located near the San Francisco Zoo.

Now that you have a flavor of what to find in each section of the city, it's time to get a more detailed look. Each neighborhood profile includes the following information:

- Monthly rents gathered from the *San Francisco Sunday Examiner and Chronicle* classified section. These represent averages and can vary.

- Demographics cited from *UPCLOSE San Francisco Bay Area 1991* (Up Close Publishing, 1991).

- Crime statistics, as interpreted from the San Francisco Police Department figures for 1998 (**www.ci.sf.ca.us/police**). Categories are:

  - Below average: Fairly safe

  - Average: Still safe, but take precautions

  - Above average: Watch your back and belongings

- Street parking availability, as based on my own experience and informal interviews with residents, is categorized as:

  - Good: You will always find something, usually near your destination

  - Moderate: You will find parking, but you may have to circle the block a few times

  - Difficult: Think about public transportation

BERNAL HEIGHTS

Located on a hill rising above the Mission District and Noe Valley, this neighborhood has lower-than-average city rents and a diverse population of younger, creative types. You will find a small-town quaintness here, reflected in the architecture of Queen Anne cottages and Victorian bungalows and also in the bustling main street with an eclectic mix of small shops and cafés. This neighborhood offers city living with many suburban charms.

Bordered by: Cesar Chavez (Army) Street, San Jose Avenue, U.S. 101, and Interstate 280

Bus lines: 9X, 12, 14, 14L, 14X, 23, 24, 27, 49, 67

Main street: Cortland Avenue between Mission and Bocana Streets

BERNAL HEIGHTS

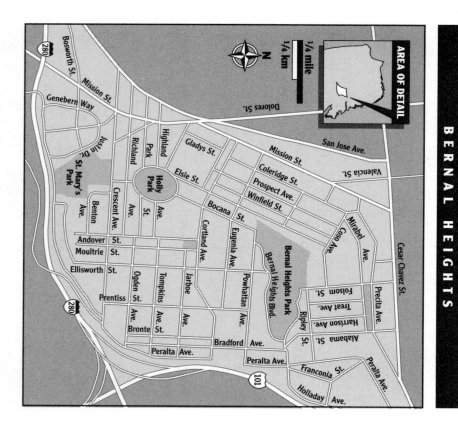

AREA OF DETAIL

1/4 mile
1/4 km

N

BERNAL HEIGHTS NEIGHBORHOOD RESOURCES

Community Organization

Bernal Heights
Neighborhood Center
515 Cortland Avenue
(415) 206-2140 or 648-0330

Post Office

30 29th Street
(800) 275-8777

Library

Bernal Heights Library
500 Cortland Avenue
(415) 695-5160

Recreation Center

St. Mary's Park Recreation Center
On Crescent Avenue at Murray Street
(415) 695-5006

Parks

Bernal Heights Park
Bernal Heights Boulevard at
Folsom Street

Holly Park
Holly Park Circle on Elsie Street

St. Mary's Park
Crescent Avenue at Benton Avenue

Worship

St. Anthony's Catholic Church
3215 Cesar Chavez (Army) Street
(415) 647-2704

St. John the Evangelist
Episcopal Church
1661 15th Street
(415) 861-1436

St. Kevin's Catholic Church
704 Cortland Avenue
(415) 648-5751

Bank

Bank of America
433 Cortland Avenue
(650) 615-4700

Supermarkets/Grocery Stores

All-American Meat Market
615 Cortland Avenue
(415) 647-4776

Bernal Heights Produce
800 Cortland Avenue
(415) 282-7308

The Good Life Grocery
448 Cortland Avenue
(415) 648-3221

JC Supermarket
820 Cortland Avenue
(415) 648-4656

Safeway
3350 Mission Street
(415) 826-2866

Cleaners/Laundromats

Bell's Cleaners
629 Cortland Avenue
(415) 285-3239

Bill's Whirl-O-Mat
600 Cortland Avenue
(415) 282-5912

Cortland One Hour Cleaners
331 Cortland Avenue
(415) 282-3700

Health Club

Navarro's Gym
3470 Mission Street
(415) 550-1694

Video Rentals

Four Star Videos
402 Cortland Avenue
(415) 641-5380

Video Oasis
448 Cortland Avenue
(415) 648-3569

Shoe Repair

Alexander's Shoe Repair
3296 Mission Street
(415) 648-4947

Hardware Stores

Cole Hardware
3312 Mission Street
(415) 647-8700

Goodman's Lumber Company
445 Bayshore Boulevard between
Cesar Chavez (Army) Street and
Alemany Boulevard
(415) 285-2800

BERNAL HEIGHTS NEIGHBORHOOD STATISTICS

Average Monthly Rent

Studio: $775 to $1,100

One-bedroom: $950 to $1,500
Two-bedroom: $1,400 to $2,200

Ethnic/Racial Distribution

White: 38%

African American: 10%

Asian: 22%

Hispanic: 30%

Median Age: 33

Gender Distribution

Male: 50%

Female: 50%

Renters: 51%

Crime

Violent crime: Average with aggravated assault having the most
incidents

Property crime: Below average,
with auto theft having the most
incidents

Street Parking

Permit required: No

Availability: Moderate

Local Newspaper

Noe Review, (415) 641-8926

DOWNTOWN/UNION SQUARE/CIVIC CENTER

This neighborhood is a blend of the upscale Union Square shopping district, socially distressed Tenderloin community, and San Francisco city government. The lines between these communities are usually clear but sometimes blur. The division is clear when you cross the street from the luxurious San Francisco Hilton hotel in Union Square and find yourself in the midst of a homeless congregation on the other side. But if you wander up Hayes Street from the elegant Opera House, what at

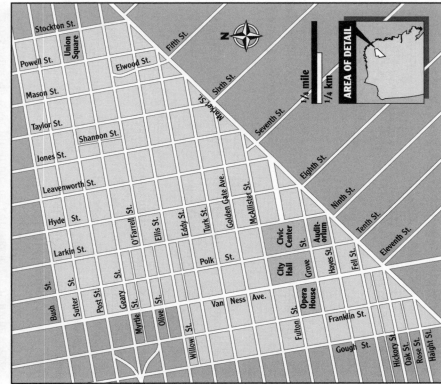

DOWNTOWN/UNION SQUARE/CIVIC CENTER

first appears to be a bad neighborhood quickly turns into a hip commercial strip with specialty shops, art galleries, cafés, and restaurants.

The Union Square residential neighborhood is full of sturdy old apartment buildings built in a time when no detail was too extravagant. Their elegant exterior architecture disguises poor interior maintenance. Many residents are elderly and have been there from better times or have relocated because of housing subsidies. The Academy of Art is located here, so you will find a young artist population that brings a hip accent to the community. In the nearby Tenderloin, a growing Asian immigrant population has made its home here. Their presence and small businesses, such as markets and restaurants, have improved the neighborhood slightly. Even so, it is still considered one of the worst neighborhoods in the city, and the visible signs are prostitutes and drunks loitering in the streets.

The Civic Center neighborhood is home to San Francisco city government and the homeless. Surrounding city hall are cultural and civic landmarks such as Davies Symphony Hall, War Memorial Opera House, Herbst Theater, and the San Francisco Main Library. Nearby Hayes Street between Franklin and Webster is a perfect example of a once-shabby neighborhood that has been redeveloped into a thriving commercial strip.

Bordered by: Bush Street, Stockton Street, Market Street, Gough Street, Ellis Street, and Van Ness Avenue

Bus lines: 2, 3, 4, 5, 8, 21, 27, 30, 31, 38, 38L, 42, 45, 47, 49, 76

Main streets: Van Ness Avenue and Market Street (this is a shopping district with many commercial streets)

DOWNTOWN/UNION SQUARE/CIVIC CENTER NEIGHBORHOOD RESOURCES

Community Organizations

Tenderloin Neighborhood Development Corporation
201 Eddy Street
San Francisco, CA 94102
(415) 776-2151

Union Square Association
323 Geary Street, Suite 710
San Francisco, CA 94102
(415) 781-7880

Post Office

1400 Pine Street or
121 Stockton Street (inside Macy's)
(800) 275-8777

Library

San Francisco Main Library
100 Larkin Street
(415) 557-4400

Recreation Center

Tenderloin Rec Center
570 Ellis Street
(415) 292-2162

Park

Union Square Park
At Stockton, Post, Powell, and
Geary Streets

Worship

Advent of Christ the King
Episcopal Church
261 Fell Street between Franklin
and Gough Streets
(415) 431-0454

First Baptist Church of California
1800 Market Street
at Octavia Street
(415) 863-3382

Glide Memorial
United Methodist Church
330 Ellis Street
(415) 771-6300

St. Boniface Catholic Church
133 Golden Gate Avenue
(415) 863-7515

Banks

Bank of America
One Powell Street
(650) 615-4700

Coast Federal Bank
1201 Market Street at 8th Street
(415) 241-8700

United Savings Bank
711 Van Ness Avenue
(415) 928-0700

Supermarkets/Grocery Stores

There are too many small corner
grocery stores in this neighborhood
to list them all.

Bread and Butter Market
888 O'Farrell Street at Polk Street
(415) 563-8985

City Hall Market
424 Hayes Street
(415) 863-1372

Hayes Valley Supermarket
580 Hayes Street
(415) 431-3527

Sutter Fine Foods
988 Sutter Street
(415) 776-7079

Pharmacies

A-P Pharmacy
1000 Larkin Street at Post Street
(415) 673-9130

Merrill's Drug Center
Market Street near 7th Street
(415) 431-7240

Walgreens
790 Van Ness Avenue
292-4899; and 500 Geary Street
673-8411

Cleaners/Laundromats

There are too many Laundromats and cleaners scattered about this neighborhood to list them all.

Abell Martinizing
441 Eddy Street
(415) 776-6662

Apple Cleaners
849 Leavenworth Street
(415) 776-9391

Dry Clean Image
455 Market Street
(415) 882-7351

Golden Launderette
445 Leavenworth Street
(415) 885-1144

Hyde-O'Farrell Dry Cleaners and Finished Laundry
467 Hyde Street
(415) 474-3523

Health Clubs

Central YMCA
220 Golden Gate Avenue
(415) 885-0460

In Shape
371 Hayes Street
(415) 241-0203

Muscle System (men only)
364 Hayes Street
(415) 863-4701

Video Rental

Wherehouse
1303 Van Ness Avenue
(415) 346-1978

Shoe Repair

Anthony's Shoe Service, Inc.
30 Geary Street
(415) 781-1338

Hyde Shoe Repair
112 Hyde Street
(415) 474-5622

ShoeWiz
865 Market Street
San Francisco Shopping Center
(415) 546-6986

Hardware Stores

Double Eagle Hardware
530 O'Farrell Street
near Jones Street
(415) 673-6724

Cole Hardware
70 Fourth Street
(415) 777-4400

Haji's Hardware
1170 Sutter Street
(415) 885-6321

DOWNTOWN/UNION SQUARE/CIVIC CENTER NEIGHBORHOOD STATISTICS

Average Monthly Rent

Studio: $600 to $850

One-bedroom: $1,100 to $1,325

Two-bedroom: $1,275 to $1,600

Ethnic/Racial Distribution

White: 52%

African American: 14%

Asian: 26%

Hispanic: 8%

Median Age: 39

Gender Distribution

Male: 64%

Female: 36%

Renters: 98%

Crime

Violent crime: Above average, with robbery having the most incidents

Property crime: Above average, with larceny having the most incidents

Street Parking

Permit required: No, but mostly parking meters

Availability: Difficult

Local Newspaper

None

GLEN PARK/DIAMOND HEIGHTS

Glen Park is the place to go if you want quiet living yet proximity to freeways and public transportation that will get you to work. This is a

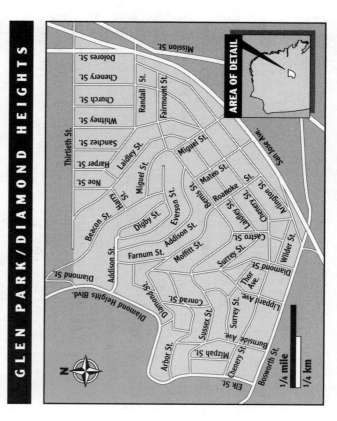

GLEN PARK/DIAMOND HEIGHTS

homey community, with narrow, winding, tree-lined streets, tucked between Bernal Heights and Diamond Heights. You will find the best of both worlds here—city living with suburban touches.

Bordered by: San Jose Avenue, 30th Street, Bosworth Street, and Elk Street

Bus lines: 26, 35, 44, 52

Main street: Chenery Street, from Diamond Street to Castro Street

GLEN PARK/DIAMOND HEIGHTS NEIGHBORHOOD RESOURCES

Community Organizations

Glen Park Association
P.O. Box 31292
San Francisco, CA 94131

Glen Park Neighbors
333 Bryant Street, Suite 220
San Francisco, CA 94107

Post Office

Diamond Heights Station
5265 Diamond Heights Boulevard
(800) 275-8877

Library

Glen Park Branch of the Library
653 Chenery Street
(415) 337-4740

Recreation Center

Glen Park Rec Center
70 Elk Street
(415) 337-4705

Parks

Dorothy Erskine Park
On Bosworth Street
at Burnside Avenue

George Christopher Playground
Off Diamond Heights Boulevard at
Gold Mine Street

Glen Canyon Park
On O'Shaughnessy Boulevard and
Elk Street

Walter Haas Playground
On Diamond Street at Beacon Street

Worship

Shepherd of the Hills
Lutheran Church
Diamond Heights Boulevard at
Addison Street
(415) 586-3424

St. Francis Episcopal Church
399 San Fernando Way
(415) 334-1590

St. Phillips Catholic Church
725 Diamond Street
(415) 282-0141

Banks

Bank of America
5268 Diamond Heights Boulevard
(415) 615-4700

California Federal Bank
2895 Diamond Street
(800) 843-2265

Supermarkets/Grocery Stores

Church Produce
1795 Church Street
(415) 282-1153

Diamond Supermarket
2815 Diamond Street
(415) 587-8851

Safeway
Diamond Heights Shopping Center
5290 Diamond Heights Boulevard
(415) 824-7744

Shoe Repair

Alexander's Shoe Repair
3296 Mission Street
(415) 648-4947

Glen Park Shoe Repair
2912 Diamond Street
(415) 334-0826

Hardware Store

Glen Park Hardware
685 Chenery Street
(415) 585-5761

Cleaners/Laundromats

Diamond Heights Cleaners
5214 Diamond Heights Boulevard
(415) 285-2252

Ernie's Laundromat
636 Chenery Street
(415) 585-6911

Glen Park Cleaners
701 Chenery Street
(415) 239-8247

Tina's Laundromat
636 Chenery
(415) 585-6911

Health Club

SOL Gym
2838 Diamond Street
(415) 334-7697

Video Rental

Diamond Video
5214 Diamond Heights Boulevard
(415) 550-1087

GLEN PARK/DIAMOND HEIGHTS NEIGHBORHOOD STATISTICS

Average Monthly Rent

Studio: $950 to $1,250

One-bedroom: $1,200 to $1,400

Two-bedroom: $1,475 to $2,200

Ethnic/Racial Distribution

White: 38%

African American: 10%

Asian: 22%

Hispanic: 30%

Median Age: 39

Gender Distribution

Male: 64%

Female: 36%

Renters: 98%

Parking

Permit required: Yes

Crime

Violent crime: Below average, with robbery having the most incidents

Property crime: Below average, with auto theft having the most incidents

Availability: Moderate

Local Newspaper

Noe Review, (415) 648-5898

HAIGHT-ASHBURY/COLE VALLEY

This community has a lively, nonconformist atmosphere. It was the 1960s mecca for America's hippies and was the center of the counter-culture

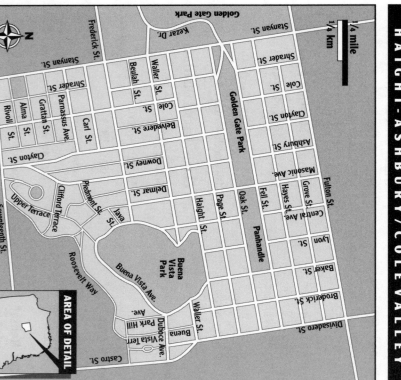

movement. It still retains some of that '60s flavor along Haight Street, where a new wave of Gen X hippies hang outside of funky secondhand clothing stores and paraphernalia shops. For more traditional living, Cole Valley is just south of Haight Street; the streets are narrow and tree-lined, and parking is impossible. Cole Valley has a small, quaint business district, so you never have to venture to the griminess of the Haight. The Haight-Ashbury/Cole Valley neighborhoods are situated near Golden Gate Park, Buena Vista Park, and the Panhandle, which are great areas for outdoor recreation and relaxation. University of California-San Francisco and its hospital are also nearby. If you make this your home, you'll share the community with young, rebellious student types, old hippies, drug dealers, and the avant garde. Living here is sure to be an experience.

Bordered by: Divisadero Street, Buena Vista Avenue, Stanyan Street, and Fulton Street

Bus lines: 6, 7, 22, 24, 33, 37, 43, 66, 71

Main streets: Haight Street, from Masonic to Stanyan Streets; in Cole Valley, Cole Street from Waller to Carl Streets

HAIGHT-ASHBURY/COLE VALLEY NEIGHBORHOOD RESOURCES

Community Organization

Haight-Ashbury
Neighborhood Council
P.O. Box 170518
San Francisco, CA 94117
(800) 275-8777

Post Office

Clayton Street Station
554 Clayton Street

Library

1833 Page Street near Cole Street
(415) 666-7155

Recreation Center

Hamilton Rec Center
1900 Geary Street at Steiner Street
(415) 292-2008

Parks

Buena Vista Park
Haight and Lyon Streets

Corona Heights Park
Castro and 15th Streets

Richard Gamble Memorial Park
Cole and Carl Streets

Worship

All Saints Episcopal Church
1350 Waller Street
(415) 621-1862

Hamilton United Methodist
Church
1525 Waller Street
(415) 566-2416

St. Agnes Catholic Church
1025 Masonic Street
(415) 487-8560

Supermarkets/Grocery Stores

Alpha Market
960 Cole Street
(415) 564-8910

Cala Foods
690 Stanyan Street
(415) 752-3940

Diamond Supermarket
199 Parnassus Avenue
(415) 664-3034

Haight Ashbury Produce
1615 Haight Street
(415) 861-5672

Haight Natural Foods
1621 Haight Street
(415) 487-1540

Real Food Company
1023 Stanyan Street
(415) 564-2800

Say Cheese and Food
856 Cole Street
(415) 665-5020

Pharmacy

Val-Grin Drug Store
925 Cole Street
(415) 661-1216

Cleaners/Laundromats

Cole Cleaners
947 Cole Street
(415) 566-8841

Lucky Cleaners
1300 Haight Street
(415) 621-7867

New Russ Cleaners
701 Schrader Street
(415) 750-9590

Parkview Launderette
618 Stanyan Street
(415) 566-9040

Prosperity Cleaners
912 Cole Street
(415) 566-9040

Quality Wash and Dry
1431 Haight Street
(415) 431-1330

Health Club

Cole Valley Fitness
957 Cole Street
(415) 665-3330

Video Rentals

Into Video
1439 Haight Street
(415) 864-2346

Video Nook
858 Cole Street
(415) 731-6265

Shoe Repair

Elite Shoe Repair
1614 Haight Street
(415) 863-3260

Hardware Stores

Cole Hardware
956 Cole Street
(415) 753-2653

Roberts Hardware
1629 Haight Street
(415) 431-3392

HAIGHT-ASHBURY/COLE VALLEY NEIGHBORHOOD STATISTICS

Average Monthly Rent

Studio: $900 to $1,100

One-bedroom: $1,000 to $1,500

Two-bedroom: $1,800 to $2,200

Ethnic/Racial Distribution

White: 76%

African American: 10%

Asian: 10%

Hispanic: 4%

Median Age: 32

Gender Distribution

Male: 57%

Female: 43%

Renters: 82%

Crime

Violent crime: Average, with aggravated assault having the most incidents

Property crime: Average, with auto boost having the most incidents

Street Parking

Permit required: Yes

Availability: Difficult

Local Newspaper

Haight-Ashbury Free Press (www.webcom.com/haight)

LAKESHORE

Though this neighborhood appears to be mostly residential, it is the home of San Francisco State University and its population of college students. San Francisco State offers on-campus housing, which is a good thing, because the area does not have many apartment buildings. If you choose to live in this part of the city, you will enjoy Lake Merced and Harding Park, two recreational areas that have, among other things, golf, biking, and running. It is also home to one of the nicest shopping centers in the city, Stonestown Galleria. This mall has a Nordstrom anchor store and quality shops such as Ann Taylor

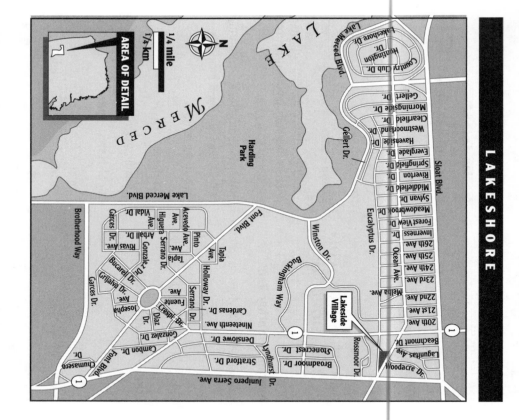

and Banana Republic. If you do not end up living here, you are sure to visit the neighborhood for sports or shopping.

Bordered by: Junipero Serra Boulevard, Sloat Boulevard, and Ocean Avenue

Bus lines: 17, 18, 28, 28L, 29, 88, M

Main street: There is no clearly defined street; Stonestown Galleria and Lakeside Village offer shopping and strolling.

LAKESHORE NEIGHBORHOOD RESOURCES

Community Organization

Lake Merced Hill Association
1150 Lake Merced Boulevard
San Francisco, CA 94132

Post Office

565 Buckingham Way
(800) 275-8777

Library

155 Winston Drive at 19th Avenue
(415) 337-4780

Recreation Center

Ocean View Recreation Center
Capitol Avenue and
Montana Street
(415) 337-4710

Parks

Lake Merced
Lake Merced Boulevard

Pine Lake Park
Crestlake Drive at Paraiso Place

Worship

First United Presbyterian Church
1740 Sloat Boulevard
(415) 681-5780

Church of the Incarnation
(Episcopal)
1750 29th Avenue
(415) 564-2324

Lakeside Presbyterian Church
19th Avenue and Eucalyptus Drive
(415) 564-8833

Lutheran Church of Our Savior
Junipero Serra Boulevard and
Garfield Street
(415) 586-7890

St. Cecilia's Catholic Church
2555 17th Avenue
(415) 664-8481

St. Stephen's Catholic Church
601 Eucalyptus Drive
(415) 681-2444

Temple Baptist Church
3355 19th Avenue
(415) 566-4080

Temple United Methodist Church
1111 Junipero Serra Boulevard
(415) 586-1444

West Portal Lutheran Church
200 Sloat Boulevard
(415) 661-0242

Banks

Bank of America
1007 Taraval Street
1515 Sloat Street (inside the
Lakeshore Plaza Lucky)
245 Winston Drive
(650) 615-4700

Bank of the West
495 Buckingham Way
(415) 665-5252

Cleaners/Laundromats

Lakeshore Cleaners
1513 Sloat Boulevard
(415) 753-5458

Stonestown Cleaners
285 Winston Drive
(415) 564-5881

Video Rentals

Blockbuster Video
1503 Sloat Boulevard
(415) 753-1404
1770 Ocean Avenue
(415) 333-3468

Shoe Repair

Lakeshore Shoe Service
1553 Sloat Boulevard
(415) 664-1344

Hardware Store

Lakeshore Lock and Hardware
1583 Sloat Boulevard
(415) 665-5300

LAKESHORE NEIGHBORHOOD STATISTICS

Average Monthly Rent

Studio: not available
One-bedroom: $1,100 to $1,350
Two-bedroom: $1,500 to $2,000

Ethnic/Racial Distribution

White: 64%
African American: 8%

California Federal Bank
3146 20th Avenue
(800) 843-2265

Glendale Federal
2499 Ocean Avenue
(415) 586-9292

Wells Fargo Bank
599 Buckingham Way
(415) 396-3221

World Savings and Loan
1595 Sloat Boulevard
(415) 242-1534

Supermarkets/Grocery Stores

Lucky Food Center
1515 Sloat Boulevard
(415) 681-4300

Parkside Farmer's Market
555 Taraval Street
(415) 681-5563

Petrini's Stonestown Market
255 Winston Drive
(415) 753-0189

Safeway
730 Taraval Street
(415) 665-4136

Pharmacies

Thrifty Drug Store
445 Taraval Street
(415) 564-9437

Walgreens
2550 Ocean Avenue
(415) 587-9111

Asian: 20%

Hispanic: 8%

Median Age: 38

Gender Distribution

Male: 41%

Female: 59%

Renters: 75%

MARINA/COW HOLLOW

The Marina was created on landfill for the Pan Pacific Expo back in 1915. Because of this, it sustained some of the worst damage in the 1989 Loma Prieta earthquake. But that doesn't stop it from being a

Crime

Violent crime: Below average, with robbery having the most incidents

Property crime: Average, with larceny having the most incidents

Street Parking

Permit required: Yes

Availability: Good

Local Newspaper

None

MARINA/COW HOLLOW

AREA OF DETAIL

San Francisco Bay

Fort Mason

Van Ness Ave.
Franklin St.
Gough St.
Octavia St.
Laguna St.
Lombard St.
Greenwich St.
Filbert St.
Union St.
Green St.
Moscone Rec. Center
Buchanan St.
Webster St.
Fillmore St.
Steiner St.
Pierce St.
Scott St.
Divisadero St.
Broderick St.
Baker St.

Marina Blvd.
Beach St.
North Point St.
Bay St.
Mallorca Wy.
Toledo Wy.
Alhambra St.
Capra Wy.
Avila St.
Cervantes Blvd.
Rico Wy.
Casa Wy.
Ritero Wy.
Prado St.

Marina-Green Park

Yacht Harbor
Marina Blvd.
Jefferson St.
Beach St.
North Point St.
Bay St.
Francisco St.
Chestnut St.
Richardson Ave.
Lyon St.

101

1/4 mile
1/4 km

popular community for young, white-collar singles and couples who pay some of the highest rents in the city. This attraction could be its proximity to the Marina Green, a grassy open space bordering the San Francisco Bay from Fort Mason to the Golden Gate Bridge. There is always a flurry of athletic activity along here, including jogging and rollerblading. It gets especially active on the weekends with sunbathers, kite-flyers, and volleyball enthusiasts. Another attraction could be the active day and night life along Chestnut Street, which has many bars, boutiques, and cafés. The residential portion of the neighborhood consists of well-tended streets lined with elegant Mediterranean-style buildings, some with views of the bay. This is the place to be if you want to experience hip, yuppie, urban living.

Bordered by: Van Ness Avenue, Green Street, Lyon Street, and Marina Boulevard

Main street: Chestnut Street, between Fillmore and Divisadero Streets

Bus lines: 22, 28, 30, 30X, 43, 76

MARINA NEIGHBORHOOD RESOURCES

Community Organizations

Marina Neighborhood Association
3727 Fillmore Street, #201
San Francisco, CA 94123

Cow Hollow Neighbors in Action
2742 Baker Street
San Francisco, CA 94123

Recreation Center

Moscone Center
1800 Chestnut
at Buchanan Street
(415) 292-2006

Park

Marina Green
Along Marina Boulevard between
Laguna and Baker Streets

Post Office

2055 Lombard Street
3749 Buchanan Street
(800) 284-0755

Library

1890 Chestnut at Webster Street
(415) 292-2006 or 292-2150

Worship

Calvary Presbyterian Church
2515 Fillmore Street
at Jackson Street
(415) 346-3832
www.churchnet.org/churchnet/calvary

St. Mary the Virgin
Episcopal Church
2325 Union Street
(415) 921-3665

St. Vincent de Paul Catholic Church
2320 Green Street
(415) 922-1010

Banks

Bank of America
2200 Chestnut Street
(650) 615-4700

Citibank
2197 Chestnut Street
(415) 923-1123

Great Western Bank
2166 Chestnut Street
(800) 782-8875

Home Savings of America
2750 Van Ness Avenue
(415) 474-5052

Wells Fargo Bank
2055 Chestnut Street
(415) 396-4507

World Savings and Loan
2298 Chestnut Street
(415) 346-9658

Supermarkets/Grocery Stores

Marina Super
2323 Chestnut Street
(415) 346-7470

Real Foods
3060 Fillmore Street
(415) 567-1540

Safeway
15 Marina Boulevard
(415) 563-4946

Pharmacies

Burton's Pharmacy
2016 Chestnut Street
(415) 567-1166

Walgreens
2125 Chestnut Street
(415) 567-9322
Divisadero and Lombard Streets
(415) 931-6415

Cleaners/Laundromats

B & M Launderesse
2371 Chestnut Street
(415) 921-0405

Fine Arts Cleaners
2379 Chestnut Street
(415) 885-4416

Launderland (Laundromat)
3320 Fillmore Street
(415) 921-7813

The Laundry Basket
2228 Chestnut Street
(415) 567-9888

Walnut Cleaners
2266 Chestnut Street
(415) 921-0495

Health Clubs

24 Hour Fitness
3741 Buchanan Street
(415) 563-3535

Marina Club
3333 Fillmore Street
(415) 563-3333

Asian: 10%

Hispanic: 4%

Median Age: 38

Gender Distribution

Male: 42%

Female: 58%

Video Rentals

Captain Video
2398 Lombard Street
(415) 921-2839

Hardware Store

Fredericksen Hardware
3029 Fillmore Street
(415) 292-2950

Renters: 85%

Crime

Violent crime: Average, with robbery having the most incidents

Property crime: Average, with larceny having the most incidents

MARINA NEIGHBORHOOD STATISTICS

Average Monthly Rent

Studio: $1,000 to $1,350

One-bedroom: $1,375 to $2,200

Two-bedroom: $2,400 to $2,750

Street Parking

Permit required: Yes

Availability: Difficult

Ethnic/Racial Distribution

White: 84%

African American: 2%

Local Newspaper

Marina Times, (415) 928-1398

MISSION DISTRICT

The Mission District was once prime land for the Ohlone Native Americans and then for Spanish missionaries. Today it is known as a Latino neighborhood with gang activity and high crime, especially at night. But change is coming to the northern part of the district, thanks to a continugency of artists, musicians, and lesbians who are calling this low-rent

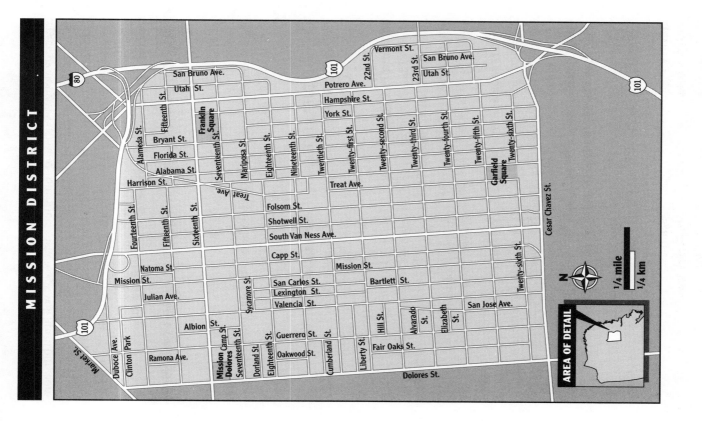

neighborhood home. North Mission is becoming quite the artsy scene, especially along Valencia and 16th Streets, where you will find a burgeoning restaurant scene, grunge cafés, secondhand bookstores, and plenty of thrift shops. The Women's Building serves, among others things, as a meeting place for progressive and radical political groups that tend to congregate in this part of town. This is a great neighborhood for those seeking a bohemian living experience.

Bordered by: Market Street, Dolores Street, Cesar Chavez (Army) Street, and U.S. 101

Bus lines: 12, 14, 14L, 22, 26, 27, 33, 49, 53

Main streets: Valencia Street, from 16th Street to about 19th Street, and 16th Street, from Dolores to Valencia Streets

MISSION DISTRICT NEIGHBORHOOD RESOURCES

Community Organizations

Inner Mission Neighbors
2922 Mission Street, Suite 106
San Francisco, CA 94110
(415) 826-7319

North Mission Association
286 Guerrero Street
San Francisco, CA 94103

Post Office

1198 South Van Ness Avenue at
23rd Street
(800) 275-8777

Library

3359 24th Street
(415) 695-5090

Recreation Center

Mission Rec Center
2450 Harrison Street (gym)
745 Treat Avenue (theater arts and cultural programs for kids)
(415) 695-5012 or 695-5014

Park

Mission Dolores Park
Dolores Street at 18th Street

Worship

Golden Gate Lutheran Church
601 Dolores Street at 19th Street
(415) 647-5050

Mission Dolores Catholic Church
3321 16th Street
(415) 621-8203

St. John the Evangelist Episcopal Church
1661 15th Street
(415) 861-1436

St. Matthew's Lutheran Church
3281 16th Street at Dolores Street
(415) 863-6371

Banks

Bank of America
2701 Mission Street
(650) 615-4700

Wells Fargo Bank
2595 Mission Street
(415) 396-8103

Supermarket/Grocery Store

Safeway
2020 Market Street
(415) 861-7660

Pharmacies

Walgreens
1979 Mission Street
(415) 558-8905
2712 Mission Street
(415) 285-9100

Cleaners/Laundromats

Fabri Care Dry Cleaners
2345 Mission Street
(415) 647-2345

Mission Quick Cleaners
3270 24th Street
(415) 285-5313

Launderland Laundromat
3800 24th Street
(415) 282-9839

Laundryworld Laundromat
2799 24th Street
(415) 648-5081

Health Clubs

See Upper Market or Noe Valley listings.

Video Rentals

See Upper Market or Noe Valley listings.

Shoe Repair

Mission Shoe Repair Shop
3174 22nd Street
(415) 285-3767

Montano Shoe Repair
199 Guerrero Street
(415) 626-7638

Hardware Store

Cole Hardware
3312 Mission Street
(415) 647-8700

MISSION DISTRICT NEIGHBORHOOD STATISTICS

Average Monthly Rent

Studio: $700 to $875

One-bedroom: $900 to $1,200

Two-bedroom: $1,650 to $2,200

Ethnic/Racial Distribution

White: 28%

African American: 8%

Asian: 14%

Hispanic: 50%

Median Age: 31

Gender Distribution

Male: 51%

Female: 49%

Renters: 87%

Crime

Violent crime: Above average, with robbery having the most incidents

Property crime: Above average, with larceny having the most incidents

Street Parking

Availability: Moderate

Permit required: Yes, in most but not all areas

Local Newspaper

New Mission News, (415) 695-8702

NOB HILL

For over a century, this has been the home of San Francisco high society. But scattered among the luxurious high-rises are affordable apartment buildings housing working professionals. The many professionals who live here enjoy the proximity to work in the Financial District as well as restaurants and shopping in Chinatown and on Polk Street. The steep hills that comprise this neighborhood offer excellent Stairmaster-like workouts, so there is hardly a need for a health club membership. Some attractions in this neighborhood are Grace Cathedral and the famous Fairmont Hotel.

Bordered by: Bush Street, Powell Street, Broadway, and Van Ness Avenue

Bus lines: 1, 27

Main streets: California Street, between Powell and Polk Streets, and Polk Street, between California and Broadway Streets

NOB HILL NEIGHBORHOOD RESOURCES

Community Organizations

Nob Hill Association
588 Sutter Street, #433
San Francisco, CA 94102
(415) 546-8917

Nob Hill Neighbors
1525 Grant Avenue
San Francisco, CA 94133

Post Office

1400 Pine Street

867 Stockton Street (in Chinatown)
(800) 275-8777

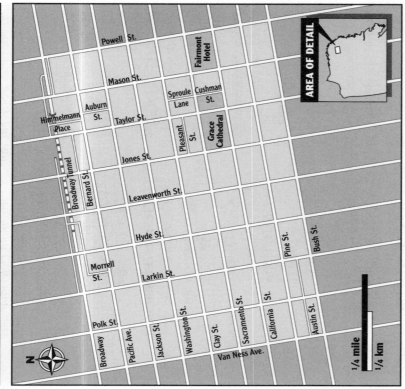

Library

Chinatown Branch
1135 Powell Street
(415) 274-0275

Recreation Center

Chinese Recreation Center
1199 Mason Street
(415) 292-2017

Park

Huntington Square Park
On Taylor Street across from Grace
Cathedral

Worship

First St. John United Methodist
Church
1600 Clay Street at Larkin Street
(415) 474-6219

Grace Cathedral Episcopal Church
1100 California Street
(415) 749-6310

Notre Dame Des Victoires Catholic
Church
566 Bush Street
(415) 397-0113

Pharmacies

Fairmont Hotel Pharmacy
801 Powell Street
at California Street
(415) 362-3000

Walgreens
1524 Polk Street
(415) 673-4809

Cleaners/Laundromats

Cable Car Cleaners
1398 California Street
(415) 928-0219

Clean Express Coin Laundry
(Laundromat)
1566 Hyde Street

Larkin Street Laundromat
1868 Larkin Street

Marvel Cleaners
1501 California Street
(415) 775-0897

Top Elegance Cleaners
1156 Taylor Street
(415) 931-8963

Health Clubs

Chinatown YMCA
855 Sacramento Street
(415) 576-9622

Club One
950 California Street
(415) 397-6363

Video Rental

Video Movie Center II
1414 California Street
(415) 775-5505

Old First Presbyterian Church
1751 Sacramento Street at Van
Ness Avenue
(415) 776-5552

Old St. Mary's Catholic Church
660 California Street
(415) 288-3800

Banks

American Savings Bank
1500 Polk Street
(415) 749-6535

Bank of America
1640 Van Ness Avenue
(650) 615-4700

California Federal Bank
1541 Polk Street
(800) 843-2265

Wells Fargo Bank
1560 Van Ness Avenue
(415) 396-4595

Supermarkets/Grocery Stores

Cala Foods
Hyde and California Streets
(415) 776-3650

Le Beau Nob Hill Market
1263 Leavenworth Street
(415) 885-3030

Nob Hill Produce
1000 Hyde Street
(415) 441-2220

Whole Foods
1765 California Street
(415) 674-0500

Shoe Repair

Crazy Cobbler Shoe Repair
1042 Hyde Street
(415) 776-5033

Hardware Store

Brownie's Hardware
1552 Polk Street
(415) 673-8900

NOB HILL NEIGHBORHOOD STATISTICS

Average Monthly Rent

Studio: $750 to $1,350

One-bedroom: $900 to $1,700

Two-bedroom: $1,600 to $2,600

Ethnic/Racial Distribution

White: 44%

African American: 2%

Asian: 50%

Hispanic: 4%

Median Age: 38

Gender Distribution

Male: 52%

Female: 48%

Renters: 88%

Crime

Violent crime: Above average, with robbery having the most incidents

Property crime: Average, with larceny having the most incidents

Street Parking

Permit required: Yes

Availability: Difficult

Local Newspaper

Nob Hill Gazette, (415) 227-0190

NOE VALLEY

It could be a slice of small-town America along 24th Street: mothers strolling their babies, yuppie singles walking their dogs, couples holding hands and window-shopping. Welcome to Noe Valley, one of San Francisco's best-kept secrets. Up the hill from the Castro, this neighborhood offers a respite from the hustle and bustle of the city below. This is a place where small business is king and corporate chain stores and restaurants are practically nonexistent (Walgreens and Thrifty drug stores have opened as well as Starbucks Coffee). Noe Valley is a tight-knit, friendly community with a small-town feel. Residents are hip and progressive, interested in the environment and a good latte.

Bordered by: Diamond Heights Blvd., Dolores Street, 30th Street, Portola Drive, and 21st Street

Bus lines: 24, 48, J

Main street: 24th Street, between Castro Street and Church Street.

NOE VALLEY NEIGHBORHOOD RESOURCES

Community Organizations

Friends of Noe Valley
3922 22nd Street
San Francisco, CA 94114

Noe Valley Neighborhood Association
995 Duncan Street
San Francisco, CA 94131

Post Office

4083 24th Street
(800) 275-8777

Library

451 Jersey Street near Castro Street
(415) 695-5095

Recreation Center

Upper Noe Recreation Center
285 Day Street at Sanchez Street
(415) 695-5011

Worship

Bethany United Methodist Church
1268 Sanchez Street
(415) 647-8393

Holy Innocents Episcopal Church
455 Fair Oaks Street
(415) 824-5142

St. James Catholic Church
1086 Guerrero Street
(415) 824-4232

St. Paul's Catholic Church
221 Valley Street
(415) 648-7538

St. Philip's Catholic Church
725 Diamond Street
(415) 282-0141

Banks

Bank of America
4098 24th Street
(650) 615-4700

Coast Federal Bank
3998 24th Street
(415) 285-3040

Wells Fargo Bank
4023 24th Street
(415) 550-0128

Supermarkets/Grocery Stores

Bell Markets
3950 24th Street
(415) 648-0876

Jim and Sons Produce
3813 24th Street
(415) 647-0755

Mikeytom Market
1747 Church Street
(415) 826-5757

Real Food Company
3939 24th Street
(415) 282-9500

Pharmacies

Thrifty Drugs
4045 24th Street
(415) 648-8660

Walgreens
1333 Castro Street
(415) 826-8998

Cleaners/Laundromats

Best Cleaners and Laundry
3783 24th Street
(415) 648-2378

Launderland Coin-Op Laundry
3800 24th Street
(415) 282-9839

Suzie's Laundry Service
3812 24th Street
(415) 647-1597

Health Club

Back Room Yoga and Bodyworks
1199 Sanchez Street
(415) 821-2979

Video Rentals

West Coast Video
1201 Church Street
(415) 648-0300

Shoe Repair

The Wooden Heel
4071 24th Street
(415) 824-9399

Hardware Store

Tuggey's Hardware
3885 24th Street
(415) 282-5081

NOE VALLEY NEIGHBORHOOD STATISTICS

Average Monthly Rent

Studio: $875 to $1,100

One-bedroom: $1,000 to $1,500

Two-bedroom: $1,700 to $2,250

Ethnic/Racial Distribution

White: 72%

African American: 6%

Asian: 10%

Hispanic: 12%

Median Age: 34

Gender Distribution

Male: 54%

Female: 46%

Renters: 66%

Crime

Property crime: Average, with auto boost having the most incidents

Violent crime: Below average, with aggravated assault having the most incidents

Street Parking

Permit required: No

Availability: Difficult

Local Newspaper

Noe Valley Voice, (415) 821-3324 or www.noevalleyvoice.com

NORTH BEACH/TELEGRAPH HILL

This once Italian immigrant community is still known as San Francisco's "Little Italy" even though the predominant ethnic group today is Asian. There is still an abundance of Italian restaurants, cafés, pastry shops, and delis. This neighborhood is conveniently located near the Financial District, two main bridges, and the freeways. North Beach was home to the Beat generation, and landmarks such as City Lights Bookstore and Vesuvio Bar remain. The Beats were around in the 1950s, writing poetry and pro-

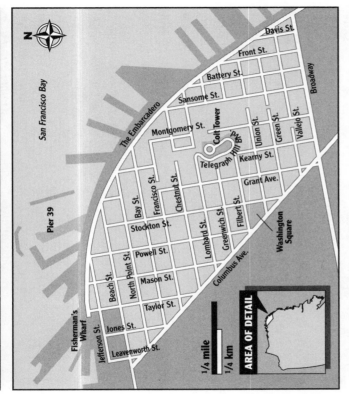

North Beach/Telegraph Hill map showing San Francisco Bay, Fisherman's Wharf, Pier 39, Coit Tower, Telegraph Hill, Washington Square, and surrounding streets including Davis St., Front St., Battery St., Sansome St., The Embarcadero, Montgomery St., Kearny St., Grant Ave., Columbus Ave., Broadway, and others. Includes compass (N), scale (1/4 mile, 1/4 km), and Area of Detail inset.

testing against conformity. Instead of Beats, today your neighbors might be Gen Xers, hippies, and the occasional artist mixed in with some professionals. This is a nonconformist neighborhood with a lot of pizzazz.

Bordered by: Columbus Avenue, Broadway, and the Embarcadero

Bus lines: 15, 30, 39, 41, 42, 45

Main streets: Columbus and Grant Avenues

NORTH BEACH/ TELEGRAPH HILL NEIGHBORHOOD RESOURCES

Telegraph Hill Dwellers
P.O. Box 330159
San Francisco, CA 94133
(415) 255-6799

Community Organizations

North Beach Neighbors
P.O. Box 330115
San Francisco, CA 94133

Post Office

North Beach Post Office
1640 Stockton Street
(800) 275-8777

Library

North Beach Library
2000 Mason Street
(415) 274-0270

Recreation Center

North Beach Pool and Playground
Powell and Lombard Streets
(415) 274-0200

Park

Washington Square Park
Stockton, Union, Columbus, and
Filbert Streets
(415) 421-0809

Worship

St. Peter and Paul Catholic Church
666 Filbert Street
(650) 615-4700

Banks

Bank of America
1445 Stockton Street
701 Grant Avenue (in Chinatown)
(415) 982-1344

Bank of the West
580 Green Street
(415) 433-6110

Bayview Federal Bank
1435 Stockton Street
(415) 396-2748

Wells Fargo Bank
468 Columbus Avenue
(415) 396-2741

1160 Grant Avenue
(415) 396-2741

Supermarkets/Grocery Stores

Nature Stop
1336 Grant Avenue
(415) 398-3810

Rossi's Supermarket
627 Vallejo Street
(415) 986-1068

Safeway
350 Bay Street
(415) 781-4374

Pharmacies

Walgreens
320 Bay Street
(415) 296-0108

1344 Stockton Street
(415) 981-6244

Laundromats/Cleaners

Doowash Laundromat and Café
817 Columbus Avenue
(415) 885-1222

Francisco Launderette
1901 Stockton Street
(415) 989-5934

Little Bubbles Coin Wash
Laundromat
1535 Grant Avenue
(415) 398-2247

Price Cleaners
800 Bay Street
(415) 885-1717

Tower Laundromat
1800 Stockton Street
(415) 421-2021

Health Clubs

24 Hour Fitness
350 Bay Street
(415) 395-9595

Bay Club
150 Greenwich Street
(415) 433-2200

North Point Health Club
2310 Powell Street
(415) 989-1449

Video Rentals

Blockbuster Video
350 Bay Street
(415) 982-4800

Film Yard Video
1610 Stockton Street
(415) 392-4255

North Beach Video
1398 Grant Avenue
(415) 398-7773

Shoe Repair

Galletti Brothers
Shoe Repair
427 Columbus Avenue
(415) 982-2897

Hardware Store

Tower Hardware
1300 Grant Avenue
(415) 788-1188

NORTH BEACH/
TELEGRAPH HILL
NEIGHBORHOOD
STATISTICS

Average Monthly Rent

Studio: $900 to $1,300

One-bedroom: $1,200 to $2,200

Two-bedroom: $1,675 to $3,000

Ethnic/Racial Distribution

White: 50%

African American: 5%

Asian: 45%

Median Age: 38

Gender Distribution

Male: 52%

Female: 48%

Renters: 83%

Crime

Violent crime: Average, with robbery having the most incidents

Property crime: Average, with larceny having the most incidents

Street Parking

Permit required: Yes

Availability: Difficult

Local Newspaper

North Beach NOW, (415) 391-1043

PACIFIC HEIGHTS/LOWER PACIFIC HEIGHTS

Like its neighbor the Marina District, Pacific Heights caters to a young, educated, dog-loving, professional crowd who enjoys outdoor sports and hanging out in the cafés on Union and Fillmore Streets. Pacific Heights is known as an upscale neighborhood and lives up to its reputation off of Union Street near the Presidio, where mansions are inhabited by the old, moneyed elite. The views from this part of town are great and so is the shopping along Union Street, with its many boutiques and specialty stores. Lower Pacific Heights is just over a hill south of Union Street. It centers around Fillmore Street, with its shops, restaurants, and services. This part is also very yuppie but not as upscale. The further south you go on Fillmore Street, the grittier the neighborhood becomes. Pacific Heights and Lower Pacific Heights are for those who want clean-cut living with no surprises.

Bordered by: Union Street, Van Ness Avenue, California Street, Presidio Avenue, and Lyon Street

Bus lines: 1, 22, 41, 45

Main streets: Union Street, between Van Ness Avenue and Fillmore Street, and Fillmore Street, between Jackson and California Streets

PACIFIC HEIGHTS/LOWER PACIFIC HEIGHTS

PACIFIC HEIGHTS/LOWER PACIFIC HEIGHTS NEIGHBORHOOD RESOURCES

Community Organization

Pacific Heights Residents Association
2585 Pacific Avenue
San Francisco, CA 94115
(415) 922-3572

Post Office

2055 Lombard Street
(800) 275-8777

Libraries

Presidio Branch
3150 Sacramento Street
(415) 292-2155

Golden Gate Valley Branch
1801 Green Street
(415) 292-2195

Western Addition Branch
1550 Scott Street
(415) 292-2160

Recreation Centers

Presidio Heights Playground
Clay Street near Walnut Street
(415) 292-2005

Parks

Allyne Park
Corner of Green and Gough Streets

Alta Plaza Park
Jackson and Steiner Streets

Lafayette Park
Washington Street between Gough
and Laguna Streets

Worship

Calvary Presbyterian Church
2515 Fillmore at Jackson Street
(415) 346-3832

Congregation Sherith Israel
2266 California Street
(415) 346-1720

St. Mary the Virgin
Episcopal Church
2325 Union Street
(415) 921-3665

St. Dominic's Catholic Church
2390 Bush Street
(415) 567-7824

St. Vincent de Paul Catholic Church
2320 Green Street
(415) 922-1010

Banks

Bank of America
1995 Union Street
2310 Fillmore Street
(650) 615-4700

Wells Fargo Bank
1900 Union Street
(415) 396-4890
2100 Fillmore Street
(415) 396-4453

Supermarkets/Grocery Stores

California Street Creamery
2413 California Street
(415) 929-8610

City Pantry
2190 Union Street
(415) 923-9771

Mollie Stone's Market
2435 California Street
(415) 567-4902

Self Service Wash Center
(Laundromat)
2434 California Street

Union French Cleaners
1718 Union Street
(415) 923-1212

Mayflower Market
2498 Fillmore Street
(415) 346-1700

Pacific Heights Market
1971 Fillmore Street
(415) 921-9300

The Straw Jar and the Bean
(Natural/Organic Food Store)
2047 Fillmore Street
(415) 922-3811

Thriftway Market
2174 Union Street
(415) 922-4545

Pharmacy

Walgreens
1899 Fillmore Street
(415) 771-1568

Cleaners/Laundromats

Best Cleaners
1699 Union Street
(415) 292-4073

Italy Cleaners
2502 Clay Street
(415) 673-7525

Pacific Heights Cleaners
2437 Fillmore Street
(415) 567-5999

Health Clubs

In Shape
3214 Fillmore Street
(415) 922-3700

Pacific Heights Health Club
2358 Pine Street
(415) 563-6694

Video Rentals

Castro Video
2410 California Street
(415) 441-3111

Wherehouse
2083 Union Street
(415) 346-0944

See Western Addition listing for Blockbuster Video.

Shoe Repair

SF Boot and Shoe Repair
2448 Fillmore Street
(415) 567-6176

Hardware Stores

Fillmore Hardware
1930 Fillmore Street
(415) 346-5240

Fredericksen Hardware
3029 Fillmore Street
(415) 292-2950

Pacific Heights Hardware
2828 California Street
(415) 346-9262

PACIFIC HEIGHTS/LOWER PACIFIC HEIGHTS NEIGHBORHOOD STATISTICS

Median Age: 38

Gender Distribution

Male: 50%

Female: 50%

Renters: 84%

Average Monthly Rent

Studio: $775 to $1,400

One-bedroom: $1,200 to $1,900

Two-bedroom: $2,100 to $2,800

Ethnic/Racial Distribution

White: 84%

African American: 4%

Asian: 8%

Hispanic: 4%

Crime

Violent crime: Average, with robbery having the most incidents

Property crime: Average, with auto boost having the most incidents

Street Parking

Permit required: Yes

Availability: Difficult

Local Newspaper

New Fillmore, (415) 931-0515

POTRERO HILL

This neighborhood is becoming very trendy, attracting artists, computer people, hip couples with kids, and others who enjoy quiet residential living, great views, and a sunny microclimate. The main retail area is along 18th Street, where the true community spirit can be felt. Among the many gathering spots and watering holes is Farley's Café, where locals enjoy their coffee and papers. You are sure to run into your neighbors browsing at Christopher Books or enjoying a treat at the Daily Scoop Ice Cream Shop. There has been a recent boom in loft construction that is attracting neighborhood entrepreneurs looking for live/work space. The only problem with this cozy neighborhood is its proximity to housing projects, making crime a problem.

Bordered by: Cesar Chavez (Army) Street, 3rd Street, U.S. 101, and 16th Street

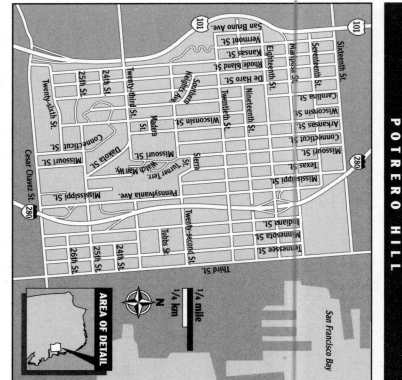

Bus lines: 19, 22, 53

Main street: 18th Street, between York and Alabama Streets

POTRERO HILL NEIGHBORHOOD RESOURCES

Community Organization

Lower Potrero Hill Neighborhood Association
934 Minnesota Street
San Francisco, CA 94107

Post Office

4083 24th Street
(800) 275-8777

Library

1616 20th Street
near Connecticut Street
(415) 695-6640

Recreation Center

801 Arkansas Street at 22nd Street
(415) 695-5009

Park

Esprit Park
On Minnesota Street between
18th and 22nd Streets

Worship

St. Gregory's Episcopalian Church
500 De Haro Street
(415) 255-1552

St. Peter's Catholic Church
1200 Florida Street
(415) 282-1652

St. Teresa's Catholic Church
390 Missouri Street
(415) 285-5272

Bank

Bank of America
680 8th Street (inside Potrero
Design Center)
(650) 615-4700

Supermarkets/Grocery Stores

Good Life Grocery
1524 20th Street
(415) 282-9204

Safeway
2300 16th Street
(415) 575-1120

Pharmacy

Walgreens
1189 Potrero Avenue
(415) 647-0368

Cleaners/Laundromat

Billy's Cleaners and Whirlomat
Laundry
1503 20th Street
(415) 826-0422

Health Club

World Gym
260 De Haro Street
(415) 703-9650

Video Rental

Dr. Video
1521 18th Street
(415) 826-2900

Shoe Repair

See Mission District for listings.

Hardware Store

See Mission District for listings.

POTRERO HILL NEIGHBORHOOD STATISTICS

Average Monthly Rent

Studio: $800 to $1,200

One-bedroom: $1,450 to $1,700

Two-bedroom: $1,750 to $2,250

Ethnic/Racial Distribution

White: 58%

African American: 22%

Asian: 8%

Hispanic: 12%

Median Age: 35

Gender Distribution

Male: 54%

Female: 46%

Renters: 61%

Street Parking

Permit required: No

Crime

Violent crime: Average, with robbery having the most incidents

Availability: Good

Property crime: Average, with auto
theft having the most incidents

Local Newspaper

Potrero View, (415) 824-7516

PRESIDIO HEIGHTS/LAUREL HEIGHTS

This is a pristine community neighboring the city's newest national park,
the Presidio. Thanks to the meticulous care and respect former Presidio
army base residents gave to this neighborhood, Presidio Heights/Laurel
Heights is one of the truly civilized areas left in the city. Wealthier residents live in beautifully maintained mansions overlooking acres of eucalyptus trees that fill Presidio National Park. For the rest of us, there are
equally nice apartments for rent that, if available, can cost a bundle.

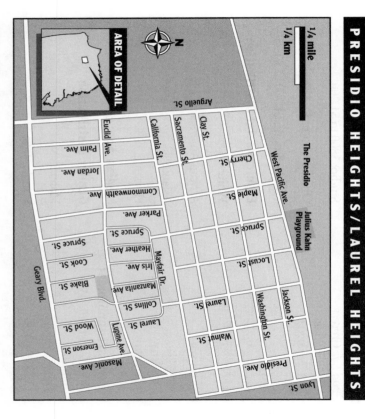

Retail activity is concentrated along Sacramento Street (between Lyon and Spruce Streets) and also along California Street near California Pacific Medical Center.

Bordered by: West Pacific Avenue, Arguello Boulevard, Geary Boulevard, Masonic Avenue, and Presidio Avenue

Bus lines: 1, 2, 4, 28, 28L, 33, 38, 38L, 43, 44

Main streets: Sacramento Street, between Lyon and Spruce Streets, and Laurel Village Shopping Center at the 3000 block of California Street

PRESIDIO HEIGHTS/ LAUREL HEIGHTS NEIGHBORHOOD RESOURCES

Community Organization

Presidio Heights Association of Neighbors
P.O. Box 29503
San Francisco, CA 94129

Post Office

950 Lincoln Boulevard
(800) 275-8777

Library

3150 Sacramento Street
(415) 292-2155

Parks/Playgrounds

Laurel Hill Playground
Euclid Avenue at Blake Street

Julius Kahn Playground
Jackson Street at Spruce Street

Worship

Congregation Emanu-El
2 Lake Street
(415) 751-2535

Park Presidio
United Methodist Church
4301 Geary Boulevard
(415) 751-4438

St. James Episcopal Church
4620 California Street
(415) 751-1198

Banks

Bank of America
3565 California Street
(650) 615-4700

Citibank
3296 Sacramento Street
(415) 922-0403

Wells Fargo Bank
3431 California Street
(415) 544-5063

Supermarkets/Grocery Stores

Cal-Mart Supermarket
3585 California Street
(415) 751-3516

Laurel Super Mart
3445 California Street
(415) 752-0179

PRESIDIO HEIGHTS/LAUREL HEIGHTS NEIGHBORHOOD STATISTICS

Average Monthly Rent

Studio: $925 to $1,750

One-bedroom: $1,250 to $2,150

Two-bedroom: $1,800 to $2,400

Ethnic/Racial Distribution

White: 74%

African American: 6%

Asian: 16%

Hispanic: 4%

Median Age: 36

Gender Distribution

Male: 47%

Female: 53%

Renters: 74%

Crime

Violent crime: Below average, with robbery having the most incidents

Property crime: Below average, with larceny having the most incidents

Street Parking

Permit required: Yes

Availability: Moderate

Local Newspaper

None

Pharmacy

Walgreens
3601 California Street
at Spruce Street
(415) 668-3555

Cleaners/Laundromats

Locust Cleaners
3587 Sacramento Street
(415) 346-9271

Peninon French Laundry
and Cleaners
3707 Sacramento Street
(415) 751-9200

Sacramento Wash and Dry
3200 Sacramento Street
(415) 922-8899

Veteran's Deluxe Cleaners
3300 Sacramento Street
(415) 567-6585

Health Club

Pinnacle Fitness Club
3200 California Street
(415) 440-2242

Video Rentals

California Video Express
4355 California Street
(415) 752-8504

Shoe Repair

Cobblers Bench Shoe Repair
3308 Sacramento Street
(415) 567-3555

Hardware Store

Hardware Unlimited
3326 Sacramento Street
(415) 931-9133

RICHMOND DISTRICT

This used to be a graveyard district, but the bodies have been moved to Colma to make room for the living. Today, the Richmond District is a solid middle-class neighborhood with a diverse ethnic population, great restaurants, convenient shopping, and low crime. The Inner Richmond along Clement Street reflects the influence of a growing Asian population and is sometimes referred to as the "New Chinatown." In fact, Asians replaced a significant Russian population that settled here after the revolution. If you choose to live in the Richmond, you will have access to Presidio National Park as well as Golden Gate Park. The University of San Francisco campus is near the Inner Richmond; Lincoln Park Golf Course, one of the nicest public courses in the city, is in the Outer Richmond. The weather is usually foggy in this part of town.

Bordered by: Fulton Street, Masonic Avenue, Geary Boulevard, Arguello Boulevard, Lake Street, 32nd Avenue, Clement Street, and 48th Avenue

Bus lines: 1, 2, 28, 28L, 29, 31, 33, 38

Main streets: Clement Street, between Arguello and 8th Avenue, and Geary Boulevard, between 9th and 25th Avenues

RICHMOND DISTRICT NEIGHBORHOOD RESOURCES

Community Organizations

Richmond Community Association
240 4th Avenue
San Francisco, CA 94118

Lincoln Park Neighborhood
Association
270 32nd Avenue
San Francisco, CA 94121
(415) 221-4959

Post Offices

Geary Station
5654 Geary Boulevard

Golden Gate Station
3245 Geary Boulevard
(800) 275-8777

Library

351 9th Avenue
near Clement Street
(415) 666-7165

Recreation Center

Richmond Playground
California Street and 18th Avenue
(415) 666-7013

Park

Mountain Lake Park
Lake Street between 8th
and 12th Avenues

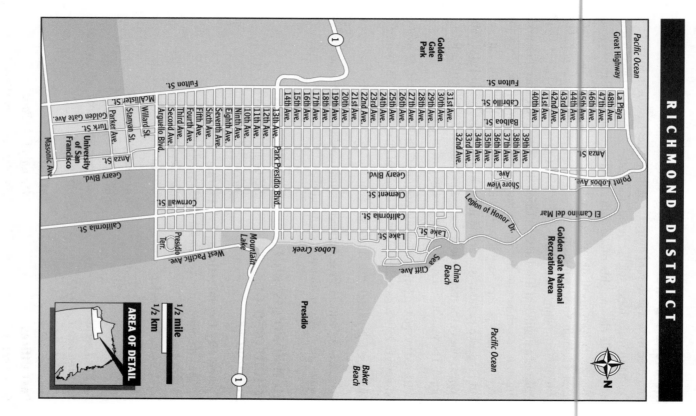

AREA OF DETAIL

1/2 mile
1/2 km

N

Worship

Congregation Beth Sholom
1301 Clement Street
(415) 221-8736

First United Lutheran Church
6555 Geary Boulevard
(415) 751-8101

Pine United Methodist Church
426 33rd Avenue
(415) 387-1800

St. Ignatius Catholic Church
650 Parker Avenue
(415) 422-2188

St. Peter's Episcopal Church
420 29th Avenue
(415) 751-4942

Banks

Bank of America
5500 Geary Boulevard
(650) 615-4700

Bank of the West
801 Clement Street
(415) 387-1425

California Federal Bank
4455 Geary Boulevard
(800) 843-2265

Glendale Federal Bank
6100 Geary Boulevard
(415) 387-5112

Great Western Bank
5600 Geary Boulevard
(800) 782-8875

Wells Fargo Bank
5455 Geary Boulevard
(415) 396-3645

Supermarkets/Grocery Stores

Appel & Dietrich Fine Food Market
6001 California Street
(415) 221-7600

Cala Foods
4041 Geary Boulevard
(415) 221-9191

Fruit Basket
661 Clement Street
(415) 221-0656

Seven-Eleven Food Store
900 Clement Street
(415) 668-3537

State Market
4751 Geary Boulevard
(415) 752-3466

Pharmacies

Evergreen Pharmacy
5601 Geary Boulevard
(415) 221-0065

Hall's Pharmacy
6157 Geary Boulevard
(415) 751-1320

Health Clubs

Pinnacle Fitness Center
3200 California Street
(415) 440-2242

Richmond YMCA
360 18th Avenue
(415) 668-2060

Video Rentals

Blockbuster Video
5240 Geary Boulevard
(415) 668-2675

California Video Express
4355 California Street
(415) 752-8504

Wherehouse
3301 Geary Boulevard
(415) 751-3711

Shoe Repair

Geary Shoe Repair
5430 Geary Boulevard
(415) 387-1268

Geary Shoe Repair and Service
6242 Geary Boulevard
(415) 221-6101

Hardware Stores

Standard Plumbing and Hardware
1019 Clement Street
(415) 221-1888

Bay View Hardware
6114 Geary Boulevard
(415) 221-4764

Joe's Pharmacy
5199 Geary Boulevard
(415) 751-2326

Rite-Aid Pharmacy
5280 Geary Boulevard
(415) 668-2040

Walgreens
719 Clement Street
(415) 668-3939
5411 Geary Boulevard
(415) 752-6727

Cleaners/Laundromats

Aurora Clean Center Laundromat
1744 Clement Street
(415) 752-0909

Certified Cleaners
2601 Clement Street
(415) 752-0659

Clean X-Press
5211 Geary Boulevard
(415) 221-3388

Geary Cleaners
5911 Geary Boulevard
(415) 751-9218

Lux Cleaners & Shoe Repair
531 Geary Street
(415) 752-6228

Qualitech Cleaners
5754 Geary Boulevard
(415) 668-1175

RICHMOND DISTRICT NEIGHBORHOOD STATISTICS

Average Monthly Rent

Studio: $800 to $1,000

One-bedroom: $1,100 to $1,600

Two-bedroom: $1,650 to $2,250

Ethnic/Racial Distribution

White: 44%

African American: 4%

Asian: 48%

Hispanic: 4%

Median Age: 34

Gender Distribution

Male: 46%

Female: 54%

Renters: 70%

Crime

Violent crime: Average, with robbery having the most incidents

Property crime: Average, with larceny having the most incidents

Street Parking

Permit required: Yes

Availability: Moderate to difficult

Local Newspaper

None

RUSSIAN HILL

This hilly community was named after the Russian seal hunters and traders who are buried there. Russian Hill is located between North Beach and Pacific Heights. Instead of the morbid burial ground it used to be, it is a hip, yuppie neighborhood with great shops and views. Polk Street, from Union Street to California Street, is the main commercial strip with local bars, ethnic restaurants, and gourmet grocery stores. South of California Street is the Polk Gulch, once the heart of gay San Francisco. Today it is the second most prominent gay community next to the Castro. Compared to the coziness on the north side, the south side of Polk shows a grittier scene including drugs and prostitution.

Bordered by: Columbus Avenue, Broadway, and Van Ness Avenue

Bus lines: 19, 41, 42, 45, 49

Main street: Polk Street, between Union and California Streets

RUSSIAN HILL NEIGHBORHOOD RESOURCES

Community Organization

Russian Hill Neighbors
2040 Polk Street
San Francisco, CA 94109
(415) 267-0575

Post Office

Nearby ones are in North Beach and Marina District.

Library

Nearby ones are in North Beach and Marina District.

Recreation Center

Nearby ones are in North Beach and Marina District.

Park

Russian Hill Park
On Bay Street between Hyde and Larkin Streets

Worship

See North Beach, Nob Hill, or Pacific Heights listings.

Bank

Coast Federal Savings and Loan
1850 Polk Street
(415) 928-6400

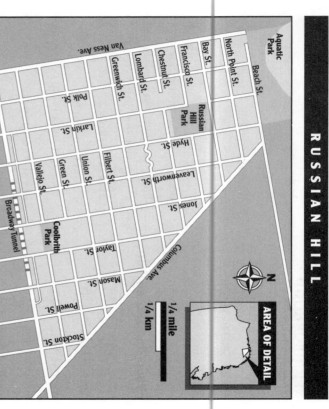

Supermarkets/Grocery Stores

Big Apple Grocery Express
1650 Polk Street
(415) 775-9090

Food Warehouse
1732 Polk Street
(415) 292-5659

Grand Meat Company
1806 Polk Street
(415) 885-5030

Polk and Green Produce Market
2222 Polk Street
(415) 776-3099

Polk & Vallejo Market
2150 Polk Street
(415) 673-4176

Real Food Company
2140 Polk Street
(415) 673-7420

Pharmacies

Home Drug Co.
1200 Union Street
(415) 474-0281

Walgreens
1524 Polk Street
(415) 673-4809
2254 Polk Street
(415) 474-9750

Cleaners/Laundromats

Holiday Cleaners
1850 Polk Street
(415) 928-5707

Michael's Cleaners
2235 Polk Street
(415) 771-0660

Missing Sock Laundromat
1958 Hyde Street
(415) 673-5640

Silk Tech Cleaners
2221 Polk Street
(415) 474-1120

Health Club

Karate One
1830 Polk Street
(415) 474-3322

Video Rentals

Movie Magic
1590 Pacific Avenue
(415) 771-1290
2325 Polk Street
(415) 775-3735

Shoe Repair

Frank's Shoe Repair
1561 Polk Street
(415) 775-1694

Hardware Store

Brownie's Hardware
1552 Polk Street
(415) 673-8900

RUSSIAN HILL NEIGHBORHOOD STATISTICS

Average Monthly Rent

Studio: $900 to $1,600

SOUTH OF MARKET

South of Market (SoMa) is quickly redeveloping from a rundown warehouse district into a hip place to live and work. Warehouses and industrial spaces are being transformed into live/work lofts, trendy restaurants, art galleries, and nightclubs. Many of life's conveniences have come to this part of town, including food stores like Costco and Trader Joe's and factory outlet stores. There is also a plethora of auto repair shops and auto bodywork garages. If you choose to live in SoMa, you will feel like you have a lot of elbow room. This part of town is still not densely populated like most of San Francisco. Parking won't be a problem, but your car getting stolen will. Crime is still high because of the population of vagrants who live on the streets. But it's the price you pay if you want to live on the cutting edge in a neighborhood that is about to explode with exciting development. The new modern art museum, Yerba Buena Gardens, and, coming soon, a baseball stadium, are signs of what to expect. The newly redesigned CalTrain station on 4th and Townsend Streets is a convenient way to get to the Peninsula. SoMa is quickly becoming one of the city's most vibrant new neighborhoods.

Renters: 80%

Crime

Violent crime: Average, with robbery having the most incidents

Property crime: Average, with larceny having the most incidents

Street Parking

Permit required: Yes

Availability: Difficult

Local Newspaper

None

One-bedroom: $1,250 to $2,200

Two-bedroom: $2,250 to $2,750

Ethnic/Racial Distribution

White: 48%

African American: 1%

Asian: 50%

Hispanic: 1%

Median Age: 40

Gender Distribution

Male: 46%

Female: 54%

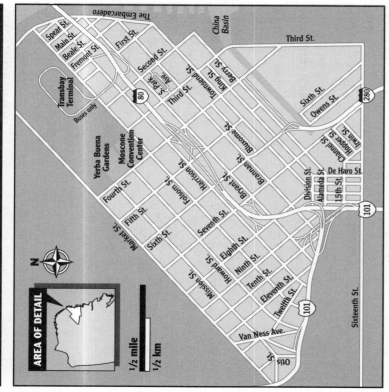

Bordered by: 16th Street, U.S. 101, Market Street, 4th Street, Folsom Street, and the Embarcadero waterfront

Bus lines: 9, 12, 14, 14L, 15, 19, 22, 26, 27, 30, 42, 45, 76

Main street: A main street has not been established, but there are pockets of activity, and it will take some exploring on your part. South Park at 2nd and Bryant Streets is like a Parisian square lined with cafés and restaurants and in the center is a playground and grassy area to hang out. Around 11th and Folsom Streets is a thriving nightlife scene with Slim's performance club, Hamburger Mary's burger joint, and the DNA Lounge. Streets closer to Market Street have convenience stores and clothing shops.

SOUTH OF MARKET NEIGHBORHOOD RESOURCES

Community Organization

South of Market Neighborhood Association

737 Folsom Street, #314
San Francisco, CA 94107

Post Offices

1600 Bryant Street

180 Steuart Street (at Rincon Center)
(800) 275-8777

Library

The closest one is the Main Library at Civic Center.

Recreation Center

270 6th Street
(415) 554-9532

Park

South Park
Between 2nd and 3rd Streets and Brannan and Bryant Streets

Worship

St. Patrick's Catholic Church
756 Mission Street
(415) 421-3730

Banks

Bank of America
501 Brannan Street
(650) 615-4700

Wells Fargo Bank
301 3rd Street
(415) 396-2005

Supermarkets/Grocery Stores

Bayside Market
120 Brannan Street
(415) 227-0151

Costco
450 10th Street
(415) 626-4288

Museum Parc Market
725 Folsom Street
(415) 543-9753

Rainbow Grocery
1745 Folsom Street
(415) 863-0621

Trader Joe's
555 9th Street
(415) 863-1292

Pharmacy

Costco
450 10th Street
(415) 626-4341

Cleaners/Laundromats

Brain Wash Café and Laundromat
1122 Folsom Street
(415) 431-9274

Museum Parc Cleaners
707 Folsom Street
(415) 777-1088

Health Clubs

24 Hour Fitness
303 2nd Street
(415) 543-7808

Club One Museum Parc
350 3rd Street
(415) 512-1010

Gold's Gym
1001 Brannan Street
(415) 552-4653

Video Rentals
South Beach Video
151 Brannan Street
(415) 882-9953

Shoe Repair
Magic Shoe Repair
345 3rd Street
(415) 512-7123

Hardware Stores
Cole Fox Hardware
70 4th Street
(415) 777-4400

Hundley Hardware Co.
617 Bryant Street
(415) 777-5050

SOUTH OF MARKET NEIGHBORHOOD STATISTICS

Average Monthly Rent
Studio: $775 to $1,200

One-bedroom: $1,100 to $2,000

Two-bedroom: $1,300 to $2,500

Ethnic/Racial Distribution

White: 30%

African American: 20%

Asian: 38%

Hispanic: 12%

Median Age: 45

Gender Distribution

Male: 67%

Female: 33%

Renters: 96%

Crime

Violent crime: Above average, with robbery having the most incidents

Property crime: Above average, with larceny having the most incidents

Street Parking

Permit required: Yes, in a few areas

Availability: Good

Local Newspaper

None

SUNSET

The Sunset District extends from Stanyan Street all the way out to the ocean and is divided into Inner and Outer Sunset. The Inner Sunset is a lively part of town, home of the University of California,

San Francisco, and neighbor to Golden Gate Park. Unlike its residential, family-oriented Outer Sunset sister, this neighborhood has lots of single young residents and many convenient local businesses. Neighborhood lifestyle resembles that of the Marina District and Pacific Heights, except there is more of a diversity of people: university students and young married couples, artsy types, and ethnic residents. If you choose to live here, you will enjoy all the recreational activities Golden Gate Park has to offer and lots of neighborhood camaraderie.

The Outer Sunset starts at about 19th Avenue and ends at the beach. It is mostly tracts of single-family, attached homes. Many families live in this part of town but more single professionals are moving in because of the availability of affordable places to rent. Access to Golden Gate Park

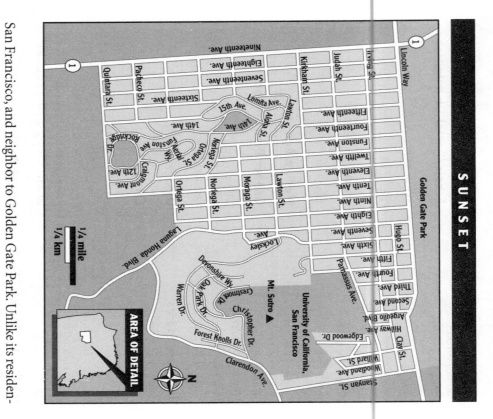

and Stern Grove Park is nearby as well as the Stonestown Galleria Shopping Center. This part of town offers quieter, suburban living while still being a part of the city.

Bordered by: Lincoln Way, Ocean Avenue, Rivera Street, Quintara Street, 10th Avenue, Ortega Street, Clarendon Avenue, and Stanyan Street

Bus lines: 6, 44, 66, 71, N Judah

Main street: Irving Street, between 5th and 9th Streets

SUNSET NEIGHBORHOOD RESOURCES

Community Organizations

Inner Sunset Neighborhood Association
1309 12th Avenue
San Francisco, CA 94122

Sunset Neighbors Unite
1831 Lincoln Way
San Francisco, CA 94122

Post Office

1317 9th Avenue
(415) 759-1901

Library

1305 18th Avenue
(415) 753-7130

Recreation Center

Sunset Recreation Center
2201 Lawton Street
(415) 753-7098

Parks

Golden Gate Park
Interior Park Belt at Stanyan and Belgrave Streets

Grandview Park
Quintara and Cragmont Streets

West Sunset Park
Bordered by Ortega and Quintara Streets and 39th and 41st Avenues

Worship

19th Avenue Baptist Church
1370 19th Avenue
(415) 564-7721

Calvary United Methodist Church
1400 Judah Street
(415) 566-3704

Christ Church Lutheran
1090 Quintara Street
(415) 664-0915

Seventh Avenue Presbyterian Church
1329 7th Avenue
(415) 664-2543

St. Anne of the Sunset Catholic Church
850 Judah Street
(415) 665-1600

Banks

Bank of America
800 Irving Street
(650) 615-4700

Wells Fargo Bank
725 Irving Street
(415) 396-4394

Supermarkets/Grocery Stores

Irving Food Mart
1636 Irving Street
(415) 661-4356

Parks Farmers Market
840 Irving Street
(415) 665-1154

Pharmacies

Dessel's Pharmacy
756 Irving Street
(415) 681-3300

Reliable Drugs
801 Irving Street
(415) 664-8800

Cleaners/Laundromats

Daya Cleaners
617 Irving Street
(415) 566-8005

Irving Laundry World
1932 Irving Street
(415) 665-0911

Health Club

MegaFlex Gym & Fitness Center
1247 9th Avenue
(415) 564-4343

Video Rentals

Le Video
1239 9th Avenue
(415) 566-3606

Shoe Repair

Sunset Shoe Repair
621 Irving Street
(415) 661-8259

Hardware Store

Progress True Value Hardware
724 Irving Street
(415) 731-2038

INNER SUNSET NEIGHBORHOOD STATISTICS

Average Monthly Rent

Studio: $825 to $1,100
One-bedroom: $900 to $1,450
Two-bedroom: $1,250 to $2,000

Ethnic/Racial Distribution

White: 48%
African American: 2%
Asian: 44%
Hispanic: 6%

Median Age: 37

Gender Distribution

Male: 47%
Female: 53%

Renters: 42%

Crime

Violent crime: Below average, with robbery having the most incidents

Property crime: Below average, with larceny having the most incidents

Street Parking

Permit required: Yes

Availability: Good to moderate

Local Newspaper

Sunset Beacon, (415) 831-0464

UPPER MARKET/EUREKA VALLEY

Also known as the Castro, this is the home of San Francisco's largest gay community. It is a well-maintained neighborhood with a great sense of pride and style. Small businesses tend to have a creative flair and cater to their market. Castro Street is the heart of this community and is always full of street life. Outside of this high-traffic area, the neighborhood can

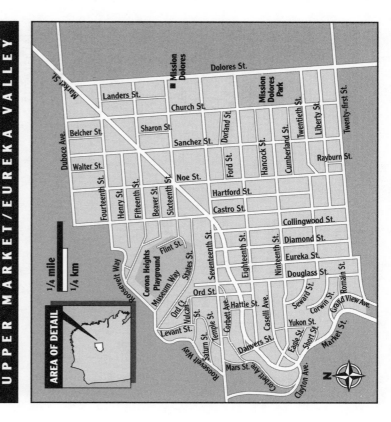

UPPER MARKET/EUREKA VALLEY

be very charming and quiet. Being gay is not a prerequisite for living here, but it does add to the experience.

Bordered by: Market Street, Dolores Street, Douglass Street, and 21st Street

Bus lines: K, L, and M streetcars

Main streets: Castro Street, between Market and 21st Streets, and Market Street, from Castro to Sanchez Streets

UPPER MARKET/EUREKA VALLEY NEIGHBORHOOD RESOURCES

Community Organization

Duboce Triangle Neighborhood Association
2235 15th Street
San Francisco, CA 94114
(415) 431-5317

Post Office

4083 24th Street
2075 Market Street
(800) 275-8777

Library

Eureka Valley
3555 16th Street
(415) 554-9445

Recreation Center

Eureka Valley Rec Center
100 Collingwood Street
at 18th Street
(415) 554-9528

Park

Mission Dolores Park
18th and Church Streets

Worship

Golden Gate Lutheran Church
601 Dolores Street
(415) 647-5050

Most Holy Redeemer Catholic Church
100 Diamond Street
(415) 863-6259

St. Aidan's Episcopal Church
101 Gold Mine Drive
(415) 285-9540

St. Francis Lutheran Church
152 Church Street
(415) 621-2635

Banks

Bank of America
501 Castro Street
(650) 615-4700

California Federal Bank
2099 Market Street
444 Castro Street
(800) 843-2265

Eureka Bank
443 Castro Street
(415) 431-6700

Supermarkets/Grocery Stores

Buffalo Whole Food and Grain Co.
598 Castro Street
(415) 626-7038

Cala Foods
4201 18th Street
(415) 431-3822

Harvest Ranch Market
2285 Market Street
(415) 626-0805

Safeway
2020 Market Street
(415) 861-7660

Seven-Eleven Food Store
3998 18th Street
(415) 552-8611

Valley Pride Market
474 Castro Street
(415) 431-1292

Pharmacies

Stadtlander's Pharmacy
4122 18th Street
(415) 434-8600

Walgreens
498 Castro Street
(415) 861-6276
1333 Castro Street
(415) 826-8998

Cleaners/Laundromats

As the Suds Turn
4172 18th Street

Castro Cleaners
4051 18th Street
(415) 552-2988

Little Hollywood Launderette
1906 Market Street
(415) 252-9357

Martinizing One Hour Cleaners
2233 Market Street
(415) 552-6035

Toni's Cleaners and Laundry
270 Noe Street
(415) 861-6993

Health Clubs

City Athletic Club
2500 Market Street
(415) 552-6680

Market Street Gym
2301 Market Street
(415) 626-4488

Muscle System
2275 Market Street
(415) 863-4700

Video Rentals

Blockbuster Video
160 Church Street
(415) 255-0600

Castro Video
525 Castro Street
(415) 552-2448

Take One Video & Laser
445 Castro Street
(415) 864-1456

Tower Video
2278 Market Street
(415) 255-5920

Shoe Repair

The Pioneer Renewer Shoe Repair
4501 18th Street
(415) 255-4576

Hardware Store

Cliff's Variety Store
479 Castro Street
(415) 431-5365

UPPER MARKET/EUREKA VALLEY NEIGHBORHOOD STATISTICS

Average Monthly Rent

Studio: $950 to $1,200

One-bedroom: $880 to $1,700

Two-bedroom: $1,500 to $2,500

Ethnic/Racial Distribution

White: 80%

African American: 5%

Asian: 7%

Hispanic: 8%

Median Age: 34

Gender Distribution

Male: 69%

Female: 31%

Renters: 79%

Crime

Violent crime: Above average, with robbery having the most incidents

Property crime: Above average, with larceny having the most incidents

Street Parking

Permit required: Yes

Availability: Difficult

Local Newspaper

San Francisco Bay Times (gay/lesbian/bi/trans newspaper for the Bay Area), (415) 227-0800

WESTERN ADDITION

This is one of San Francisco's most diverse neighborhoods. It is home to the Japanese Cultural and Trade Center, along with a Japanese-American community. Also in the neighborhood is the Center for African and African American Art, supported by a large African American population. Japantown revolves around the Cultural and Trade Center on Geary Street. South of Geary Street, the neighborhood looses some of its polish,

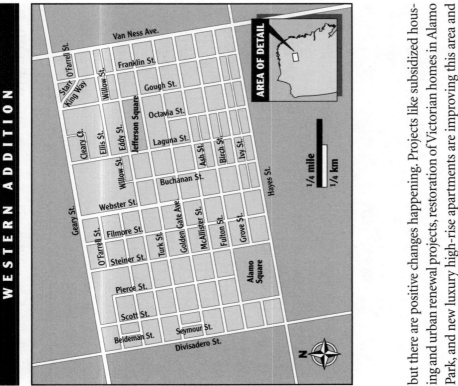

WESTERN ADDITION

but there are positive changes happening. Projects like subsidized housing and urban renewal projects, restoration of Victorian homes in Alamo Park, and new luxury high-rise apartments are improving this area and bringing in more businesses. The one downside to this part of town, especially south of Geary Street, is the higher-than-average crime due in part to the many housing projects in the area.

Bordered by: Geary Street, Van Ness Avenue, Hayes Street, and Divisadero Street

Bus lines: 5, 21, 22, 24, 31, 38, 38L, 42, 47, 49

Main street: The closest main street is Fillmore Street in Lower Pacific Heights; on Webster Street at Geary Boulevard is a business area with a Safeway and other practical services.

WESTERN ADDITION NEIGHBORHOOD RESOURCES

Community Organization

Western Addition Neighborhood Association
1948 Sutter Street
San Francisco, CA 94115

Post Office

1550 Steiner Street
(800) 275-8777

Library

1550 Scott Street at Geary Street
(415) 292-2160

Recreation Center

Hamilton
Geary and Steiner Streets
(415) 292-2008

Parks

Alamo Square
Fulton and Steiner Streets

Jefferson Square
Eddy and Gough Streets

Worship

Ebenezer Baptist Church
275 Divisadero Street
(415) 621-3996

First Friendship Institutional
Baptist Church
501 Steiner Street
(415) 431-4775

First Union Baptist Church
1001 Webster Street
(415) 929-9738

Hamilton Square Baptist Church
1212 Geary Street
(415) 673-8586

Sacred Heart Catholic Church
546 Fillmore Street
(415) 861-5460

St. Cyprian's Episcopal Church
2097 Turk Street
(415) 567-1855

St. Mark's Catholic Cathedral
1111 Gough Street
(415) 567-2020

St. Mary's Lutheran Church
1111 O'Farrell Street
(415) 928-7770

St. Paulus Lutheran Church
950 Gough Street
(415) 673-8088

Banks

See Lower Pacific Heights listings.

Supermarkets/Grocery Stores

Bell Market
1336 Post Street
(415) 771-8448

Safeway
1335 Webster Street
(415) 921-4557

Pharmacies

Walgreens
Divisadero and O'Farrell Streets
(415) 931-9971

See other Walgreens listing under the Pacific Heights section.

Cleaner/Laundromat

European Cleaners
1468 Fillmore Street
(415) 921-1900

Health Clubs

Cathedral Hill Plaza Athletic Club
1333 Gough Street
(415) 292-1741

San Francisco Athletic Club
1755 O'Farrell Street
(415) 776-2260

Video Rentals

Blockbuster Video
1493 Webster Street
(415) 771-5620

Shoe Repair

K-Shoe Service
1426 Fillmore Street
(415) 929-8422

Hardware Store

Divisadero Lock and Hardware
1649 Divisadero Street
(415) 673-5300

WESTERN ADDITION NEIGHBORHOOD STATISTICS

Average Monthly Rent

Studio: $600 to $1,000

One-bedroom: $1,150 to $1,350

Two-bedroom: $1,500 to $2,500

Ethnic/Racial Distribution

White: 38%

African American: 38%

Asian: 16%

Hispanic: 8%

Median Age: 34

Gender Distribution

Male: 53%

Female: 47%

Renters: 89%

Crime

Violent crime: Above average, with robbery having the most incidents

Property crime: Above average, with auto boost having the most incidents

Street Parking

Permit required: Yes, in some areas

Availability: Moderate to difficult

Local Newspaper

New Fillmore, (415) 931-0515

OTHER BAY AREA COMMUNITIES

If you choose to avoid fast-paced city living, there are many fine suburbs outside of San Francisco. Though these suburbs, like most, are family-oriented, some have congregations of young and single professionals. These folks typically choose suburban living because their jobs are located nearby, they want to have more open space for sports and recreation, or they want to pay less rent and get more for the rental buck. The following is an overview of three San Francisco Bay regions and their counties. I list all the communities in each county but only go into detail with those that attract a young, single, professional crowd. Contact local chambers of commerce (see Appendix B for listings) to request more information and relocation packets.

NORTH BAY

MARIN COUNTY
www.marin.org

Instead of becoming overdeveloped, this waterside county has carefully preserved its natural resources such as Mt. Tamalpais, Point Reyes National Park Seashore, Marin Headlands, and the Tennessee Valley. Communities in this region include Belvedere, Corte Madera, Fairfax, Larkspur, Marin City, Mill Valley, Novato, Ross, San Anselmo, San Rafael, Sausalito, and Tiburon.

Mill Valley

This town attracts writers and artists and therefore has a great appreciation for the arts. It hosts an annual film festival, and its Lytton Square town center has quaint galleries and boutiques. Mill Valley is situated in the shadow of Mt. Tamalpais, which has great hiking trails. The town also has a nine-hole golf course, doggie parks, and bike paths. Rents for studio apartments start at about $750, one-bedrooms at $1,400, and two-bedrooms at $1,700.

San Anselmo

This is a middle-class professional community with older homes, a town center, and over 130 antique stores dubbing itself the Antique Capital of Northern California. For outdoor enthusiasts, it is located next to Mt. Tamalpais, known for its hiking and mountain biking trails. The town has five parks, a library, and lots of outdoor recreation like tennis and softball.

San Rafael

Located halfway between San Francisco and the wine country, San Rafael is Marin's oldest city. It is also Marin's seat of county government. Attractions include a civic center designed by Frank Lloyd Wright, Mission San Rafael Arcangel, and Dominican College (est. 1890). Its downtown area is filled with quaint shops and eateries. Like everywhere else in Marin, San Rafael has many outdoor activities, including golf, baseball, biking, and hiking. Except for the Canal area, where crime is high and drugs are a problem, other parts of the town are very suburban and well kept. One-bedroom apartments start at about $875 and two-bedrooms at $1,300.

Sausalito

This is Marin County's most popular tourist spot. The commercial strip along the waterfront has many galleries, clothing boutiques, and restaurants. An easy commute to San Francisco by ferry or bus makes it a popular rental area for city workers. Rents are not cheap, however, with one-bedroom apartments averaging around $1,500 and two-bedrooms around $2,200. If you can afford it, you will be rewarded with low-stress living.

Tiburon

This is a wealthy harbor village with great views of San Francisco and Angel Island. The downtown (Main Street) is a popular weekend destination for city dwellers who bicycle over the Golden Gate Bridge to enjoy brunch at Sam's Café on the waterfront. There are many shops, galleries, and restaurants along Tiburon Boulevard. Crime is low and rents are high. A two-bedroom apartment ranges between $1,400 and $2,400 per month.

EAST BAY

ALAMEDA COUNTY
www.alameda.org

This county is located fifteen minutes to a half-hour east of San Francisco across the Bay Bridge. It is a suburban metropolis surrounded by rolling hills and recreational parks. Alameda County communities include Alameda, Albany, Berkeley, Dublin, Emeryville, Fremont, Hayward, Livermore, Newark, Oakland, Claremont/Rockridge, Eastmont, Elmhurst/ Brookfield Village, Forest Park, Fruitvale, Lakeshore/Trestle Glen, Melrose/ Seminary, Millsmont, Montclair/Piedmont Pines, Oak Knoll/Sheffield

Village, Oakmore/Diamond, Temescal, Piedmont, Pleasanton, San Leandro, Union City, Ashland/Cherryland, Castro Valley, and San Lorenzo.

Berkeley

In Berkeley, you can choose to live on the south side by U.C. Berkeley, which is like a suburban Haight-Ashbury, or on the north side, which is more residential. Life on the south side is not for the quiet soul. There is much street life along Telegraph Avenue, and the college town reputation is definitely merited. Crime is higher here due in part to a population of young street people. The north side, on the other hand, is a quieter, gentler community. For the most part, Berkeley is an extremely liberal city that attracts creative, innovative types like artists, educators, and computer professionals. Berkeley is an easy BART commute to San Francisco.

Oakland

This is an ethnically diverse city that is home to the Oakland A's baseball team, the Golden State Warriors basketball team, museums, theater, ballet, symphony, zoo, and a convention center. It is a big city just like San Francisco. Choose your neighborhood carefully, though. Crime is high in the western section, while the east and in the hills are safer. If you live here, you will enjoy affordable rents, mild weather, and lots of activities both in town and over the Bay Bridge in San Francisco. Rents for studio apartments average about $550, one-bedrooms about $750, and two-bedrooms about $1,300.

CONTRA COSTA COUNTY

Once a quiet farm community, this area has developed into an important business and commercial region. Towns include Antioch, Brentwood, Clayton, Concord, Danville, El Cerrito, Hercules, Lafayette, Martinez, Moraga, Orinda, Pinole, Pittsburg, Pleasant Hill, Richmond, San Pablo, San Ramon, and Walnut Creek.

Concord

This is a bedroom community with a thriving business district that creates thousands of white-collar jobs. Some corporations here are Bank of America and Chevron. You can shop at Sun Valley Mall, and Cal-State Hayward has a satellite campus nearby. There are also nineteen parks, golf courses, a community center, and Concord Pavilion concert hall. If you need to get to San Francisco, you're in luck—Concord has a BART station that will take you directly downtown.

Walnut Creek

Even though Walnut Creek has a large retirement community, it has been attracting many single professionals who enjoy Mount Diablo and its surrounding parklands, as well as many restaurants, bookstores, shops, and movie theaters in its downtown. There are also fifteen parks, two golf courses, two libraries, and a brand new Regional Center for the Arts. The commute to San Francisco is a pleasant and easy BART train ride.

PENINSULA

SAN MATEO COUNTY

This area covers Daly City to Menlo Park, encompassing the San Francisco International Airport. Biotechnology, industrial, and business parks are located along Highway 101, the county's main business corridor. San Mateo County communities include Atherton, Belmont, Brisbane, Burlingame, Colma, Daly City, East Palo Alto, Foster City, Half Moon Bay, Hillsborough, Menlo Park, Millbrae, Pacifica, Redwood City, San Bruno, San Carlos, San Mateo, and South San Francisco.

Burlingame

Burlingame is a peaceful bedroom community with ranch-style homes and sycamore-lined streets. San Francisco International Airport is minutes away, which is a plus if you do a lot of traveling for your job, but the noise can be intrusive at times. If you live here, you will enjoy many activities thanks to fifteen parks, tennis and basketball courts, a recreation center, and a fishing pier. Studio apartments rent for around $900 per month, one-bedroom apartments average about $1,300 per month, and two-bedrooms about $1,800.

Foster City

This pleasant and attractive town was built from scratch by a rags-to-riches orphan named Jack Foster. His success was helped by the fact that he bought a piece of land that sits on an island with three sides surrounded by water. This makes for wonderful outdoor activities along the many trails that wander the shoreline. No need to worry about fog, because the town is sheltered by hills and is close to the bay. Foster City has everything a resident could want or need, including a library, recreation center, eighteen parks, and opportunity for employment at more than six hundred businesses, including the headquarters for Visa. The neighborhood residences are a mix of apartments, townhouses, and modest homes, and crime is low.

Menlo Park

This is a clean, well-cared-for suburb with tree-lined streets, nine parks, and a popular farmer's market. This is also home to some Bay Area industry biggies like Sun Microsystems, *Sunset* magazine, and the U.S. Geological Survey. Under construction is a one-million-square-foot engineering and research park that will employ close to 3,600 people. Commutes to San Francisco can either be done by CalTrain or SamTrans buses.

Redwood City

Redwood City is an established, attractive, tree-filled city that has a port and little crime. It does not have the polish of its neighboring Menlo Park and Foster City, but it does have many of the same features. There are seven parks, two municipal swimming pools, three libraries, a nine-hole golf course, four marinas, and a farmer's market in the summer. Redwood City is known as the headquarters for software giant Oracle.

San Mateo

This city has it all: four parks, golf course, marina, farmer's market, arts center, horse racing, wildlife center, bay beach, two big shopping malls, and plenty of open space. If that is not enough for you, then an easy commute along Highways 101 and 280 will get you to San Francisco. This is a well-maintained, middle-class city that offers a comfortable lifestyle.

TEMPORARY
AND PERMANENT
JOB PLACEMENT

WHEN YOU ARE new to a city and need to find work, signing up with an employment agency is a quick and easy way to do it. Most agencies have temporary and permanent job placement departments. While the permanent job placement side searches for full-time work, the temporary side can set you up with short-term job assignments. Temp work is a great way to earn quick cash and get your foot in the door at many companies. It is not uncommon for temporary jobs to turn into full-time permanent jobs. A survey conducted by the National Association of Temporary and Staffing Services (1998) said that nearly three-quarters of temporary workers move on to permanent jobs. Be warned, though, that many employment agencies, both temporary and permanent, get mostly administrative jobs. To the college-educated, this may sound unappealing, but if you have a good attitude and some foresight, these jobs will turn into something better. I am a good example of this.

When I moved to San Francisco after graduate school, I needed to find work right away. Like most people, I had no savings to support me until the perfect job came along. I signed up with eight temp agencies with the attitude that I was happy to be working and perhaps I would find permanent work and eventually get promoted. Well, this attitude paid off. I did administrative temp work for a big bank in a very boring department. I was a hard worker, doing every menial task that was given to me with a positive attitude. I established a good reputation in my department and soon started getting more interesting and challenging projects. I developed a good working relationship with my manager and started telling her about my talents as a writer. I offered to help her with proposals and communication materials for the department. Soon she hired me for the vacant administrative assistant position I was filling as a temp. She kept using my writing skills, and, because I worked for a big bank, I was able to take that experience to a different department and into a more interesting, non-administrative position. If you cannot bear the thought of doing administrative work, there are agencies that place people in contracting positions that involve more expertise, like computers and accounting.

Now I would like to give those of you who have never used an employment agency an overview of what to expect.

The more agencies you sign up with, the better chance you have of finding work. This chapter lists only a few of the many agencies in the Bay Area. Your best bet is to supplement my agency list with the classified ads in the Sunday paper and the telephone book Yellow Pages. When you review the classified ads, you will notice that many of the listed jobs are offered through employment agencies. You can pick your agencies by how interesting you think the jobs they list are. The Yellow Pages will list all agencies in town, sometimes with a description of their services.

Once you choose your agencies, call and make appointments. You will be asked if you are interested in temporary assignments, permanent work, or both. It is recommended you register with both sides so all your bases are covered. Besides, that way you won't go through the registration process twice (temporary and permanent departments are usually run separately in the same agency). I mentioned in chapter 2 that you should call ahead to make your appointment before you move to San Francisco. This is recommended, because you may have to wait up to three weeks before meeting with an agent.

When preparing for your meeting with the agency, make sure you have several copies of your résumé to distribute. If possible, write different versions of your résumé to market yourself for different positions. For example, have a résumé that shows exactly how talented you are, a résumé that highlights your administrative skills, and a résumé that emphasizes your transferable skills.

How you look and dress is also important for these meetings. Even though you are not going to be working for the agency per se, you will be representing them when you go out on interviews or temp assignments. San Francisco is a fairly conservative city despite what you may hear. If you get a chance, have lunch in the Financial District to get an idea of what type of wardrobe professionals wear.

Arrive at the agency on time even though you will probably have to wait. Bring the Sunday newspaper classified section that lists the agency jobs that interest you. During this wait you will be asked to complete an application and show a passport for proof of U.S. residency and a driver's license for identification.

Be prepared to take a battery of tests before you even get to see an agent. Testing is a normal part of the registration and screening process, and you will probably find some of the tests laughably easy. You may be tested on your typing speed and knowledge of certain software programs such as Microsoft Word, Excel, Access, and PowerPoint. They may give you a ten-key, spelling, grammar, math, and filing tests. You will probably wonder why you went to college when you are completing your filing test, but everyone has to do it.

When you finally get to meet with an agent, he or she will review your test scores and ask you what type of job you are looking for. You can say anything you want, but they will probably tell you they fill support positions. If there is an industry you want to get into, for example advertising, the agent can focus on that.

You will then be handed some time sheets and told how the agency works. If you are temping, you will be told to call the agency once a day. I recommend calling in two times a day—first thing in the morning and then around 4 P.M. to be put on the list for the next day. For permanent work, call in once a week or when you see an interesting job listing the agency has put in the paper.

To help you select the right employment agencies to register with, ask the following questions before you schedule an appointment and/or at the time you meet with your counselor:

- *What type of job placement do you do handle—temporary, permanent, executive, or a combination?* Most agencies will have temporary and permanent placement departments, usually with different counselors working in each area. As I mentioned earlier, it is best to register in both areas so that all your bases are covered.

- *What are some typical temporary and permanent positions you fill at your agency?* If you are looking for a technical writing job and the agency mainly gets administrative jobs, then that is not a good fit. Also, be clear with the agency about what you are looking for, because if they can't help you, they may refer you to another agency that can.

- *What is the hourly rate for a temporary job at your agency?* Depending on the job, ranges will be anywhere from $10 per hour for clerical to $85 per hour for computer programmers. Here is a very general average of temp wages:

Receptionist/Clerical	$10 to $12
Administrative/Secretarial	$12 to $18
Accounting/Bookkeeping/Finance	$15 to $22
Desktop Publishing/Graphics	$17 to $20
Legal/Paralegal	$20 to $24
Medical Workers	$9 to $18
Dental Workers	$14 to $36
Technical/Systems	$30 to $85

- *What is the typical salary for a permanent job found through your agency?* This will give you an idea of the job market in the area. Salaries may appear to be high if you are not from California, but you will soon discover the high cost of living in San Francisco makes up for this. If you want a realistic look of competitive salaries in different industries, contact professional organizations or visit your local library for the information. The Internet also has Web sites with salary information. Try **jobsmart.com** for profession-specific salary surveys.

- *What skills and qualifications would make me most marketable in the workforce your agency deals with?* This will help you assess your own skills and decide where you need more training. In general, computer skills and knowledge of many software programs are always a plus in the temporary job force. Also, more specialized agencies that handle medical, dental, legal, and insurance professions may require certain licensing or experience levels.

- *How long will it take to find a temporary or permanent job once I register?* This usually depends on your skill level and the job market. Also, those people who have been registered with the agency for a while will probably get priority on temporary jobs because of their experience and reputation.

- *Who are some of your clients?* Agencies may not always reveal who their clients are. If this is the case and you have specific companies in mind you would like to work for, say, The Gap or Levi's, the agency can tell you if they are clients or perhaps refer you to the agency handling those accounts. Another option is to call the company's human resources department and ask what temp agencies they use.

- *How soon can I get an appointment with the agency?* Depending on how popular the agency is, this can range from one day to three weeks. Call early to be on the safe side.

- *How much time should be set aside for the appointment?* Registration will take about one to two hours, so plan your schedule accordingly.

- *What should I bring with me?* The state of California requires that all job applicants present a passport or other form of identification that proves eligibility to work in the United States. Besides that, agencies may ask for the following: copies of your résumé, letters of recommendation, references, driver's license or other form of identification, and school transcripts.

- *Which tests do you administer to applicants?* There will be basic evaluation tests such as math, filing, spelling, grammar, accounting, and whatever else is appropriate for the agency. There will also be tests on the computer for typing speed and knowledge of different software programs like Microsoft Word and Excel. Ask the agency which tests they administer so you can brush up ahead of time.

- *Do you offer any training or benefits?* Most agencies will offer some type of benefits and training, whether it's a discounted health plan, a software tutorial, or vacation pay after working a certain number of hours.

- *How often would I need to call in for work?* Some agencies will say to call in once every couple of days, while others are specific about the time and frequency you should check in. When you are starting out, it is better to call more frequently so the office receptionist and your counselor become familiar with you.

- *What advice do you give to your temps?* This is a great question to get insight about the temporary workforce from people who know it best. Counselors will talk to you about things like dress code and attitude. On specific assignments, they can tell you about your supervisor's personality or the experience the last temp had. This is beneficial to get you in the right frame of mind for work.

PERSONNEL AGENCIES

The following is a list of some local Bay Area personnel agencies. This list incorporates the top twenty-five agencies in the Bay Area, as named in the *1998 Book of Lists* published by the *San Francisco Business Times*. Also included are a number of agencies that answered a survey for this chapter. Remember, the phone book and newspapers are also good resources for finding agencies in the area.

ABA Staffing
2121 South El Camino Real,
Suite 605
San Mateo, CA 94403
(650) 349-9200
www.abastaff.com

Industries: Accounting, retail, general office, secretarial, banking, finance, telemarketing, sales, technical, marketing, legal, direct mail, hospitality

Benefits and training: Both

ABAR Staffing Service
595 Market Street, Suite 950
San Francisco, CA 94105
(415) 243-9700
www.abarstaffing.com

Industries: Finance, accounting, administration, sales, marketing, management, clerical, hospitality

Benefits and training: Both

Accountants On Call
44 Montgomery Street, Suite 2310
San Francisco, CA 94104
(415) 398-3366
www.aocnet.com

Industries: Finance, accounting, clerical

Benefits and training: Benefits only

Accountemps
388 Market Street, Suite 1400
San Francisco, CA 94111
(415) 434-1900
www.accountemps.com

Industries: Finance, accounting

Benefits and training: Both

Adecco International
100 Redwood Shores Parkway
Redwood City, CA 94065
(650) 610-1000
www.adecco.com

Industries: Finance, accounting, sales, management, engineering, marketing, administration, technical/systems, clerical, hospitality, executives

Benefits and training: Both

Alper & Associates Personnel Service
353 Sacramento Street, Suite 1860
San Francisco, CA 94111
(415) 397-6611
www.alperpersonnel.com

Industries: Administration, corporate, legal

Benefits and training: Both

American Technical
39899 Balentine Drive, Suite 140
Newark, CA 94560
(510) 623-3600
www.atnes.com

Industries: Finance, accounting, sales, marketing, management, engineering, administration, technical/systems, clerical, hospitality

Benefits and training: Both

AppleOne Employment Services
1515 South El Camino Real, 3rd Floor
San Mateo, CA 94402
(650) 358-8888
www.appleone.com

Industries: Finance, accounting, sales, marketing, management, technical/systems, administration, clerical, hospitality

Benefits and training: Both

ArtLinks
1450 Fourth Street, Suite 10
Berkeley, CA 94710
(510) 528-2668
www.artlinks-staffing.com

Industries: Graphic design, multimedia, publishing

Benefits and training: None

Bradford Staff, Inc.
130 Battery Street, Suite 600
San Francisco, CA 94111
(415) 362-0435
www.bradfordstaff.com

Industries: Sales, marketing, management, technical/systems, administration, clerical

Benefits and training: Both

CDI Corporation West
44 Montgomery Street
San Francisco, CA 94104
(415) 434-1841
www.cdicorp.com

Industries: Finance, accounting, sales, marketing, engineering, administration, technical/systems, clerical

Benefits and training: None

Certified Personnel

111 Pine Street, Suite 710
San Francisco, CA 94111
(415) 677-9900
www.certified-personnel.com

Industries: Finance, accounting, marketing, administration, technical, clerical, hospitality, legal

Benefits and training: Both

Corestaff/Roberta Enterprises, Inc.

180 Montgomery Street, Suite 1840
San Francisco, CA 94104
(415) 433-7624

Industries: Administration, clerical

Benefits and training: Benefits only

Diversified Personnel

1300 Clay Street, Suite 530
Oakland, CA 94612
(510) 873-8500
www.diversifiedpersonnel.com

Industries: Finance, accounting, administration, clerical

Benefits and training: Both

The Eastridge Group

311 California Street, 6th Floor
San Francisco, CA 94104
(415) 616-9710
www.sfeastridge.com

Industries: Finance, accounting, engineering, administration, technical/systems, clerical

Benefits and training: Both

Gary D. Nelson & Associates

425 California Street, Suite 600
San Francisco, CA 94104
(415) 989-9911
www.gonelson.com

Industries: Finance, accounting, engineering, administration, technical/systems, clerical, executives

Benefits and training: Both

Innovations PSI

345 California Street, Suite 1750
San Francisco, CA 94104
(415) 392-4022

Industries: Finance, accounting, administration, technical/systems, clerical, hospitality

Benefits and training: Both

Interim Personnel

44 Montgomery Street, Suite 1250
San Francisco, CA 94104
(415) 391-5979
www.interim.com

Industries: Finance, accounting, sales, marketing, administration, clerical

Benefits and training: Both

Industries: Finance, accounting, sales, marketing, management, engineering, administration, technical/systems, clerical, hospitality

Benefits and training: Both

Kelly Services, Inc.
50 California Street, Suite 2320
San Francisco, CA 94111
(415) 675-3023
www.kellyservices.com

Industries: Finance, accounting, sales, marketing, management, engineering, administration, technical/systems, clerical, hospitality

Benefits and training: Both

Key Resources Inc.
101 California Street, Suite 650
San Francisco, CA 94111
(415) 986-6700
www.keyresources.com

Industries: Finance, accounting, sales, marketing, administration, clerical

Benefits and training: Both

Madsen Staffing Services
120 Montgomery Street, Suite 2075
San Francisco, CA 94104
(415) 433-1018

Industries: Finance, accounting, sales, marketing, administration, clerical

Benefits and training: Both

McCall Staffing Services
351 California Street, Suite 1200
San Francisco, CA 94104
(415) 981-3400

Industries: Finance, accounting, administration, clerical

Benefits and training: Both

New Boston Systems
27 Maiden Lane, Suite 300
San Francisco, CA 94108
800-339-5339 (within California);
(415) 788-8488
www.newboston.com

Industries: Technical, programming, engineering, computers

Benefits and training; Benefits only

Office Team
388 Market Street, Suite 1400
San Francisco, CA 94111
(415) 434-2429
www.officeteam.com

Industries: Administration, clerical

Benefits and training: Both

Olsten Staffing Services, Inc.
120 Montgomery Street, Suite 700
San Francisco, CA 94104
(415) 433-1110
www.olsten.com

Industries: Finance, accounting, sales, engineering, marketing, administration, technical/systems, clerical, hospitality, executives

Benefits and training: Both

The People Connection

230 California Street, Suite 501
San Francisco, CA 94111
(415) 397-5517
www.people-connection.com

Industries: Administration, clerical

Benefits and training: Benefits only

ProServ

110 Sutter Street, Suite 600
San Francisco, CA 94104
(415) 781-6100

Industries: Finance, accounting, sales, management, marketing, administration, technical/systems, clerical, hospitality

Benefits and training: Both

Pro Staff Personnel Service

222 Front Street, Suite 700
San Francisco, CA 94111
(415) 986-8500
www.prostaff.com

Industries: Finance, accounting, marketing, sales, management, administration, technical/systems, clerical, hospitality

Benefits and training: Both

Remedy Intelligent Staffing

595 Market Street, Suite 1150
San Francisco, CA 94105
(415) 243-8566
www.remedystaff.com

Industries: Finance, marketing, administration, clerical, hospitality

Benefits and training: Both

Industries: Finance, accounting, sales, management, engineering, administration, technical/systems, clerical, hospitality; executives

Benefits and training: Both

The Right People

155 Montgomery Street, #1600
San Francisco, CA 94104
(415) 705-5333
www.rightpeople.com

Industries: Clerical, word processing, administrative, graphics, desktop publishing; reception

Benefits and training: Both

TAC Staffing Services

24301 Southland Drive, Suite 607
Hayward, CA 94545
(510) 786-0922
www.tacstaffing.com

Industries: Finance, accounting, engineering, administration, technical/systems, clerical

Benefits and training: Both

Talent Tree Staffing Services

343 Sansome Street, Suite 170
San Francisco, CA 94104
(415) 391-2333
www.ttree.com

Industries: Finance, accounting, sales, marketing, administration, clerical, hospitality

Benefits and training: Both

Temporary Skills Unlimited (TSU)
2380 Salvio Street, Suite 300
Concord, CA 94520
(510) 827-5627

Industries: Finance, accounting, marketing, administration, technical, clerical

Benefits and training: Both

Truex Associates
332 Pine Street, Suite 400
San Francisco, CA 94104
(415) 433-6222

Industries: Finance, accounting, engineering, management, administration, technical/systems, clerical, hospitality, executives

Benefits and training: Both

Volt Services Group
340 Pine Street, Suite 504
San Francisco, CA 94104
(415) 391-6830
www.volt.com

Industries: Finance, accounting, sales, management, executive, engineering, marketing, administration, technical/systems, clerical, hospitality

Benefits and training: Both

Western Staff Services
301 Lennon Lane
Walnut Creek, CA 94598
(510) 930-5300
www.westaff.com

Industries: Finance, accounting, management, engineering, marketing, administration, technical/systems, clerical, hospitality, executives

Benefits and training: Both

SPECIALIZED TEMPORARY EMPLOYMENT AGENCIES

DENTAL

Dental Fill-Ins Placement Agency
2027 Van Ness Avenue
San Francisco, CA 94109
(415) 771-2426

Dental Plus Medical (DPM)
490 Post Street, Suite 1701
San Francisco, CA 94102
(415) 677-0961

Dental Power
450 Sutter, Suite 2315
San Francisco, CA 94102
(415) 781-2909

INSURANCE

Insurance Personnel Service
120 Montgomery Street, Suite 2500
San Francisco, CA 94104
(415) 391-5900

The Tetsell Group
350 California Street, Suite 1750
San Francisco, CA 94104
(415) 392-4000

LEGAL

The Affiliates
388 Market Street, Suite 1420
San Francisco, CA 94111
(415) 982-2001

Chapman Williams International
300 Montgomery Street, Suite 860
San Francisco, CA 94104
(415) 392-2729

Exclusively Legal
311 California Street, Sixth Floor
San Francisco, CA 94104
(415) 616-9733

Legal Staff
433 California Street, Suite 904
San Francisco, CA 94104
(415) 433-3230

Mark Associates
300 Montgomery Street, Suite 860
San Francisco, CA 94104
(415) 392-1835

Specialists Group
655 Montgomery Street, Suite 515
San Francisco, CA 94111
(415) 421-9400

MEDICAL

Medical Center Agency
870 Market Street, Suite 650
San Francisco, CA 94102
(415) 397-9440

Medi-Quest Staffing Services
120 Montgomery Street, Suite 2075
San Francisco, CA 94104
(415) 421-7183

TECHNICAL

Manpower Technical
1390 Willow Pass Road, Suite 130
Concord, CA 94520
(925) 825-8585
www.manpower.com

PC Processors
353 Sacramento Street, Suite 600
San Francisco, CA 94111
(415) 986-2844
www.pcprocessors.com

Tech Search
2015 Bridgeway, Suite 301
Sausalito, CA 94965
(415) 332-1282
www.jobsight.com

The local phone company has a Local Talk tips line to give you information about temporary agencies. The main number is (415) 837-5050, and the choices are

1510   How a temporary agency works
1515   Information you may need
1520   Fees
1525   The interview

CHAPTER EIGHT

MORE JOB-FINDING IDEAS

IN CHAPTER 7, I talked about the different temporary and permanent job placement agencies in San Francisco. If you are new to the city and/or need to find work right away, enlisting an agency's help is probably the quickest and easiest way to do it. You can combine that method of job searching with your own efforts. However, there are many other ways to find work in San Francisco. The most obvious is to look through the newspaper classified ads. If your goal is a managerial job, then executive recruiters are a good bet. You can also research different Bay Area companies and contact them yourself. In this chapter, I will list different options for finding a job in San Francisco. I will also reference several excellent resources to help you with your own research.

EXECUTIVE RECRUITERS

Executive recruiters work with people who have held management positions, make over $40,000 a year, or are proven in their field. The following is a list of the fifteen largest contingency executive search firms in the Bay Area as ranked in the *1998 Book of Lists* published by the *San Francisco Business Times*. Many more can be found either in the Yellow Pages under "Executive Search" or researching the job-finding books listed at the end of this chapter.

Accountants Executive Search

44 Montgomery Street, Suite 2310
San Francisco, CA 94104
(415) 398-3800

Areas of specialization: Accounting and finance

Carhaghe and Gibbs Business Solutions

220 Sansome Street, Suite 800
San Francisco, CA 94104
(415) 956-6400
www.cgusa.com

Areas of specialization: Finance, accounting, professional temporaries, computer consultants

Culver Personnel Inc.

690 Market Street, Suite 200
San Francisco, CA 94104
(415) 956-9911
www.culvercorp.com

Areas of specialization: Sales and sales management, high technology, Internet hardware, software, networking, pharmaceutical, business services, industrial

Edward Bell Associates

50 First Street, Suite 320
San Francisco, CA 94105
(415) 442-0270

Areas of specialization: Accounting, finance, data processing, real estate, clerical

Major, Hagen & Africa

655 Commercial Street
San Francisco, CA 94111
(415) 956-1010

Areas of specialization: Corporate counsel, law firm partners and associates

Management Recruiters International

591 Redwood Highway, Suite 2225
Mill Valley, CA 94941
(415) 383-7044
www.mrimvca.com

Areas of specialization: Computer hardware and software, data communications, semiconductors, Internet, emerging technologies

Montgomery Resources, Inc.

555 Montgomery Street, Suite 1650
San Francisco, CA 94111
(415) 956-4242
www.montres.com

Areas of specialization: Accounting and finance

Next Step Recruiting

3130 La Selva Drive, Suite 105
San Mateo, CA 94403
(650) 577-8000
www.4nextstep.com

Areas of specialization: Software, consulting, outsourcing, sales, business products, retail management

Parker & Lynch
101 California Street, Suite 1825
San Francisco, CA 94111
(415) 956-6700
www.parkerlynch.com

Areas of specialization: Finance and accounting

Robert Grant Associates/ RGA Associates
100 Pine Street, Suite 2225
San Francisco, CA 94111
(415) 981-7424

Areas of specialization: Consumer marketing, advertising, high-tech sales, biotech, health care, hardware/software engineers

Robert Half
388 Market Street, Suite 1400
San Francisco, CA 94111
(415) 434-1900
www.roberthalf.com

Areas of specialization: Accounting, finance, banking, information systems

Sales Consultants
480 Roland Way, Suite 103
Oakland, CA 94621
(510) 569-6231
www.scsanfran.com

Areas of specialization: Sales in medical, pharmaceutical, telecommunications, chemical, environmental, business/computer projects

Search West
100 Pine Street
San Francisco, CA 94111
(415) 788-1770

Areas of specialization: Finance, accounting, human resources, energy, sales, technology, engineering, mail order, food and beverage

SmartSource Inc.
500 Ygnacio Valley Road, Suite 390
Walnut Creek, CA 94596
(510) 935-4200
www.smartsourceinc.com

Areas of specialization: Telecommunications, PC/LAN/WAN, information systems, client server

Tech Search
2015 Bridgeway, Suite 301
Sausalito, CA 94965
(415) 332-1282
www.jobsight.com

Areas of specialization: Telecommunications, software developers, CEOs, CTOs, directors of technology

COMPANY JOB LINES

Company job lines are a good way to find out if a company has job opportunities without making cold calls. Listings are usually updated weekly.

24 Hour Fitness
P.O. Box 9071
Pleasanton, CA 94566
(925) 416-3194
www.24hourfitness.com

Industry: Fitness centers

Airtouch Communications
1 California Street
San Francisco, CA 94111
(800) 282-3530
www.airtouch.com

Industry: Cellular communications

Asian Art Museum
Golden Gate Park
San Francisco, CA 94118
(415) 379-8802
www.asianart.org

Industry: Art

Bank of America
Bank of America Center
San Francisco, CA 94104
(415) 241-5023
www.bankamerica.com

Industry: Banking

Bechtel Corp.
50 Beale Street
San Francisco, CA 94105
(415) 768-4448
www.bechtel.com

Industry: Engineering, construction, development and management

Birkenstock Footprints Sandals
P.O. Box 1640
Novato, CA 94948
(415) 892-4400 ext. 622

Industry: Importer and distributor of footwear

Brøderbund Software
500 Redwood Parkway
Novato, CA 94948
(415) 382-4404
www.broderbund.com

Industry: Software developer and publisher

California Academy of Sciences
Golden Gate Park
San Francisco, CA 94118
(415) 750-7333
www.calacademy.org

Industry: Science

California School Library Association
1499 Old Bayshore Highway,
Suite 142
Burlingame, CA 94010
(415) 697-8832
www.cla-net.org

Industry: Library

California State Automobile Association

100 Van Ness Avenue
San Francisco, CA 94102
(415) 565-2194
www.csaa.com

Industry: Auto, insurance

Cellular One

651 Gateway Boulevard, Suite 1500
South San Francisco, CA 94080
(650) 827-5490
www.cellone-sf.com

Industry: Wireless communication service

Charles Schwab

101 Montgomery Street
San Francisco, CA 94104
(415) 627-7227
www.schwab.com

Industry: Brokerage and financial services

Chevron Corp.

P575 Market Street
San Francisco, CA 94104
(415) 894-2552
Richmond: (510) 242-5523
www.chevron.com

Industry: Petroleum refining

Chronicle Publishing Co.

901 Mission Street
San Francisco, CA 94103
(415) 777-8485
www.sfgate.com

Industry: Newspaper, broadcasting, and book publishing

City and County of San Francisco

44 Gough Street
San Francisco, CA 94103
(415) 557-4888
www.ci.sf.ca.us

Industry: City and county government

Clorox Co.

1221 Broadway Street
Oakland, CA 94612
(510) 271-7625
www.clorox.com

Industry: Specialty cleaners, polishes, and sanitation goods

Davies Medical Center

Castro and Duboce Streets
San Francisco, CA 94114
(415) 565-6104
www.daviesmed.org

Industry: General medical and surgical hospital

Esprit

900 Minnesota Avenue
San Francisco, CA 94107
(415) 550-3998
www.esprit.com

Industry: Women's clothing

Exploratorium

3601 Lyon Street
San Francisco, CA 94123
(415) 561-0328
www.exploratorium.edu
Industry: Science museum

Federal Job Information Center

211 Main Street
San Francisco, CA 94105
(415) 744-5627
www.clubfed.com
Industry: Federal jobs

Federal Reserve Bank of San Francisco

101 Market Street
San Francisco, CA 94105
(415) 974-3330
www.frbsf.org
Industry: Banking

Franklin Resources

777 Mariners Island Boulevard
San Mateo, CA 94404
(650) 312-JOBS (5627)
www.frk.com
Industry: Mutual funds and investment management

Gap Incorporated

1 Harrison Street
San Francisco, CA 94105
(888) 442-7562
www.gap.com
Industry: Clothing manufacturer

Genentech Inc.

1 DNA Way
South San Francisco, CA 94080
(650) 225-2580
www.gene.com
Industry: Biotechnology/biopharmaceuticals

Golden Gate Transit

1011 Andersen Drive
San Rafael, CA 94901
(415) 257-4545
www.goldengate.org
Industry: Transportation

Good Guys

7000 Marina Boulevard
Brisbane, CA 94005
(650) 615-6051 (corporate)
800-JOB-GUYS (stores)
www.thegoodguys.com
Industry: Retail consumer electronics

Gymboree Corp.

700 Airport Boulevard
Burlingame, CA 94010
(415) 579-0600
www.gymboree.com
Industry: Children's apparel and retail

Hambrecht & Quist Group

One Bush Street
San Francisco, CA 94104
(415) 399-4338
www.hamquist.com
Industry: Investment banking

Hilton Hotel
1 Hilton Square
San Francisco, CA 94102
(415) 923-5068
www.hilton.com

Industry: Hotels and hospitality

Kaiser Permanente
One Kaiser Plaza
Oakland, CA 94612
(415) 202-2500
www.ca.kaiserpermanente.org

Industry: Health care

KGO Channel 7
900 Front Street
San Francisco, CA 94111
(415) 954-7958
www.citysearch7.com/kgo

Industry: Television broadcasting

KPIX Channel 5
855 Battery Street
San Francisco, CA 94111
(415) 765-8609
www.kpix.com

Industry: Television broadcasting

KQED Channel 9
2601 Mariposa Street
San Francisco, CA 94110
(415) 553-2303
www.kqed.org

Industry: Public television station

KRON Channel 4
1001 Van Ness Avenue
San Francisco, CA 94109
(415) 561-8662
www.kron.com

Industry: Television broadcasting
station

Levi Strauss and Co.
1155 Battery Street
San Francisco, CA 94111
(415) 501-7828
www.levi.com

Industry: Clothing manufacturer

Lucasfilm
P.O. Box 2009
San Rafael, CA 94912
(415) 662-1999
www.lucasfilm.com

Industry: Film

McKesson Corp.
One Post Street, McKesson Plaza
San Francisco, CA 94104
(415) 983-8409
www.mckesson.com

Industry: Drug and toiletries distribution

NASA Ames Research Center
Nasa Mail Stop 2448
Moffet Field, CA 94035
(650) 604-8000
huminfo.arc.nasa.gov

Industry: Air and space

North Face Inc.
2013 Farallon Drive
San Leandro, CA 94577
(510) 618-3500 (ask to be connected to their job hotline)

Industry: Sporting goods

Pacific Bell and Pacific Telesis
140 New Montgomery Street
San Francisco, CA 94105
800-924-JOBS (5627)
www.pactel.com

Industry: Telephone communications and telecommunications

Pacific Gas and Electric (PG&E)
77 Beale Street
San Francisco, CA 94177
(415) 973-5195
www.pge.com

Industry: Utility company

PC World Communications
501 2nd Street
San Francisco, CA 94107
(415) 978-3100
www.pcworld.com

Industry: Computer magazines

Peet's Coffee & Tea Inc.
1400 Park Avenue
Emeryville, CA 94608
(888) 733-8715
www.peets.com

Industry: Coffee and tea retailers

PeopleSoft, Inc.
4440 Rosewood Drive
Pleasanton, CA 94588
(510) 225-3000
www.peoplesoft.com

Industry: Computer software

Safeway Inc.
5918 Stoneridge Mall Road
Pleasanton, CA 94566
(800) 988-5175
www.safeway.com

Industry: Supermarkets

San Francisco Museum of Modern Art
151 Third Street
San Francisco, CA 94103
(415) 357-4000
www.sfmoma.org

Industry: Modern art museum

San Francisco Newspaper Agency
925 Mission Street
San Francisco, CA 94103
(415) 777-7642
www.sfgate.com

Industry: Newspaper publisher

San Francisco State University
1600 Holloway Avenue
San Francisco, CA 94132
(415) 338-1871
www.sfsu.edu

Industry: Education

San Francisco Unified School District Classified Jobs
135 Van Ness Avenue
San Francisco, CA 94102
(415) 241-6162
nisus.sfusd.k12.ca.us

Industry: Teaching and education

Sierra Club
85 Second Street, 2nd Floor
San Francisco, CA 94105
(415) 977-5744
www.sierraclub.org

Industry: Environmental

Sharper Image Corp.
650 Davis Street
San Francisco, CA 94111
(415) 445-6000 (ask to be connected to their job hotline)
www.sharperimage.com

Industry: Retail

Sybase Inc.
6475 Christie Avenue
Emeryville, CA 94608
(510) 922-8494
www.sybase.com/careers

Industry: Client/server software

Transamerica Corp.
600 Montgomery Street
San Francisco, CA 94111
(415) 983-4900
www.transamerica.com

Industry: Insurance

Union Bank
350 California Street
San Francisco, CA 94104
(415) 705-7013
www.uboc.com

Industry: Banking

University of California, San Francisco Campus
3rd & Parnassus Avenues
San Francisco, CA 94143
(415) 502-5627
www.ucsf.edu

Industry: Education

U.S. Geological Survey
345 Middlefield Road
Menlo Park, CA 94025
(415) 329-4122
www.usgs.gov

Industry: Geology

U.S. Postal Service
1300 Evans Avenue
San Francisco, CA 94124
(415) 550-5534 (ext. 1)
www.usps.gov

Industry: Postal

Williams-Sonoma
3250 Van Ness Avenue
San Francisco, CA 94109
(415) 421-7900 (ask to be connected to their job hotline)
www.williams-sonoma.com

Industry: Retail cookware shops/catalog

Workforce Solutions

A Division of International
Business Machines (IBM)
425 Market Street
San Francisco, CA 94105

(415) 545-3756
www.empl.ibm.com

Industry: Computers, business
machines

PROFESSIONAL ORGANIZATIONS/
CAREER DEVELOPMENT SERVICES

The following listing contains the names of various nonprofit career
development organizations and professional societies that serve as job-
finding resources. Membership rates and services are subject to change.

Alumnae Resources

120 Montgomery Street, Suite 600
San Francisco, CA 94104

(415) 274-4747
(415) 274-4715 Fax

www.ar.org

Description: Alumnae Resources is a unique career development organization offering career planning and job-search assistance in a professional and supportive environment. They provide a comprehensive
range of services to Bay Area women and men who are seeking to
begin, advance, or change their careers.

Fee: $95 membership

What You Get: Discounts on programs and workshops, counseling ses-
sions, unlimited use of the Resource Center reference library, access to the
CareerLine touch-tone job hotline, attendance at membership support
groups, subscription to AR's quarterly newsletter and calendar, and more.

Note: Call or write for a newsletter/calendar and see for yourself what
they offer. There are also orientations of the center several times a week.

Chamber of Commerce Job Forum

465 California Street, 9th Floor
San Francisco, CA 94104

(415) 392-4520
www.sfchamber.com

Description: The Job Forum is a unique community service aimed at helping people help themselves in their job search. The emphasis is on intelligently planning and conducting a job-finding campaign. The Forum is neither a placement service nor an employment agency.

Fee: None

How It Works: Every Wednesday evening, from 6:30 P.M. to 8:30 P.M., a rotating panel of four experts from business, academia, and government volunteer their time to discuss a wide variety of individual job-finding problems. Attendees are welcome to discuss their own situations in open session. Attendees are also encouraged to exchange with one another any helpful job information they may have. Typical topics include newcomers to the community, recent graduates, job information sources, voluntary or involuntary termination.

Note: Call or write the Chamber of Commerce for an informational brochure.

Experience Unlimited

3120 Mission Street
San Francisco, CA 94102
(415) 695-6500
www.edd.cahwnet.gov

Description: This service is sponsored by the California State Employment Development Department. It offers career counseling, testing, résumé assistance, and workshops. They also have job listings and computerized job matching.

Fee: Free, but requires volunteer time at the center

International Association of Business Communicators (IABC)

San Francisco Chapter
One Hallidie Plaza, Suite 600
San Francisco, CA 94102
(415) 773-9654 (Infoline)
(415) 433-3400 (membership info)
www.iabc.com

Description: This is an organization of Bay Area communications professionals whose mission is to help members develop professional and ethical excellence and contribute more effectively to their organizations and their communities. It offers valuable contact with other communication professionals through regular meetings, awards competitions, seminars, and other projects.

Fee: $246 membership

What You Get: Membership includes a subscription to *Communication World* magazine, biweekly *Leads* job listings, discounts on monthly programs, professional development seminars and round-tables.

Note: IABC events are open to the public and can be found on the IABC Web site or by calling the Infoline phone number listed. Also, you can request a sample issue of *Leads*, the twice-monthly job listing newsletter.

LifePlan Center

53rd Street, Suite 324
San Francisco, CA 94103
(415) 546-4499
(415) 777-1396 (fax)
www.lifeplancenter.org

Description: A nonprofit organization dedicated to men and women in their fifties, sixties, and seventies who are in transition as they address changes in their work and personal lives.

Fee: $70 membership

What You Get: Bimonthly newsletter and calendar, orientation to the center, peer guidance, resource network, women's and men's forums, work strategies, access to the resource center including job listings, and discounts on workshops and programs.

Note: This is an independent project of Alumnae Resources. Call or write for a newsletter and calendar.

Media Alliance

814 Mission Street, Suite 205
San Francisco, CA 94103
www.media-alliance.org
(415) 546-6334 (general info)
(415) 546-6491 (classes)

Description: This is a nonprofit organization that serves media and communications professionals. It is also an advocacy organization for media issues such as media access and professional responsibility.

Fee: $55 standard membership plus $25 for JobFile Access. Check out their Web site for other membership options.

What You Get: Quarterly class brochure, discounts on classes, discounted health insurance, and JobFile with access to listings of Bay Area media jobs. Many reputable Bay Area companies list their jobs here. Listings fall into categories such as freelance, permanent/full-time, and internships.

Note: Ask about volunteering your services in exchange for free classes.

National Writers Union

Local 3 San Francisco Bay Area
337 17th Street, Suite 101
Oakland, CA 94612
(510) 839-1248
(415) 979-5522 (Technical Writing Job Hotline)
www.igc.apc.org/nwu/

Description: The National Writers Union (NWU) is an innovative labor union committed to improving the economic and business concerns of freelance writers through the collective strength of its members. Members include journalists, novelists, biographers, historians, poets, commercial writers, and technical writers. Some union activities include handling grievances, working with journalists and their contracts, helping book authors get fair contracts, and operating a Writers Job Hotline with available technical and business writing jobs.

Fee: $50 to $95, based on a sliding scale according to what you earn as a writer and length of membership

What You Get: Membership in the NWU is open to all qualified writers, published and unpublished. Membership includes *American Writer*, a quarterly newsletter; invitations to forums, seminars, and workshops; contract assistance, access to an agent database, discounted health plan, and more.

Association for Women in Communications (AWC)

120 Village Square, Suite 143
Orinda, CA 94563
(510) 253-1784 (office)
(510) 253-8685 Job Hotline (members only)

Description: AWC, formerly Women in Communications (WICI), is an international organization with more than seven thousand members and eighty chapters. The Bay Area chapter has a membership of over three hundred women representing all areas of the communications industry. AWC is dedicated to professional development through an annual conference and local educational programs and awards.

Fee: $180

What You Get: Use of the AWC Job Bank hotline, the *Bridge* monthly chapter newsletter, the *Matrix* national monthly newsletter, membership directories, and monthly events featuring high-profile speakers.

WORLD WIDE WEB RESOURCES

The following list of Internet job-finding resources for the San Francisco Bay Area is not complete. Some Web sites offer their own specific services, and others link to different resources related to your job search.

CareerMosaic
(www.careermosaic.com)

Jobsmart.Org
(www.jobsmart.org)

Bay Area Jobs
(www.bayareacareers.com)

Yahoo San Francisco Bay Area Employment
(www.sfbay.yahoo.com/employment)

Internet Online Career Center
(www.occ.com)

San Francisco Chronicle *and* **Examiner** *Job Classifieds*
(www.sfgate.com)

Opportunity NOCs
(www.opportunitynocs.org)
This is a weekly publication of job openings and information in the nonprofit sector.

CHAPTER NINE

GETTING INVOLVED IN THE CITY

SAN FRANCISCO IS a major metropolitan city, and it offers its residents countless activities that are fun, safe, and social. Getting involved in the city by joining a health club or professional organization, by volunteering, or by taking a class will enable you to meet people who share similar interests while doing something you enjoy. Before you know it, your social calendar will be filled seven nights a week. Here are a few things to remember before joining a club or organization, especially if a fee is involved:

Make sure you are doing something you enjoy. If you join Encore (the young professionals' group that supports the ballet) but you hate the ballet, then you are not going to click with the true ballet enthusiasts there. You are better off joining the museum club because you love modern art.

Make sure your involvement will help you meet your goals in some way. For example, by joining a gym you will be able to work toward your goal of losing ten pounds. By taking a class in personal finance you will be able to plan for your financial future. Perhaps you have used the services of the Red Cross and you want to give back to that organization by volunteering your time.

Understand any commitment it may involve. This is especially true if you decide to volunteer or take a class. Nonprofit organizations depend on their volunteers, and many require a once-a-week, six-month commitment to start out. If you are taking a class, make sure your schedule allows you to be there, on time, the once or twice a week it may meet.

So do your research. Contact organizations and clubs and ask for information, visit the facilities, request guest passes, check out homepages, and put your name on mailing lists.

HEALTH AND FITNESS

The city of San Francisco could be considered one big health club. Climbing the hills is as effective as a Stairmaster workout. You can find countless books about the glorious bike trails all around the Bay Area, like the ride from San Francisco over the Golden Gate Bridge and into Sausalito. And for a funky experience, join a tai chi session at Washington Square Park in North Beach—you'll be balancing on one leg with almost a hundred Chinese neighbors.

San Francisco and the Bay Area have many healthy workout opportunities, including quality health clubs and sports clubs. Once you get to know the area, you will discover more opportunities to stay fit and meet friends. Request newsletters from sports clubs to find out what they do. Health clubs will usually let you try out their facilities for free before joining. Health club fees vary depending on special promotions being run or, in some cases, whom you happen to talk to. Make sure you negotiate for the best deal.

HEALTH CLUBS IN THE BAY AREA

Joining a health club is a good way to interact with others while staying in shape. It can put some routine in your life during the period of uncertainty and change that comes from your move to the Bay Area. You may be doing temporary work at a different company each week, but you can escape to the same health club and start recognizing familiar faces. The following is a list of health clubs and their offerings.

24 Hour Fitness
Various locations
800-24-WORKOUT
(800-24-967-5688)
www.24hourfitness.com

24 Hour Fitness has the most locations throughout San Francisco and the Bay Area. Each location offers different amenities. These fitness centers are the most affordable, and they constantly run membership specials. Ask for free passes.

Amenities: Aerobics, weight machines, free weights, cardio, and more, depending on the site

Bay Club

150 Greenwich Street
San Francisco, CA 94111
www.sfbayclub.com

or

555 California Street
(Bank of America Center)
San Francisco, CA 94104
www.bayclubbofa.com
(415) 433-2550 (Membership)

This is an upscale yuppie health club with excellent facilities.

Amenities: Greenwich Street—Pool, racquetball, squash, aerobics, tennis, sun deck, parking, social activities; Bank of America Center—Cardio, free weights, machine weights, aerobics, women's workout area, steam room, sauna, hot tub, massage, spa, personal trainer, laundry, towel service, tanning, parking

Club One

Various locations
(415) 288-1000
www.clubone.com

Club One has several locations throughout San Francisco and the Bay Area. Each location offers different amenities. They also have a reciprocity program with other sport, tennis, and golf clubs in the area. Check out their Web site for membership information and club details.

Amenities: Cardio, aerobics, free weights, machine weights, personal trainer, pool, racquetball courts, tennis courts, laundry, towel service, steam room, child care

Cole Valley Fitness

957 Cole Street
San Francisco, CA 94117
(415) 665-3330

This is a basic neighborhood, no-frills gym.

Amenities: Cardio, free weights, machine weights, personal trainers

Crunch Fitness

1000 Van Ness Avenue
San Francisco, CA 94109
(415) 931-1100
www.crunchfitness.com

This is a 30,000-square-foot state-of-the-art facility that strives to create an environment where members don't feel self-conscious about their bodies.

Amenities: Aerobics, cardio, machine weights, free weights, indoor rockclimbing, boxing, yoga, personal training, massage, sauna, discounted parking

Embarcadero YMCA

169 Steuart Street
San Francisco, CA 94105
(415) 957-9622
www.embarcaderoymca.org

Modern, clean facilities with classes and equipment for every fitness level. Cardio machines, like Stairmasters, look out on the Bay, which makes for a great after-work stress release.

Amenities: Cardio, aerobics, free weights, machine weights, pool, racquetball, squash, basketball, massage, towel service, personal trainer, volleyball, steam room, sauna, Jacuzzi, sun deck

Golden Gateway Tennis and Swim Club

370 Drumm Street
San Francisco, CA 94111
(415) 616-8800
www.ggtsc.com

This is San Francisco's only outdoor tennis and swimming club located in the financial district.

Amenities: Tennis, swimming, massage, personal training, cardio, machine weights, free weights, towel service, steam room, sauna, sun deck, parking, laundry, social activities

Gorilla Sports

2450 Sutter Street
San Francisco, CA 94105
(415) 474-BOXX
or
2324 Chestnut Street
San Francisco, CA 94123
(415) 292-8470
www.gorillasports.com

A unique workout facility that challenges its members by offering diverse and innovative programs like boxing, tae kwon do, and spinning.

Amenities: Machine weights, free weights, boxing, spinning, and yoga classes

In Shape at Andre's

3214 Fillmore Street
San Francisco, CA 94123
(415) 922-3700
or
371 Hayes Street
San Francisco, CA 94102
(415) 241-0203

These are neighborhood exercise classes where you pay by the class and come when you want.

Amenities: Aerobics, spinning, body conditioning

Marina Fitness Club

3333 Fillmore Street
San Francisco, CA 94123
(415) 563-3333

This is the Marina District's neighborhood gym.

Amenities: Aerobics, cardio, machine weights, free weights, sauna, steam room, towel service, personal trainers, sun deck

Mission Cliffs

2295 Harrison Street
San Francisco, CA 94110
(415) 550-0515
www.mission-cliffs.com

This is an indoor climbing gym with walls reaching up to 55 feet high. Different instruction programs are available for all levels. There are also weight equipment and saunas.

Amenities: Climbing wall, cardio, free weights, machine weights, sauna, towel service, personal trainers

Pacific Heights Health Club

2358 Pine Street
San Francisco, CA 94115
(415) 563-6694

Another neighborhood gym located in an old Victorian home. There are separate workout areas for men and women.

Amenities: Cardio, free weights, machine weights, personal trainers, towel service

Pinnacle Fitness

Various locations
(510) 838-4960
www.fitnessclub.com

There are six locations in San Francisco and the Bay Area.

Amenities: Cardio, free weights, machine weights, aerobics, boxing, swimming, basketball, steam room, towel service, personal trainers, circuit training

San Francisco Tennis Club

645 5th Street
San Francisco, CA 94107
(415) 777-9000

This is an upscale club with banquet facilities, restaurant, pro shop, car wash, and other amenities. Tennis lessons are available.

Amenities: Tennis, aerobics, machine weights, free weights, spa, massage, cardio, personal trainer, social activities, towel service, steam room, sauna, hot tub, parking

HEALTH CLUBS OUTSIDE SAN FRANCISCO

Following is a list of health clubs in the Bay Area outside of San Francisco. Some of the clubs located in San Francisco mentioned in the previous list may also have facilities outside the city.

Alameda Athletic Club

1226 Park Street
Alameda, CA 94501
(510) 521-2001

Amenities: Cardio, machine weights, free weights, aerobics, private women's gym, personal trainers, sauna, Jacuzzi, tanning, massage

Bay-O-Vista Swimming and Tennis

1881 Astor Drive
San Leandro, CA 94577
(510) 357-8366

Amenities: Pool, tennis, machine weights, free weights, aerobics, social activities, steam room, sauna, basketball, parking

The Beach

4701 Doyle Street
Emeryville, CA 94608
(510) 428-1221
www.emerybeach.com

They have two sand courts and two hard courts to play indoor volleyball.

Amenities: Volleyball, cardio, parking

City Rock Gym Indoor Climbing Center

1250 45th Street
Emeryville, CA 94608
(510) 654-2510
www.cityrock.com

Amenities: Climbing wall, cardio, free weights, machine weights, personal trainers

Club Sport

7090 Johnson Drive
Pleasanton, CA 94566
(925) 463-2822
www.club-sport.com

Amenities: Tennis, swimming, rock wall, boxing, racketball, basketball, volleyball, aerobics, personal trainers, massage, tanning, hair salon, social events, classes, child care

Mariner Square Athletic Club

2227 Mariner Square Loop
Alameda, CA 94501
(510) 523-8011
www.gomsac.com

Amenities: Racquetball, swimming, basketball, free parking, aerobics, cardio, free weights, machine weights, steam room, sauna, massage, Jacuzzi, personal trainers, salon services, towel service

Nautilus of Marin

1001 Fourth Street
San Rafael, CA 94945
(415) 485-1001

They have four locations in Marin. Call to find the best location and amenities for your needs.

Amenities: Cardio, aerobics, weights, personal trainers, racketball, basketball, steam, sauna, massage, tanning, parking

Walnut Creek Sports & Fitness Club

1908 Olympic Boulevard
Walnut Creek, CA 94549
(510) 932-6400

Amenities: aerobics, cardio, weights, pool, racketball, massage, sauna, personal trainers, child care, parking

SPORTS CLUBS

If sports is your game, San Francisco is the place to get involved at any level. There are social sports clubs and competitive sports clubs. All will give the newcomer to San Francisco an opportunity to meet others who share the love of sports. I list below some of the more well-known sports clubs. Participate in a club meeting or event, and if you don't think it's a good fit, use it as a resource to find out about other sports clubs.

Adventurous Woman Sports

www.adventurous.com

This is a company that offers sports training and classes for women taught by women. Their various classes and clinics are held throughout the Bay Area and include billiards, golf, scuba, tennis, rollerblading, and more. Check out their Web site for a more detailed list. No membership fee. Just pay by the class.

Cal Adventures

5 Haas Clubhouse
Strawberry Canyon Recreation Area
Berkeley, CA 94720
(510) 642-4000
(510) 642-7707 Hotline
calbears.berkeley.edu/recsprts/caladv

This is an outdoor education program of the University of California-Berkeley. You do not have to be affiliated with Berkeley to join their classes, trips, or take advantage of their equipment and boat rental.

World Gym

5651 Paradise Drive
Corte Madera, CA 94925
(415) 927-9494
www.worldgym.com

Amenities: Cardio, free weights, machine weights, aerobics, steam room, tanning, personal trainers

Cal Sailing and Windsurfing Club

Across from the Berkeley Marina (foot of University Avenue)
Berkeley, CA 94710
(510) 287-5905
www.well.com/user/csc/

This club offers low-cost instruction on sailing and windsurfing. Open houses are on the first weekend of the month and include free sailboat rides. Memberships are a steal at $45 for three months, which entitles you to unlimited lessons and equipment use.

Dolphin Swim and Boat Club

502 Jefferson Street (foot of Hyde Street)
San Francisco, CA 94109
(415) 441-9329
www.dolphinclub.org

When you see those crazy people swimming in the San Francisco Bay, you can bet they are members of the Dolphin Club. Membership to this aquatics club is $340 for one year and includes access to the clubhouse showers, sauna, and lockers. It's a no-frills organization that doesn't offer instruction or training but sponsors competitive open-water swims and holds parties and swimmer appreciation dinners. Membership also includes use of kayaks, skiffs, and other vessels in the boat club and a quarterly newsletter. For more information, attend a club meeting held the third Wednesday of every month.

Golden Gate Sports and Social Club

1766 Union Street
San Francisco, CA 94123
(415) 921-1233
www.sscus.com

The Sports and Social Club offers coed football, volleyball, floor hockey, soccer leagues, and even ballroom dancing. There are three levels (recreational, intermediate, and competitive), so anyone can join. Playing the sport is the tough part. Afterwards, teams enjoy socializing at the many bars and restaurants that offer club member discounts. Membership costs around $35.

Golden Gate Triathlon Club

1500 Sansome Street
San Francisco, CA 94111
(415) 434-4482 hotline
www.ggtc.org

The club has coached track workouts, swim clinics, and bike rides. Members train for the many different area triathlons. Join one of their social gatherings on the first Monday of the month. Call their hotline or check out their Web site for details. Membership is $45.

Masters Swimming

Masters swimming is a coached, organized workout for triathletes, competitive swimmers, and fitness swimmers. Masters swimming is about personal achievement and self-improvement, and we could all use a little of that. The following is a short list of where to find Masters swimming in San Francisco:

South End Rowing Club, (415) 776-7372

Embarcadero YMCA, (415) 957-9622

University of San Francisco, (415) 422-6247

Dolphin Club, (415) 441-9329

Contact local health clubs and pools to find more selection. For online information, check out the Masters swimming Internet site at **www.usms.org.**

Mission Bay Golf Club

1200 Sixth Street
San Francisco, CA 94107
(415) 431-7888

If golf is your game, this club is a great way to improve your swing and meet other players of all levels. The $100 membership includes discounts at golf courses, on lessons, and buckets of balls. The club also has many tournaments and events for all levels as well as social events such as a monthly party, which includes a free golf clinic.

SAGA North

P.O. Box 14384
San Francisco, CA 94114
(415) 995-2772

San Francisco Bay Area's Gay and Lesbian Ski Club organizes numerous ski trips during the season as well as summer outings like hiking and water skiing.

San Francisco Recreation and Parks Department
Adult Softball

(415) 753-7023

These are city-run adult men's, women's, or coed softball leagues held in the spring and summer. You can pull together your own team and register it for a $405 fee or, if you are solo, put your name and level of experience on a players list so a team manager can contact you. People who play adult softball are from all walks of life, and their ages range from twenties to forties.

San Francisco Recreation and Parks Department
Women's Volleyball and Basketball

(415) 753-7031

Volleyball season is October through December, and basketball is January through May. There are three levels of play, from entry to advanced. Team league fees are about $175 for volleyball and $375 for basketball. If you want to join a team instead of putting one together, place your name on a list and team captains will contact you if they are looking for players. There are also drop-in volleyball and basketball teams at various recreation centers in the city. The crowd is working class and professional women in their mid-twenties and thirties.

San Francisco Ski Club

(415) 337-9333 (Hotline)
www.sfskiclub.org

This is an organized, active club whose activities aren't limited to skiing. There are tons of social and sports events year-round, such as hikes, barbecues, white-water rafting, wine tastings, movie nights, camping, baseball games, and, of course, skiing. Membership is $60.

Sierra Club Chapter Activities

San Francisco Bay Chapter
2530 San Pablo Avenue, Suite I
Berkeley, CA 94702
(510) 848-0800
www.sierraclub.org

You don't have to be a Sierra Club member to enjoy their chapter activities. In fact, Sierra Club membership does not include the activities schedule of the San Francisco Bay Chapter. The 75-page booklet (costs around $5) is filled with hikes, bike rides, backpacking trips, canine hikes, and social events.

South End Rowing Club

500 Jefferson Street
San Francisco, California 94109
(415) 776-7372
www.south-end.org

This is a nonprofit athletic organization founded in 1873 for handball players, rowers, open-water swimmers, runners, and gym enthusiasts. There are numerous club events throughout the year like the New Year's Day Alcatraz Swim Party and their annual St. Patrick's Day bash. The Club is open to the public two days a week for a day use fee of $6.50. Membership is $255 annually plus a one-time $100 processing fee.

BICYCLING CLUBS

The San Francisco Bay Area has many scenic places to ride your bike. There are also many bicycle clubs for competitive racers, fitness buffs, and social cyclists. The following is a list of some San Francisco and Bay Area bike clubs. There is also local bicycling information on the Web, **www.cycling.org or xenon.stanford.edu/~rsf/mtn-bike.html.**

Berkeley Bicycle Club

P.O. Box 817
Berkeley, CA 94701
(510) 527-3222 (Hotline)

This is a fun yet serious bunch of ten-speed racers who hold group rides and train for different races. It publishes a funky newsletter called the *Berkeley Bicycle Club Pneusletter* and holds regular meetings and rides.

Different Spokes

P.O. Box 14711
San Francisco, CA 94114
spoker@backdoor.com

Different Spokes is a recreational bicycling club for the gay community and its friends. The organization has been around since 1982 and currently has over 240 active members.

Fremont Freewheelers

P.O. Box 1868
Fremont, CA 94538
(510) 888-3787 (Hotline)
home.earthlink.net/~mpolakoff

These are mountain bikers who train for races and ride for fun. They have regular Wednesday night pizza rides and Friday morning training rides. There are also many weekend recreational rides that can have a coffee or ice cream theme. Monthly club meetings give you an opportunity to get more involved with the group. Membership is under $20. Call for a copy of the club newsletter, the *Spoke'n Truth*.

San Francisco Bicycle Coalition

1095 Market Street, Suite 215
San Francisco, CA 94103
(415) 431-BIKE
www.sfbike.org

This is an activist and social group for bike riders in the city. There are committees that fight for safer roads and better bike lanes. Membership in the group gets you the *Tubular Times* newsletter with a list of the group's planned activities, a survival kit with bike maps and safety items, and discounts at area bike shops. Many members are bike messenger types and artists.

Single Cyclists

P.O. Box 656
Kentfield, CA 94904
(415) 459-2453 (Hotline)
www.best.com/~harry5/SC/

Single Cyclists is a singles social club of bicyclists who participate in a variety of mountain and road cycle rides, weekend trips, parties, dances, cultural performances, and other events in the San Francisco Bay Area. The over nine hundred members are about evenly divided between men and women. The monthly newsletter has a calendar of events that features bike rides of all levels as well as social events. Annual membership is $30.

Wombats

P.O. Box 757
Fairfield, CA 94978
(415) 459-0980 (Hotline)
www.wombats.org

Wombats stands for Women's Mountain Bike and Tea Society, a 1,200-member group of women who enjoy cycling. It was established to help women overcome obstacles when taking up the sport of cycling. It is for women who want to mountain bike but don't like competition, can't keep up with "the guys," don't know much about the equipment, and want to get better at riding before going out alone. Membership is around $25 per year. For more information, call the hotline or check out their homepage.

RUNNING CLUBS

If running is your passion, you are not alone. There are many running clubs and races to participate in the Bay Area. A few are listed below, but for an even more comprehensive list, pick up the *California Schedule*, available at sporting goods stores or by calling the magazine at (415) 472-7223 or visiting their Web site at **www.theschedule.com**. The staff is very friendly and can help you find a good group.

Bay Area Distance Runners

(415) 626-1380

This group offers marathon training for gays/lesbians/friends.

Dolphin South End Runners (DSE)

(415) 978-0837 (Hotline)
www.hulaman.com/dse.html

San Francisco's largest running club with over four hundred members. There is both competitive and recreational running as well as socials, potlucks, and civic volunteer events. Ask to see a copy of their newsletter. There are minimal charges for event participation. Annual dues are around $15 and race entry fees are around $3. There are regular weekly track workouts, weekly runs and walks, special club runs, and special events, including Bay to Breakers.

East Bay Striders

(510) 428-1200 (Hotline)
tornado.sfsu.edu

This group offers weekly workouts in Berkeley along with competitions and weekend runs.

Fleet Feet

2086 Chestnut Street
San Francisco, CA 94123
(415) 921-7188

Fleet Feet is a store that sells running shoes and clothes. If you are able to run five miles, then join them for weekly runs in the Marina District.

Hash Harriers

(415) 334-4274 (Hotline)

This is an outrageous running club with the emphasis on drink. Weekly fun runs are followed by gatherings at local watering holes.

Hoy's Sports

1632 Haight Street
San Francisco, CA 94117
(415) 252-5370

Impala Racing Team for women and Hoy's Racing Team for men are competitive running teams with organized workouts. Participants train for trail, marathon, and other types of races.

San Francisco Frontrunners

(415) 978-2429 (Hotline)

This is a social and competitive running club for gays, lesbians, and bisexuals, but it is open to all. There are usually two weekly runs, one during the week and one on the weekend. Running distance ranges from one to five miles, and on weekends there is a one-mile walk.

CULTURAL AND SOCIAL ORGANIZATIONS

San Francisco is a cultural mecca with critically acclaimed symphony, ballet, and opera companies and world-renowned museums. The many arts organizations are committed to getting young professionals involved and keeping them interested through clubs and activities. The following is a list of some of the many art and social organizations in town.

ArtPoint

M. H. de Young Memorial Museum
Golden Gate Park
San Francisco, CA 94118-4598
(415) 750-7607
www.famsf.org

Membership fee: $75 per year

Description: ArtPoint, formerly Junior Arts Council (JAC), supports two fine arts museums in San Francisco: the M. H. de Young Memorial Museum, which houses an American collection, and the California Palace of the Legion of Honor, which houses a European collection. Membership includes free entry to both museums, private tours of new exhibits, downtown gallery tours, benefits, cocktail parties, dinner parties, and visits to private collections.

Bravo!

San Francisco Opera
301 Van Ness Avenue
San Francisco, CA 94102
(415) 565-3285
www.sfopera.com

Membership fee: $60 per year

Description: This is an organization of young professionals who support the San Francisco Opera. Bravo! club hosts a variety of events, pre-performance receptions, and fund-raising benefits for the San Francisco Opera while educating its membership about the world of opera. Membership includes free admission with a guest to the Trio Series pre-performance receptions, lectures, preferential seating, and discounted tickets.

Encore!

San Francisco Ballet
455 Franklin Street
San Francisco, CA 94102
(415) 553-4634
www.sfballet.org

Membership fee: $60 per year

Description: This is a young professional's organization that supports the San Francisco Ballet through performance attendance, volunteer involvement, and financial support. Membership includes invitations to ballet performances and pre- and post-event socials like cocktail parties or dinners. These events and socials are all an additional but discounted cost.

Commonwealth Club

595 Market Street
San Francisco, CA 94105
(415) 597-6700
www.commonwealthclub.org

Membership fee: $110 per year

Description: This is a public affairs speaking forum that holds a variety of meetings (breakfasts, lunches, dinners, receptions) at which speakers discuss issues of the day. Besides formal lectures, the club sponsors a number of special events each month that allows members the opportunity to socialize in a more informal atmosphere. Group visits to cultural and sporting events, tours of local companies and research facilities, wine tastings, and restaurant outings are a few of the activities. Membership includes the publication *The Commonwealth*.

Contemporary Extension

San Francisco Museum of Modern Art
151 Third Street
San Francisco, CA 94103
(415) 357-4086
www.sfmoma.org

Membership fee: $50 per year plus $55 per year regular museum membership

Description: This is a dynamic group of young professionals between the ages of 25 and 40 who share an interest in modern art and have a desire to take an active role in supporting the museum. Membership includes special museum tours; visits to artists' studios, local galleries, and private collections; and cocktail receptions. The only requirement to join is a regular museum membership.

Film Arts Foundation

346 9th Street, Second Floor
San Francisco, CA 94103
(415) 552-8760
www.filmarts.org

Membership fee: $35 per year

Description: This is the largest regional organization of independent filmmakers in California. Services and facilities available to members include a monthly newsletter, use of the editing room, seminars and workshops, a resource library, a viewing room, a group legal plan, and more.

San Francisco Chamber of Commerce

465 California Street, Ninth Floor
San Francisco, CA 94104
(415) 392-4520
www.sfchamber.com

Membership fee: $375 per year

Description: The Chamber of Commerce is a nonprofit organization representing area businesses. Its mission is to attract, develop, and retain business in San Francisco. Members include over 1,800 companies and individuals. There are monthly business development activities like luncheons, after-hour networking socials, and committees. The $375 individual membership fee is steep, but if you are planning on freelancing, the exposure through this organization is worth it. A budget-minded option is to bypass a formal membership and attend events at a higher nonmember price.

Scholastics

San Francisco School Volunteers
65 Battery Street, Third Floor
San Francisco, CA 94111
(415) 274-0250
www.sfsv.org

Membership fee: None

Description: The Scholastics is a group of young professionals who support public education. They hold fund-raisers and are volunteer readers in the classroom.

Symphonix

San Francisco Symphony
Davies Symphony Hall
San Francisco, CA 94102
(415) 552-8000 (ext.500)
www.sfsymphony.org

Membership fee: $50 per year

Description: Symphonix, one of the San Francisco Symphony's eleven volunteer leagues, is for young professionals interested in supporting the symphony. Membership includes discounts on dinners and concerts planned once a quarter, a quarterly newsletter, quarterly membership meetings with a musical program, and invitations to members-only events.

Toastmasters International

(949) 858-8255
www.toastmasters.org

Membership fee: None

Description: Toastmasters is a program that helps develop public speaking skills. It is also a good way to meet people and professional contacts. Call the national headquarters phone number for a listing of Toastmasters groups in the area or browse their Web site.

The World Affairs Council of Northern California

312 Sutter Street, Second Floor
San Francisco, CA 94108
(415) 982-2541
www.wacsf.org

Membership fee: $55 per year

Description: The council has over 11,000 members and offers over two hundred programs a year on current and important foreign policy issues. The general membership includes a subscription to the newsletter Spotlight, use of the library, invitations to special members-only events, and reduced admission to all events. Events include dinners with diplomats, lectures from top U.S. CEOs, and forums on important domestic and international issues.

SINGLES ACTIVITIES

Contrary to popular belief, San Francisco is home to plenty of single men and women interested in dating and finding the right partner. I'm not saying being single is easy in this city—it's not easy anywhere. But there are opportunities to meet other singles through safe, fun, non-threatening groups and socials. The following are some of the more popular ones.

Calvary Presbyterian Church

2515 Fillmore Street
San Francisco, CA 94115
(415) 346-3832
www.churchnet.org/churchnet/calvary

They have a social group for singles in their twenties and thirties. Activities include retreats, bike rides, barbecues, Friday night get-togethers, and much more. Call the church for a calendar.

Jewish Community Federation

121 Steuart Street
San Francisco, CA 94105
(415) 777-0411
(415) 436-0711 Hotline
www.jewishsf.com (resource guide to Jewish life in the Bay Area)

The Young Adults Division has an active membership of over four hundred people plus a mailing list of around two thousand. A quarterly calendar lists weekly events. A popular event is Blue Monday, which is a dinner party held once a month in different restaurants. Also, First Friday Shabbat dinners are held in private homes. Five committees, including a Newcomers Committee, are responsible for the programs. The age range is twenty-one to thirty-nine.

Lafayette Orinda Presbyterian Church

49 Knox Drive
Lafayette, CA 94549
(510) 283-8890 Singles Hotline
www.lopc.org

This church has one of the most well-known singles clubs in the Bay Area. Singles are grouped according to age range, and the hotline has information about the various events, social activities, and volunteer opportunities on the calendar. Sunday night is a "welcome night" for prospective members.

Mile High Adventures & Entertainment

74 New Montgomery Street, Suite 150
San Francisco, CA 94105
(415) 974-5776 or (888) 414-4FUN
www.pacificfun.com

This is a singles social club, not a dating service. There are over three thousand members in the Bay Area and there are three chapters in San Ramon, San Francisco, and Mountain View. There are fifty to sixty scheduled activities each month, like hikes, museum visits, dinners, and weeklong vacations to Hawaii. The median age is mid- to late thirties. Call to schedule a membership interview and find out the costs.

San Francisco Ski Club

(415) 337-9333 (Hotline)
www.sfskiclub.org

As mentioned earlier, this is a year-round ski and social club for active single adults over twenty-one. It offers sports-oriented individuals the opportunity to participate in recreational activities in a relaxed, comfortable atmosphere.

Single Cyclists

P.O. Box 656
Kentfield, CA 94904
(415) 459-2453 (Hotline)
www.best.com/~harry5/SC/

Also mentioned earlier, Single Cyclists is a singles social club with over nine hundred members who do activities like bicycling, parties, dances, cultural performances, and other events in the San Francisco Bay Area.

Singles Supper Club

P.O. Box 60518
Palo Alto, CA 94306
(650) 327-4645
www.best.com/~ssc

The Singles Supper Club is a dining and social club serving single professionals between the ages of twenty-five and fifty-five. Events revolve around dining but could also include other activities such as the theater and tennis. Call to find out about upcoming events and costs.

Stanford Bachelors

P.O. Box 2345
Stanford, CA 94305
www.stanfordbachelors.org

The Stanford Bachelors is a nonprofit group consisting of Stanford Alumni. The members volunteer their time to organize fundraising social events all over the Bay Area. Profits from such events go to support Stanford related charities. The crowd age is in the mid-thirties to forties.

St. Dominic's Young Adults Group

2390 Bush Street
San Francisco, CA 94115
(415) 567-7824
www.stdominics.org

A Catholic singles group of young professionals in their twenties and thirties. Meetings are held every Wednesday evening at 7:30 P.M. in the Parish Hall. Monthly activities include hikes, social events, and service opportunities.

St. Vincent De Paul Young Adults Group

2320 Green Street
San Francisco, CA 94123
(415) 522-9242 (Hotline)

A Catholic singles group comprised of young professionals between the ages of twenty-four and forty. Activities include biweekly meetings, volunteer events, social activities, and choir. Meetings are every second and fourth Monday of the month. Young adults also meet for Mass at 5:15 P.M. on Sunday evenings.

Tennis Matchmakers

2929 Russell Street
Berkeley, CA 94705
(510) 548-6240

The focus of Tennis Matchmakers is social tennis for single, professional people. Events are held at the best private tennis clubs in the Bay Area and include a mixed doubles format followed by a catered dinner party. Membership is free, but an entry fee is charged for each event. All age and skill levels are welcome. Tennis Matchmakers is a member of the United States Tennis Association (USTA).

VOLUNTEER OPPORTUNITIES

Volunteer activities are an excellent way to meet people, make a difference, use your talents, and learn new skills. The following list of local volunteer and nonprofit organizations in the city will get you started.

American Red Cross

Bay Area Chapter
85 Second Street, 7th Floor
San Francisco, CA 94105
(415) 427-8000
www.redcross.org/ca/bayarea

Mission: A volunteer-led humanitarian organization that provides relief to victims of disaster and helps people prevent, prepare for, and respond to emergencies

Volunteer activities: Assistance to disaster victims, emergency relief, and special fund-raising events

Enterprise for High School Students

450 Mission Street, Suite 408
San Francisco, CA 94105
(415) 896-0909
www.enterprise4youth.org

Mission: Help high school students prepare for job opportunities through career apprenticeships and a job referral program

Volunteer activities: Volunteer mentors act as adult role models, developing positive one-on-one relationships with students in order to support them throughout their job search and to assist with career exploration.

Hands On San Francisco

660 Market Street, Suite 401
San Francisco, CA 94104
(415) 263-8949
www.hosf.org

Mission: Hands On San Francisco is a nonprofit volunteer organization that helps concerned individuals with busy schedules meet dire community needs through organizing, promoting, and directing service projects that bring them in touch with food banks, AIDS groups, homeless shelters, youth organizations, community centers, environmental groups, and many other organizations.

Volunteer activities: You can get involved in the areas of fund raising, marketing, managing projects, and volunteering for projects. Some past projects on the calendar were Special Olympics, Hamilton Family Center Shelter, and Habitat for Humanity. Call to be put on the mailing list and get more information. Every month, new volunteers are required to attend a thirty-minute orientation.

Friends of the Urban Forest

512 2nd Street, Fourth Floor

San Francisco, CA 94107

(415) 543-5000

Mission: This is San Francisco's citizen urban forestry organization. They offer financial, technical, and practical assistance to individuals and neighborhood groups who wish to plant and care for trees.

Volunteer activities: Tree plantings occur every weekend and sometimes during the week. This could involve activities like digging and tree maintenance. Train to be a Planting Leader or Tree Tour Guide.

Little Brothers/Friends of the Elderly

481 O'Farrell Street

San Francisco, CA 94102

(415) 771-7957

Mission: To alleviate loneliness and isolation of homebound elders in San Francisco through friendship visits by volunteers and social parties.

Volunteer activities: Visiting the elderly, putting together gift packages, joining the book club.

Project Open Hand

730 Polk Street, 4th Floor

San Francisco, CA 94109

(415) 447-2300

www.openhand.org

Mission: To provide hot meals and groceries to people with AIDS in San Francisco and the East Bay.

Volunteer activities: Volunteers are always needed to help prepare, package, and deliver meals and groceries, as well as help with special projects and events.

Raphael House

1065 Sutter Street
San Francisco, CA 94109
(415) 474-4621
www.raphaelhouse.org

Mission: Work with families to help them overcome the immediate crisis of homelessness and provide a safe, structured environment in which they can work to resolve other difficult problems related to their homelessness.

Volunteer activities: Preparing meals for residents, tutoring children.

San Francisco Maritime National Historical Park

Fort Mason, Building 201
San Francisco, CA 94123
(415) 556-1613
www.nps.gov/safr or www.maritime.org

If you are a seafarer at heart, then volunteer for the Maritime Park. They are always looking for docents and other volunteers interested in rigging, living history, woodworking, welding, artifact preservation, and more. You could be doing carpentry on the walking-beam ferry Eureka or rigging on the historic Balclutha.

San Francisco Society for the Prevention of Cruelty to Animals (SPCA)

2500 16th Street
San Francisco, CA 94103
(415) 554-3000
www.sfspca.org

Mission: This is a charitable animal-welfare organization dedicated to protecting and providing for animals in need, fostering an awareness of their importance in our lives, and finding a loving home for every animal taken into the shelter. If you love animals but your lifestyle or landlord doesn't allow pets, this is a great place to volunteer. It is a very committed bunch who are involved.

Volunteer activities: Adoption counselor, adoption outreach, dog walkers, cat and dog socializers, animal behavior, animal-assisted therapy, humane education.

VOLUNTEER CENTERS

The Bay Area has a network of Volunteer Centers that serve nonprofit organizations, individuals, city agencies, and civic groups by promoting volunteerism throughout the community. They provide referral services for connecting people with a wide variety of volunteer opportunities in San Francisco's diverse nonprofit community. You can attend an orientation of the center or request a copy of their *Volunteer Opportunities* newsletter. Also, a Board Match Plus program (**www.boardmatchplus.org**) matches people with nonprofit organizations in need of new board members. The following volunteer centers serve as resources for volunteer opportunities in the nonprofit community.

San Francisco Volunteer Center

425 Jackson Street
San Francisco, CA 94111
(415) 982-8999
www.volunteercentersf.org

Volunteer Center of Alameda County

1904 Franklin Street, Suite 211
Oakland, CA 94612
(510) 419-3970
www.vcac.org

Volunteer Center of Contra Costa County

1820 Bonanza Street, Suite 100
Walnut Creek, CA 94596
(510) 472-5760
www.meer.net/users/taylor/volcenc.htm

Volunteer Center of Marin County

650 Las Gallinas Avenue
San Rafael, CA 94903
(415) 479-5660

Volunteer Center of San Mateo County

800 South Claremont, Suite 108
San Mateo, CA 94402
(650) 342-0801
www.webgal.com/sanmateo/volunteer.shtml

EDUCATION/CLASSES

The following is a list of places to take classes or pursue a degree.

Academy of Art College

79 New Montgomery Street
San Francisco, CA 94105
800-544-ARTS
www.academyart.edu

This is a professional college that offers education and training in several fields of art and design. Choose from Bachelor of Fine Arts (BFA) programs, certificate programs, and nondegree programs. The course selection is outstanding.

Berkeley Extension

55 Laguna Street
San Francisco, CA 94102
(510) 642-4111
www.unex.berkeley.edu:4243

This is an extension of the University of California, Berkeley, campus. Quarterly catalogs are chock-full of classes in everything from art and design to travel study. You will find certificate and study programs in areas like business administration, publishing, and accounting.

City College of San Francisco

50 Phelan Avenue
San Francisco, CA 94112
(415) 239-3000
www.ccsf.cc.ca.us

This community college offers associate degrees and a credit certificate curricula. Noncredit classes are also available for those who want to brush up on a skill or pursue an interest.

California Culinary Academy

625 Polk Street
San Francisco, CA 94102
800-BAY-CHEF
www.baychef.com

This is the premier cooking school in San Francisco. Serious foodies train here and go on to work as chefs in some of the Bay Area's finest restaurants. There is a sixteen-month Professional Chef Training program, Baking and Pastry Arts Certification program, and many consumer programs for those of us who find cooking a great pastime. Call to request a catalog.

Golden Gate University

536 Mission Street
San Francisco, CA 94105
(415) 442-7800
www.ggu.edu

Degree and nondegree courses of study are offered. The campus is fully equipped with libraries, computer labs, telecommunications lab, student lounge, and bookstore. Undergraduate, graduate, and law school courses are available. There are also campuses in the East Bay, North Bay, and Silicon Valley.

HomeChef Cooking School

3501 California Street
San Francisco, CA 94118
(415) 668-3191

This school offers cooking classes that teach quick and easy dishes. Attend either lecture/demonstrations or hands-on workshops. The Basic Cooking program is thirteen lessons on the basics, starting with stocks and broths and leading up to menus for entertaining. There are also individual classes, such as cooking for couples, tamale workshop, Spanish tapas, and how to write a cookbook.

Learning Annex

291 Geary Street, #510
San Francisco, CA 94102
(415) 788-5500
www.thelearningannex.com

The Learning Annex offers a most eclectic mix of classes and hosts some surprising speakers. You will find classes in everything like the Celestine Prophecy Workshop, Massage for Couples, How to Become a Private Eye, Comedy Writing, and more. In the past, popular personalities like M. Scott Peck have been featured.

Media Alliance

841 Mission Street, Suite 205
San Francisco, CA 94103
(415) 546-6334
www.media-alliance.org

Media Alliance is a nonprofit advocacy organization that serves media professionals. It was started in 1975 by a group of Bay Area journalists to unite local media professionals and the community to change the way media professionals do business. Though their mission statement seems political, their services are very practical. If you are interested in writing, journalism, communications, public relations, advertising, or film, this is a good organization to join. They also offer a good selection of writing, editing, publishing, and Macintosh classes.

San Francisco Conservatory of Music Extension

1201 Ortega Street
San Francisco, CA 94122
(415) 759-3429
www.sfcm.edu

The San Francisco Conservatory Extension Division is dedicated to enhancing adult lives through music. Some classes offered include Jazz Harmony and Theory, Singing Handel's Messiah, Piano, and Voice.

San Francisco State University

1600 Holloway Avenue
San Francisco, CA 94132
(415) 338-1111
www.sfsu.edu

The University has undergraduate, graduate, certificate, academic, and credential programs.

San Francisco State University

College of Extended Learning

425 Market Street

San Francisco, CA 94105

800-987-7700

www.cel.sfsu.edu

San Francisco State offers continuing professional education in the heart of the Financial District. Over twenty programs such as Multimedia and Global Business are taught on evenings and weekends.

WORLD WIDE WEB RESOURCES

CitySearch7
(www.citysearch7.com)

This Web site is sponsored by local ABC affiliate channel 7. Search under *Community* for volunteer resources.

Idealist
(www.idealist.org)

Idealist is an online resource for nonprofit and community organizations and the people they serve. Idealist allows organizations—whether they have Web sites or not—to enter and update information about their services, volunteer opportunities, job openings, internships, upcoming events, and any material or publications they have produced. There are over 14,000 organizations in 120 countries using Idealist.

San Francisco is an athletic town. Because of year-round good weather, any sport can be pursued, from sailing to rollerblading. San Francisco also knows how to host some fun charity foot races that attract the most seasoned runners as well as social strollers. The following is just a few of the many runs and walks you should look out for in the local newspapers:

UNIQUE SAN FRANCISCO RACES

RACE	HELD IN:	DESCRIPTION
First Run	New Year's Eve	This is promoted as the alternative New Year's Eve celebration. The race begins at the stroke of midnight, ringing in the new year. Afterwards they have an alcohol-free celebration.
Zoo Run	January	Supports the San Francisco Zoo
Hoolihans to Hoolihans	March	Hoolihans is a popular bar with locations in San Francisco and Sausalito. The run is from the Sausalito location, over the Golden Gate Bridge, to the San Francisco location. This race benefits the Edgewood Children's Center for emotionally disturbed children.
Gimme Shelter	April	This is the biggest corporate-sponsored event in the city benefiting the St. Vincent de Paul Society.
Bay to Breakers	May	San Francisco's most famous and popular race sponsored by the local newspaper. Participants can dress in costume, run tied together as a centipede, or just walk and soak it all in.
San Francisco Marathon	July	Every city has one.
Corporate Challenge	September	This race is held in the Financial District where the business crowd shed their suits for a good cause.
Hillstride	October	This is a fun walk over seven of San Francisco's steepest hills. It benefits the Pacificare Foundation.
Race to the Far Side	November	Benefiting the California Academy of Sciences, this is a fun race sponsored by Far Side cartoon creator Gary Larson. This race attracts close to 10,000 participants, many who dress up as their favorite Far Side character.

CHAPTER TEN

SOMETHING FOR NOTHING

SAN FRANCISCO, one of the world's most popular travel destinations, is now your place to call home. Quality entertainment, fabulous restaurants, and countless activities are yours for the taking—if you have the bucks to spend. But fun can still be had even if your wallet tells you otherwise. The following is a list of free things to do in San Francisco.

FREE MUSEUM DAYS

Asian Art Museum

75 Tea Garden Drive
Golden Gate Park
(415) 379-8801
www.asianart.org

This is one of the largest museums in the Western world devoted exclusively to the arts and cultures of Asia. Their permanent collection represents over forty Asian countries spanning six thousand years of history. Free the first Wednesday of the month.

Cable Car Museum

1201 Mason Street
(415) 474-1887
www.sfcablecar.com

All the city's cable car cables run out of this building. On display are various mechanical devices, such as grips, tracks, trucks, cables, and brake mechanisms. It also houses antique cable cars, including the oldest cable car in the world dating back to 1873. Admission is always free.

California Academy of Sciences

Music Concourse Drive off John F. Kennedy Drive
Golden Gate Park
(415) 750-7145
www.calacademy.org

The California Academy of Sciences includes the Natural History Museum, Steinhart Aquarium, and Morrison Planetarium. Free the first Wednesday of the month.

Center for the Arts

Yerba Buena Gardens
Center for the Arts Galleries
701 Mission Street
(415) 978-ARTS
www.yerbabuenaarts.org

This is an independent arts complex with galleries and a theater that have programs emphasizing the diverse artists and communities of the San Francisco Bay Area. Free the first Thursday of the month from 6 P.M. to 8 P.M.

Chinese Historical Society Museum

650 Commercial Street near Montgomery Street
(415) 391-1188

Artifacts and photos tracing the history of Chinese Americans. Always free.

M. H. de Young Museum

10th and Fulton Streets
Golden Gate Park
(415) 863-3330
www.famsf.org

This museum houses an acclaimed collection of American art as well as exhibitions of African, Oceanic, textile, and pre-Columbian art from the Americas. The museum is free the first Wednesday of every month.

Exploratorium

3601 Lyon Street
(415) 563-7337
www.exploratorium.edu

Great hands-on science fun for kids and adults alike. Free the first Wednesday of every month.

Federal Reserve Bank

101 Market Street
(415) 974-2000
www.frbsf.org

"The World of Economics" is a block-long, hands-on exhibit of economic principles and history. Different computers give you the power to raise or lower interest rates and even make presidential decisions while showing how it affects the economy. There is also a bank tour of the checks and cash departments. Always free.

Fort Mason Center Museums

Intersection of Marina Boulevard and Buchanan Street

Fort Mason Center was a military site for over two hundred years. Today the former barracks house about fifty resident nonprofit groups. Among these groups are the following four fine museums:

The Mexican Museum, (415) 441-0404

Museo ItaloAmericano (**www.well.com/user/museo**), (415) 673-2200

San Francisco African-American Historical and Cultural Society, (415) 441-0640

San Francisco Craft and Folk Art Museum, (415) 775-0990

These museums are free the first Wednesday of the month.

The Jewish Museum

121 Steuart Street
(415) 543-8880
www.jewishmuseumsf.org

The Jewish Museum of San Francisco is dedicated to fostering an understanding of Judaism within the context of contemporary American society. It is a forum for exploring both contemporary Jewish identity and the ongoing cul-

tural and intellectual contributions of the American Jewish community. Free the first Monday of each month.

Musée Mechanique

Cliff House
1090 Point Lobos Avenue
(415) 386-1170

This antique mechanical arcade has the largest collection of coin-operated musical instruments in the world. Always free.

Museum of the City of San Francisco

2801 Leavenworth Street
The Cannery, Third Level
(415) 928-0289
www.sfmuseum.org

Rotating exhibits feature the rise of the city of San Francisco from its origins as a Spanish garrison, to its renown as a Gold Rush boom town, to world attention as the famous "Earthquake City." Always free.

Palace of the Legion of Honor

34th Avenue at Clement Street

Lincoln Park
(415) 863-3330
www.famsf.org

The newly renovated majestic marble building looks like it just dropped in from Paris. The Palace is home to a collection of four

The Mario Botta-designed building is a work of art in itself. Visit the modern and contemporary art collections and exhibits for free the first Tuesday of each month.

San Francisco Zoo

1 Zoo Road at Sloat Boulevard and 45th Avenue
(415) 753-7080
www.sfzoo.com

Animal exhibits, children's zoo, and a carousel. Free the first Wednesday of each month.

Wells Fargo Historical Museum

420 Montgomery Street
(415) 396-2619
www.wellsfargo.com

Artifacts from the Old West and authentic stagecoaches. Always free.

thousand years of ancient and European art from artists like El Greco, Rembrandt, Manet, Monet, and Degas. A visit will help satisfy a Louvre craving. Free the second Wednesday of each month.

San Francisco Maritime National Historical Park Museum

900 Beach Street in Aquatic Park
(415) 556-3002
www.maritime.org

On display is maritime history dating back to the Gold Rush era up to World War II. There are ship models, nautical artifacts, and a maritime bookstore. Always free.

San Francisco Museum of Modern Art

151 Third Street
(415) 357-4000
www.sfmoma.org

FREE CONCERTS

Many public plazas and churches hold free concerts, usually during the summer months when the weather is pleasant.

Old St. Mary's Cathedral

660 California Street
(415) 288-3840
members.aol.com/dovecsp/oldstmarys_sf

Free noontime concerts on Tuesdays and Thursdays featuring so-loists, bands, pianists, and other performers.

Community Music Center

544 Capp Street
(415) 647-6015
www.sfmusic.org

Features musical lectures and performances.

Stern Grove Outdoor Concerts

Sloat Boulevard at 19th Avenue
(415) 252-6252
www.sterngrove.org

Features quality musical entertainment and dance concerts every Sunday afternoon from mid-June until mid-August. Past programs featured the San Francisco Opera, Ballet, and Symphony.

People in Plazas

(415) 362-2500
www.citysearch.com/sfo/ marketstreet

The Market Street Association produces a summer concert series of Bay Area musicians who perform in various plazas on and near Market Street, a main artery that runs from the Ferry Building to the Castro. Music ranges from country to Cajun.

San Francisco Jazz Festival

(415) 398-5655

Offers free jazz concerts throughout the summer months at several locations in the financial district. Contact them for more information about the Transamerica Redwood Park Series, Levis Plaza Music Series, and Jazz in July at the Embarcadero Center.

FREE LESSONS

TENNIS LESSONS

(415) 292-2006

Year-round beginner, intermediate, and advanced tennis lessons at outdoor public courts in the Marina District neighborhood.

SWING DANCING

Mark Hopkins Hotel

California and Mason Streets
(415) 616-6916

Enjoy breathtaking views and free swing dancing lessons every Tuesday night at the Top of the Mark lounge on the 19th floor of the Mark Hopkins hotel.

Café Du Nord

2170 Market Street
San Francisco, CA 94114
(415) 861-5016
www.cafedunord.com

Every Sunday night at 8 P.M. this popular Upper Market club attracts all kinds of swing dance enthusiasts for free lessons taught by a cross-dressing instructor. Beat the 8 P.M. cover charge by arriving a little earlier.

COOKING LESSONS

Sur La Table

77 Maiden Lane
San Francisco, CA 94108
(415) 732-7900

Become an assistant to the cooking instructor. You will get hands-on practice by helping with food preparation and observing the lesson during class time. The benefits are free attendance plus minimum-wage payment for your work. The downside is you have to do the dishes, including pots and pans, as well as serve and clean up after paying class members.

FREE TOURS

NEIGHBORHOOD WALKING TOURS

The Friends of the San Francisco Public Library offer free neighborhood walking tours. This is an excellent way to get acquainted with different neighborhoods in the city and their history. Tours take about one-and-a-half hours and only group reservations are needed. Neighborhood tour themes include:

- Art Deco Marina
- Cathedral Hill's Churches
- Haight-Ashbury
- Mission Murals
- North Beach
- Pacific Heights Mansions
- Roof Gardens and Open Spaces
- Victorian San Francisco

Call (415) 557-4266 for information, or send a self-addressed, stamped envelope for a schedule to City Guides, Friends of the San Francisco Public Library, Main Library, San Francisco, CA 94102. Schedule also available at branch libraries or on the Internet at **www.hooked.net/~jhum.**

GOLDEN GATE PARK TOURS

The Friends of Recreation and Parks is an organization that supports the city's biggest park, Golden Gate Park. Every Saturday and Sunday from

May to October, this organization offers free historical walking tours of Golden Gate Park, Stern Grove, and other celebrated parks and squares. The West End Tour features the Golden Gate Park stables and a restored windmill. The Strawberry Hill Tour teaches the history of Stow Lake and offers spectacular views. For a schedule and reservations, call (415) 750-5105 or visit their Web site at **www.frp.org.**

OTHER PARK ACTIVITIES

The Golden Gate National Recreation Area includes 114 square miles of coastal wilderness, city waterfront, and historical landmarks. A quarterly calendar lists dozens of free activities offered in San Francisco and outlying areas. Some happenings are

- Pier Crabbing: Learn about equipment, bait, regulations, and other important aspects of crabbing in the bay.

- Presidio National Cemetery Walk

- Beginning Birding in the Marin Headlands

For more information, contact the Golden Gate National Recreation Area at (415) 556-0560, or write to them at Fort Mason, Building 201, San Francisco, CA 94123. Or visit their Web site at **www.nps.gov/goga.**

Mt. Tamalpais

Mt. Tamalpais State Park Hikes
801 Panoramic Highway
Mill Valley, CA 94941
(415) 388-2070
cal-parks.ca.gov

The Mt. Tamalpais Interpretive Association leads free Saturday, Sunday, and moonlight hikes through Mt. Tamalpais State Park.

FREE ENTERTAINMENT

FAIRS AND FESTIVALS

During the summer, San Francisco neighborhood fairs and festivals happen almost every weekend. The music, entertainment, and people watching are free. Contact the San Francisco Convention and Visitors Bureau for more information at (415) 391-2000 or check out their Web site at

www.sfvisitor.org. Following are four popular San Francisco fairs and festivals.

North Beach Fair

North Beach is San Francisco's Little Italy. The neighborhood's main shopping street, Grant Avenue, becomes a street vendor's mall full of handmade crafts like jewelry and pottery. Famed Washington Square Park has a petting zoo, pony rides, and many juggling acts and puppet shows.

Union Street Festival

Union Street is the main artery in Pacific Heights, San Francisco's yuppie neighborhood. This festival is colorful, classy, and civilized. You will find crafts, great shops, and boutiques along the street.

Haight-Ashbury Fair

The opposite of the Union Street Festival is the Haight-Ashbury Fair. Tie-dye and grunge mix with the scent of incense and ethnic foods. Enjoy loud bands and lots of young energy. If a flashback to the '60s is what you are looking for, this fair is it.

Filmore Festival

The highlight of the Fillmore Festival is the excellent jazz performances. The crowd is a mix of artsy folks and yuppies. This is a pleasant, mellow affair.

SHAKESPEARE IN THE PARK

(415) 422-2221

If you have never seen a Shakespeare play performed on stage, don't miss out on Shakespeare in the Park, held every September. It plays in Golden Gate Park just west of the Conservatory of Flowers.

OPERA IN THE PARK

(415) 864-3330

For over twenty years the San Francisco Opera has held a weekend in September of free opera in Golden Gate Park. It is usually the first Sunday after the season opening.

FREE LECTURES AND LITERARY EVENTS

Book readings are stimulating, interesting, and free. The following bookstores publish monthly newsletters with calendars of events that go beyond an author simply reading his or her work. You can also enjoy concerts, lectures, book clubs, and even singles events. Visit the bookstore, get on their mailing list, and ask about any frequent buyer discounts. Also check the book review section of the Sunday *San Francisco Examiner and Chronicle* newspaper for weekly events.

A Clean Well-Lighted Place for Books

Opera Plaza
601 Van Ness Avenue
San Francisco, CA 94102
(415) 441-6670
www.bookstore.com

They host top authors of the moment for readings and discussion. There is a frequent-buyer discount program, and books can be purchased on their Web site.

Alexander Book Company

50 Second Street
San Francisco, CA 94105
(415) 495-2992

This is an old-fashioned, full-service independent bookstore in downtown San Francisco. Alexander Book Company holds noontime readings for the Financial District and South of Market crowd they serve. There is a women's book club that also meets at lunch time. The *Alexander Book Column* newsletter has articles, reviews, and lists of upcoming events.

Book Passage

51 Tamal Vista Boulevard
Corte Madera, CA 94925
(800) 999-7909
www.bookpassage.com

They publish a nice, hearty newsletter packed full of readings, events, and classes. Classes and seminars are led by well-known authors like Anne

Lamott, Mary Morris, and Peter Mayle. They also organize writing conferences on topics like Travel Writing and Mystery Writing.

Booksmith

1644 Haight Street

San Francisco, CA 94117

(415) 863-8688

www.booksmith.com

They publish a schedule of free readings that have attracted authors like Marianne Faithfull and Brett Easton Ellis.

Borders Books and Music

400 Post Street

San Francisco, CA 94102

(415) 399-1633

www.borders.com

Not only does this place have book readings, panel discussions, and reading groups, it also holds music events. Past guests have included Bruce Hornsby and Judy Collins.

California Historical Society

678 Mission Street

San Francisco, CA 94105

(415) 357-1860

www.calhist.org

Every Thursday there is a free program by a local author or architect on a California-themed historical subject.

Cody's Books

2454 Telegraph Avenue

Berkeley, CA 94704

(800) 479-7744

www.codysbooks.com

Cody's has been a Berkeley institution for over forty years. The store has a calendar full of book and poetry readings and even provides sign-language interpreters for these events. There are also several book clubs like their Spanish and Travel book clubs.

San Francisco Main Library

Civic Center
San Francisco, CA 94102
(415) 557-4400
sfpl.lib.ca.us

Spend some time exploring the new Main library. Tours are conducted daily and there is usually a free exhibition or two—like portraits of lesbian families or the examination of the internment of Japanese-Americans during World War II. In conjunction with special exhibits there may be videos, performances, or educational lectures.

Stacey's

581 Market Street
San Francisco, CA 94105
(415) 421-4687
www.staceys.com

Their events are geared toward the lunch and after-work business crowd. They host a variety of fiction, business, and technical authors. They also have a book club that discusses the classics. Sign up for their free literary license for discounts on every purchase.

FREE PERFORMING ARTS

Be an usher or volunteer for the performing arts and you won't miss great theater, dance, and music events because of their cost. Call the theater way ahead of time and ask if they need ushers or other volunteers for a show. A good resource for local arts events is the *San Francisco Arts Monthly*, a free newspaper available at many locations or by calling (415) 543-6110. Here are some local theaters to contact:

Center for the Arts Theater

700 Howard Street
(415) 978-ARTS
www.yerbabuenaarts.org

Features contemporary dance and performances.

Cowell Theater

Fort Mason Center
Intersection of Marina Boulevard
and Buchanan Street
(415) 441-3400

Features contemporary dance and theater.

Curran Theater
445 Geary Street
(415) 474-3800
Features Broadway-style performances.

Magic Theater
Fort Mason Center
Intersection of Marina Boulevard and Buchanan Street, Building D
(415) 441-8822
Features plays.

Golden Gate Theater
1 Taylor Street
(415) 474-3800
Features Broadway theater.

Herbst Theater
401 Van Ness Avenue
(415) 621-6600
Features concerts and lectures.

Louise Davies Symphony Hall
201 Van Ness Avenue at Grove Street
(415) 864-6000
Features symphony concerts.

Orpheum Theater
1192 Market Street
(at Hyde and 8th Streets)
(415) 474-3800
Features Broadway theater.

Marines Memorial Theater
609 Sutter Street
(415) 771-6900
Features dance and theater.

Theater on the Square
450 Post Street
(415) 433-9500
Features theater.

War Memorial Opera House
301 Van Ness Avenue
(415) 864-3330
Features ballet and opera.

FREE HAIRCUTS

Be a hair model at San Francisco's better salons and get a great haircut. Check the local phone book for the many salons the city has. Some of the bigger names include Vidal Sassoon, Architects & Heroes, Yosh for Hair, and Henrik + Company.

CHAPTER ELEVEN

THINGS TO DO
ON THE WEEKENDS

THE BAY AREA has many fun things to do on the weekends, both in the city of San Francisco and out of town. The city has theaters, cinemas, museums, shopping, festivals, expos, and more. Just over the Golden Gate and Bay bridges are wonderful biking and hiking trails, beaches, national parks, and the wine country. Even if you are new to the city, there is no excuse for being bored. Participate in a tree planting with Friends of the Urban Forest, visit the San Francisco Museum of Modern Art, hang out at the Marina Green and watch a volleyball game, or check the *San Francisco Examiner and Chronicle* newspaper's Sunday "pink pages" for a calendar of things going on in the area.

This chapter will highlight activities and attractions in San Francisco and the Bay Area. The first part will list activities around the city that are a little touristy but a lot of fun. The second part will name interesting places to visit out of town. You will soon be running out of weekends before running out of things to do.

AROUND THE CITY

San Francisco is an entertainment playground, with many things happening in and around the city all the time. Many activities have already been mentioned throughout the book. I will now list some popular local attractions. The more time you spend exploring San Francisco, the more cool things you will discover.

TOURIST STUFF

Pier 39 at (415) 705-5500,
www.pier39.com

Fisherman's Wharf

The Cannery at (415) 771-3112,
www.thecannery.com

Ghirardelli Square at
(415) 775-5500

San Francisco residents should familiarize themselves with these four tourist attractions. You never know when friends and family will be coming to town and will want the grand tour. When these attractions are not packed with tourists, they can be very fun. Pier 39 is home to a colony of sea lions that lounge on the marina dock slips. There is also

- San Francisco's tourist industry generates an average of $14 million of business per day in the city.
- Estimated daily spending per visitor is $130.
- Visitor spending contributes more than $5 billion annually to the local economy.
- The most international visitors come from the following countries: Japan, Germany, United Kingdom, Canada, France, Taiwan, Australia/New Zealand, South Korea, and Italy.
- The most U.S. visitors come from the following areas: Southern California, New York, Dallas, Chicago, Seattle, Boston, Miami, Baltimore, and Washington, D.C.

an aquarium, virtual reality theater, and pinball arcade, making this area more interesting than cheesy. Fisherman's Wharf, a few blocks to the west, has many seafood restaurants, a wax museum, and lots of souvenir T-shirt shops. Both The Cannery and Ghirardelli Square, situated side by side, have nicer shops and restaurants. Ghirardelli Square, once a chocolate factory, is now an ice cream parlor and candy store. After you have checked out these tourist attractions, you can grab a cable car to Nob Hill and Union Square.

Alcatraz Island

(415) 705-5555 (Blue & Gold Fleet *Ferry Service*)

www.nps.gov/alcatraz

This legendary maximum security prison once held such notorious criminals as Al Capone and "Machine Gun" Kelly. It is now maintained by the park service and tours are led daily. Accessible only by ferry, this is one of San Francisco's most popular attractions. Advance ticket purchase is recommended.

Angel Island State Park

(415) 435-1915 (*Information*)
(415) 897-0715 (*Angel Island Company*)

www.angelisland.com

A short ferry ride from San Francisco, this undeveloped 750-acre island in the middle of the bay offers spectacular views of the city. There are many hiking and biking trails as well as campsites and picnic areas with barbecues. Tram tours, bike rentals, and sea kayaking are available.

Coit Tower

Telegraph Hill access via Lombard Street
(415) 362-0808

Built as a memorial to San Francisco's volunteer firefighters, Coit Tower, along with the Transamerica Pyramid building and Golden Gate Bridge, is one of the city's most recognizable landmarks. The lobby has incredible murals depicting Depression-era California. A ride to the top of the tower will reward you with fantastic views of the city and bay.

Mission Dolores

Dolores and 16th Streets
(415) 621-8203

Built in 1776, this is the oldest building in San Francisco. The chapel is a well-preserved reminder of the Spanish missionary days in the city. There is a small museum and an old, spooky cemetery.

The Presidio

Enter from Lombard Street, Presidio, Arguello, or Lincoln Boulevards
(415) 561-4323
www.nps.gov/prsf

A former military base, its 1,480 acres are now under the management and care of the National Park Service. There are more than a hundred scenic miles of trails for hiking, biking, and jogging. There is even an Arnold Palmer Company–managed golf course.

Golden Gate Park

Bordered by Stanyan Street, The Great Highway, Lincoln Way, and Fulton Street
(415) 831-2700
www.goldengatepark.org

This 1,017-acre park is a one-stop place for culture and recreation. It is the home to the de Young Museum, Academy of Sciences, and Asian Art Museum. It also has countless outdoor activities for all tastes, including the following:

- Tennis courts, (415) 753-7001 or 753-7100
- Bike paths
- Rollerblading
- Boating, (415) 752-0347

- Golf, (415) 751-8987

- Horseback riding,
  (415) 668-7360

- Basketball

BEACHES

San Francisco is bordered on the west by the Pacific Ocean, so it naturally has many beaches. Ocean Beach is a viewing beach—swimming is not allowed due to volatile currents. The views are exhilarating of the crashing surf and of Seal Rocks, located offshore, with its inhabitants of shorebirds and sea lions. At Baker Beach, off 25th Avenue, swimming is dangerous, but the views of the Golden Gate Bridge are breathtaking. A section of Baker Beach is set aside as a nude beach. One of the few swimming beaches in the city is China Beach at 28th Avenue and Sea Cliff.

MUSEUMS

San Francisco has its share of quality museums. The new San Francisco Museum of Modern Art is recognized around the world. The de Young Museum houses a fine collection of classical art and has hosted such traveling shows as the Monet exhibit. On a smaller scale, there are independent museums such as the Cable Car Museum and Jewish Museum. Chapter 10 lists city museums, big and small.

LOCAL ATTRACTIONS

San Francisco Zoo

1 Zoo Road (at 45th Avenue at Sloat Boulevard)
(415) 753-7080
www.sfzoo.com

The San Francisco Zoo has exhibits like the Koala Crossing, Penguin Island, and the Feline Conservation Center. There is also a fun Children's Zoo.

San Francisco Giants Baseball

800-SF-GIANTS
www.sfgiants.com

San Francisco Visitor Profile:

37 years old

$65,900 median household income

Average length of stay is 4.5 nights

81% arrived by plane

46% are first-time visitors

20% are frequent visitors who had five or more previous visits

44% are in San Francisco for vacation, 25% for business, and 30% for a convention

64% of visitors are domestic, 36% are international

84% of visitors rate their visit with a Very Satisfied rating

---

This is a top-ranked baseball team that makes for a fun afternoon at the 'Stick (Candlestick Park, also known as 3Com Park).

San Francisco 49ers Football

(415) 468-2249

www.sf49ers.com

These are the Super Bowl champs of 1995, their fifth Super Bowl win. The all-star lineup of players, including quarterback Steve Young, is not to be missed.

MOVIE THEATERS

For local movie information, check the newspapers or access it at your fingertips on the Internet at **www.citisearch7.com.** New in town is the AMC1000 theater with fourteen screens and loveseat style seating.

SHOPPING

Two very pleasant and popular shopping centers in San Francisco are the Embarcadero Center at (415) 772-0500 and San Francisco Shopping Centre at (415) 495-5656. The Embarcadero Center is located in the Financial District at the base of four consecutive high-rise office buildings. The center is open-air but sheltered from the rain. At one end is Justin Herman Plaza, which holds many outdoor concerts and events. The shops include clothing stores such as Talbots and Ann Taylor, bookstores and newsstands, home furnishing stores such as Pottery Barn, and more. The San Francisco Shopping Centre, or Nordstrom Shopping Center as it is sometimes called, is located at the foot of Powell Street near the cable-car turnaround. Majestic winding escalators lead to shops like J. Crew, Williams-Sonoma, and, of course, Nordstrom.

There are also many neighborhood shopping districts in the city, such as the South of Market factory outlets; Union Square with Neiman Marcus and Saks Fifth Avenue department stores; the Marina and Union Street neighborhoods with their boutiques and novelty shops; and Haight Street with its vintage clothing stores, incense shops, and other paraphernalia.

PLAYHOUSES

The following are some of the bigger local playhouses in the city. Some Broadway hits that have played include *Phantom of the Opera, Hello Dolly!,* and *The King and I.*

Curran Theater, 445 Geary Street, (415) 551-2000

Golden Gate Theater, 1 Taylor Street, (415) 551-2000

Orpheum Theater, 1192 Market Street, (415) 551-2000

American Conservatory Theater (A.C.T.), 415 Geary Street, (415) 749-2228 or **www.act-sfbay.org**

Marines Memorial Theater, 609 Sutter Street, (415) 441-7444

Center for the Arts Theater, 701 Mission Street, (415) 978-2787 or **www.yerbabuenaarts.org**

Club Fugazi (always plays *Beach Blanket Babylon*), 678 Green Street, (415) 421-4222 or **www.beachblanketbabylon.com**

Theater on the Square, 450 Post Street, (415) 433-9500

COMEDY CLUBS

Cobb's Comedy Club, The Cannery, 2801 Leavenworth Street, (415) 928-4320

Josie's Cabaret and Juice Joint, 3583 16th Street, (415) 861-7933

Punchline, 444 Battery Street, (415) 397-7573

OUT OF TOWN

Out of town to San Franciscans could mean anything from biking to Marin for the day or driving up to Lake Tahoe for the weekend. The following is a list of some fun things to do and fun places to go outside of the city.

BERKELEY

Berkeley Convention and Visitors Bureau

(510) 549-7040

www.berkeleycvb.com

The '60s are alive and well in Berkeley. This college town is full of funky people, bohemian cafés, and unique boutiques. The main drag of Telegraph Avenue has street vendors selling handmade jewelry and tie-dye T-shirts, and some excellent bookstores. It is an easy drive from the city and an even easier commute by BART.

CARMEL AND MONTEREY

Carmel Chamber of Commerce

(408) 624-2522 or

www.carmelcalifornia.org

Monterey Peninsula Convention and Visitors Bureau

(408) 649-1770 or

www.monterey.com

The drive from San Francisco down Highway 1 to Monterey and Carmel is breathtaking, with ocean views and dramatic cliffs. Monterey is the first stop on this scenic journey. The Monterey Aquarium on 886 Cannery Row, (408) 375-3333, is renowned for its aquatic species and presentation. Carmel is a seaside village with craft stores and cafés tucked behind lush foliage. Not to be missed is 17-Mile Drive, which winds around Pebble Beach Golf Course along the rough northern ocean with its tide pools and sea lions. A great day trip or weekend getaway.

PALO ALTO

Stanford Shopping Center
(650) 617-8585 or
www.stanfordshop.com

Stanford University
(650) 723-2300 or
www.stanford.edu

This upscale community is home to Stanford University and the posh Stanford Shopping Center. Stanford University campus has a Rodin sculpture garden and outstanding libraries like the Hoover Institution, which are open to the public. Stanford Shopping Center will rate high with shopaholics. The anchor department stores include Neiman Marcus and Bloomingdale's; the shops range from Pottery Barn to Ralph Lauren.

SACRAMENTO

Sacramento Convention and Visitors Bureau
(916) 264-7777
www.sna.com/cvb

This is the state capital of California. Attractions include Olde Towne, the California State Railroad Museum, the Governor's Mansion, Capitol Building, and a zoo.

SANTA CRUZ

Santa Cruz County Visitors Council
(408) 426-7433
(Recorded information)
(408) 425-1234

Sausalito Chamber of Commerce

(415) 332-0505 or
www.sausalito.com

These two bayfront towns across the Golden Gate Bridge are great places to hang out on a lazy weekend afternoon. Many San Franciscans ride their bikes over the bridge and into Sausalito to browse the shops and art galleries. Further along is Tiburon, home to Sam's, a waterfront bar and restaurant that attracts crowds willing to wait two hours for a table in the sun.

(Visitor information)
www.sccvc.org or
www.beachboardwalk.com

Santa Cruz is a bustling beach town with a boardwalk that has amusement parks and eateries. It is also home to University of California–Santa Cruz, which you can visit.

SAUSALITO AND TIBURON

Tiburon Chamber of Commerce

(415) 435-5633

OTHER OUT OF TOWN ATTRACTIONS

Great America

Great America Parkway
Santa Clara, CA 95052
(408) 988-1776
www.pgathrills.com

Disneyland may be in Southern California, but northerners have Great America. About a one-hour drive from the city, this amusement park has concerts, rides, and other entertainment.

Lake Tahoe

Lake Tahoe Visitors Authority
(800) AT-TAHOE
www.tahoe.com

Bay Area residents ski at Lake Tahoe in the winter and enjoy mountain biking and water sports in the summer. A four-hour drive from San Francisco, this getaway offers not only outdoor activities but also gambling on the Nevada side of the lake.

Lindsay Museum

1931 First Avenue
Walnut Creek, CA 94596
(925) 935-1978
www.wildlife-museum.org

This natural history museum highlights Contra Costa County wildlife. It has hands-on exhibits, an injured animal rehab center, and a pet lending library.

Marin Headlands

(415) 331-1540
www.marin.org

For nearly one hundred years this land was used by the Army. There are still remnants of the military bunkers and forts that helped defend the Golden Gate from 1870 through World War II. Visitors enjoy many hiking and equestrian trails that have incredible views of San Francisco.

New Marine World Themepark

Marine World Parkway
Vallejo, CA 94589
(707) 643-6722
www.freerun.com/napavalley/outdoor/marinewo/marinewo.html

A combination wildlife park and oceanarium. Ride elephants, see performances by killer whales, sea lions, tigers, and chimps.

Mono Lake

(760) 647-6595
www.monolake.org

Located in the eastern Sierras, this lake is believed to be a million years old. There is much to do here, like camping, hiking, swimming, or taking a naturalist-guided tour or moonlight tour.

Mt. Diablo State Park

(510) 837-2525
www.mdia.org

Located in Contra Costa County, this is a 19,000-acre state park. Recreation activities include camping, hiking, rock climbing, and horseback riding. There are also many ranger-led hikes and educational presentations offered by the Mt. Diablo Interpretive Association (925-927-7222).

Mt. Shasta

(800) 926-4865
www.mtshasta.com

This is a 14,162-foot inactive volcano surrounded by lush parklands. Besides hiking, camping and fishing, there are also unique things to do like hot-air ballooning, caving, dogsled rides, and gold panning.

Mt. Tamalpais State Park

Pantoll Ranger Station
(415) 388-2070
www.marin.org/npo/mttam

A short drive from San Francisco, over the Golden Gate Bridge and into Marin County, is Mt. Tam, as it is known by locals. The views are

---

An estimated 66,000 jobs in San Francisco are directly supported by tourists:

Hotel (27%)
Restaurant/bar (26%)
Entertainment/sightseeing (15%)
Retail (13%)
Airport (12%)
Local transportation (4%)
Convention/other (3%)

breathtaking, and there are many hiking and biking trails. The Sierra Club offers hikes, as does the Mt. Tamalpais Interpretive Association, (415) 388-2070, which has moonlight, weeknight, and weekend hikes through the park. Check out their public astronomy programs held under the stars.

Muir Woods

(415) 388-2595
www.nps.gov/muwo

This is a 550-acre coastal redwood forest with some trees reaching almost two hundred feet high. Though the park may seem crowded, there are back trails that offer some peace and solitude.

Oakland Zoo

(510) 632-9525
www.oaklandzoo.org

This zoo across the bay from San Francisco has more than three hundred animals organized by their respective geographic regions in settings that represent their native landscapes.

Raging Waters

Lake Cunningham Regional Park
San Jose, CA 95151
(408) 270-8000
www.raging-waters.com

A great way to escape the cold San Francisco summers is to drive out to sweltering San Jose and play in their premier water park. There are wave pools, the Pirate's Cove, and a seven-story water slide.

Stinson Beach

(415) 868-0942 (Information)
(415) 868-1922 (Weather, surf, parking info)

This is a popular beach sheltered by the cliffs of the Marin Headlands.

Tilden Park

(510) 635-0135
(510) 635-0138 (Information Line)

Tilden Park is located thirty minutes from San Francisco over the Bay Bridge. There are many attractions in this 2,000-acre wilderness-type area. There are a variety of hiking trails, Lake Anza for swimming and sunbathing, Tilden Little Farm with farm animals and vegetable gardens, old-fashioned miniature steam railroad trains, and a golf course.

Wine Country

Sonoma Wine and Visitor Center
(707) 586-3795 or
www.sonomawine.com

Napa Valley Conference and Visitors Bureau
(707) 226-7459 or
www.napavalley.com

The Sonoma and Napa wine countries are two attractions considered Northern California highlights. Both are an easy one-and-a-half hour drive from San Francisco. A trip to Napa Valley might include visits and tours of wineries like Robert Mondavi, Beringer, Sutter Home, and Sterling, to name a few of the more popular ones. Traveling further along Route 29 will take you to Calistoga, famous for its mud baths and hot springs. Route 12 leads to Sonoma, where you can take a bicycle or horseback tour of the local wineries like Kenwood, Benziger, and Sebastiani. Town center is quaint and old-fashioned, a nice place to stop and have lunch. To help plan your trip, visit www.winecountry.com for more information.

Yosemite National Park

P.O. Box 577
Yosemite, CA 95389
(209) 372-0264
(209) 372-0200 (General Park Information)
www.nps.gov

If wilderness and the great outdoors is your thing, a five-hour drive from the city will get you to this popular national park. Camping, hiking, and skiing are three of the many activities you can do alone or in ranger-led groups. Expect crowds and even traffic on the weekends, especially in the summer.

RECOMMENDED READING

Bay Area Backroads, by Doug McConnell, Jerry Emory, and Stacey Geiken (Chronicle Books, 1999). Based on a popular television program that goes off the beaten path to discover Bay Area locations and sights.

Stairway Walks in San Francisco, by Adah Bakalinsky (Wilderness Press, 1995). Features twenty-seven guided neighborhood stair walks.

San Francisco: The Ultimate Guide, by Randolph Delehanty (Chronicle Books, 1995). Contains self-guided walking tours organized around neighborhoods, historic sites, and museums.

The New San Francisco at Your Feet, by Margot Patterson Doss (Grove Press, 1991). A walker's guide to San Francisco with anecdotes and history.

Quick Escapes from San Francisco, by Karen Misuraca (Globe Pequot, 1996). There are thirty weekend trips within hours from San Francisco.

Bay Area Bike Rides, by Ray Hosler (Chronicle Books, 1994). Bike rides from Sonoma to the South Bay.

WORLD WIDE WEB RESOURCES

SFStation
(**www.sfstation.com**)
This is the hip, urban connection for art, entertainment, food, and other San Francisco happenings.

CitySearch7
(**www.citysearch7.com**)
This is the local ABC affiliate (Channel 7) homepage that lists city happenings as well as restaurants, sports, professional services, and more.

SFSidewalk
(**sanfrancisco.sidewalk.com**)
This is a guide to movies, restaurants, events, arts, and sports in San Francisco.

PART 3

RELOCATING TO THE SILICON VALLEY

CHAPTER TWELVE

SILICON VALLEY OVERVIEW

EOPLE AROUND THE world recognize the Silicon Valley as the birthplace of technology. Companies like Apple Computer, Hewlett-Packard, Novell, and Intel are just some of the industry giants that make their home in Santa Clara County. But before it was dubbed the Silicon Valley, it was known as the "Valley of the Heart's Delight." Good climate and agricultural prosperity attracted the first settlers to the area. Today good weather is still an attraction, along with an abundance of well-paying technology and related jobs.

The original inhabitants of Santa Clara County were the Ohlone Indians. They occupied the vast oak forests that surrounded the region for centuries before Spanish explorers arrived in the 1700s. Missions were then established, and local natives were put to work for the Spanish. The first civil settlement was founded in 1777 in what is now the city of San Jose. After Mexico declared its independence from Spain in 1821, California became a part of Mexico territory and remained under its rule until the Mexican-American War of 1846. After the war in 1848, California became part of the United States. The Gold Rush began in 1849, and the towns of Santa Clara County made their fortune not from prospecting, but by providing food and provisions for prospectors heading to the Sierras. After the Gold Rush, many of these prospectors decided to stay in the area and saw opportunities to work the land. The county became rich in agriculture and farming and by the early 1900s fruit and vegetable packing plants provided the manufacturing base for the area.

Also around the early 1900s the technical revolution slowly started. In 1909, Cyrus Elwell, a Stanford graduate, established Federal Telegraph

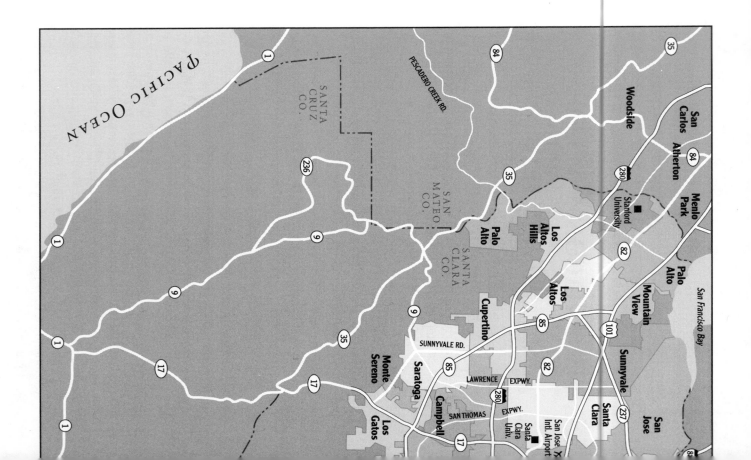

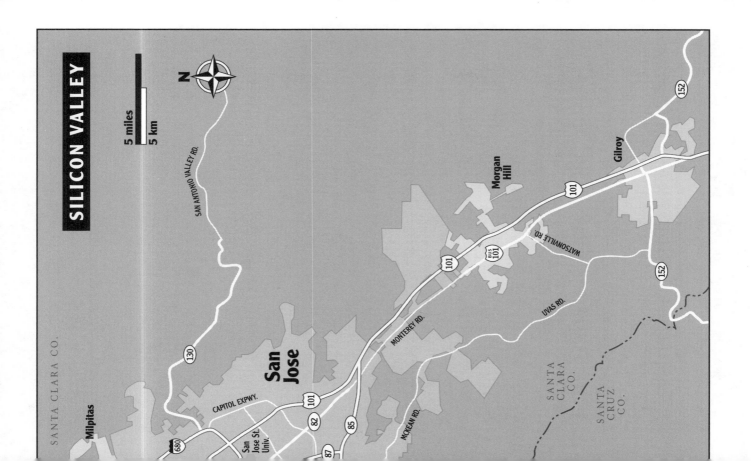

SILICON VALLEY

5 miles
5 km

N

SANTA CLARA CO.

Milpitas

San Antonio Valley Rd.

680

130

San Jose St. Univ.

CAPITOL EXPWY.

San Jose

82

101

87

85

MCKEAN RD.

MONTEREY RD.

101

UVAS RD.

BUS 101

WATSONVILLE RD.

101

Morgan Hill

SANTA CLARA CO.

SANTA CRUZ CO.

Gilroy

152

152

STATISTICS

Santa Clara County is the largest county in the San Francisco Bay Area with over 1.6 million residents.

It covers 1,312 square miles.

There are fifteen cities in Santa Clara County: (ranked by population)

1. San Jose	894,000
2. Sunnyvale	131,100
3. Santa Clara	101,900
4. Mountain View	74,700
5. Milpitas	62,600
6. Palo Alto	60,500
7. Cupertino	46,700
8. Campbell	39,700
9. Gilroy	37,450
10. Saratoga	31,100
11. Los Gatos	30,100
12. Morgan Hill	29,300
13. Los Altos	28,400
14. Los Altos Hills	8,175
15. Monte Sereno	3,420

According to the July 1997 Money magazine survey of best places to live, San Jose ranked eighth in the United States. It also has the lowest crime rate of any major city in the United States with a population of 300,000 or more.

Some San Jose firsts:

First civil settlement in California on November 29, 1777

First public school in California, San Jose Granary, 1795

First state capital on December 15, 1849

First governor of California was San Jose resident Peter H. Burnett in 1849.

First Japanese-American mayor of a large city (population 500,000 or more) was Norman Y. Mineta in 1971.

First woman mayor of a large city (population 500,000 or more) was Janet Gray Hayes in 1974.

Company in Palo Alto with financing from his alma mater. One of the company's engineers, Lee de Forrest, developed the vacuum tube that could amplify an electrical signal within airless confines. This invention established him as the founder of modern electronics. When Elwell decided to take his company to New Jersey in 1931, several engineers stayed behind and went on to establish Litton Industries and Magnavox.

A name most often associated with the development of the Silicon Valley is Frederick Terman, a professor of electrical engineering at Stanford during the 1930s. He encouraged his graduates to work for local companies or stay in the area and start their own businesses. Students like Bill Hewlett and David Packard started their own company, Hewlett-Packard, that today is a multimillion dollar corporation still going strong.

With the onset of World War II, the U.S. government began investing millions of dollars in Santa Clara County to build industrial defense plants. In San Jose, new plants were built for the production of magnesium, ferrosilicon, and plastics. The Food Machinery and Chemical Corporation (FMC) of San Jose made tanks for the Army. Joshua Hendy Iron Works, the largest manufacturer in the county, built naval landing boat engines. World War II also brought more people to the area for military service or to support the war effort. After the war ended, many of the thousands of servicemen and defense workers who came to California stayed on.

The postwar period saw rapid development of farmlands into business and residential communities with new homes, shopping centers, streets, and highways. In 1944, prominent leaders of the city of San Jose formed the Progress Committee to develop the area further. In an effort to diversify the county's manufacturing base, the County Chamber of Commerce hired a public relations representative to encourage industrial leaders nationwide to expand their businesses into Santa Clara County. Selling points included good climate, low taxes, and plenty of affordable land for new industry. The campaign ended in 1965 with great success, having attracted businesses like Ames Aerospace Laboratories, Lockheed, Shockley Transistor Corporation, Fairchild, Raytheon, Signetics, National Semiconductor, and Intel. Besides technology, other companies, like Kaiser Permanente Cement Corporation, International Minerals and Chemical Corporation, Ford Motor Company, and General Electric, built facilities in the county.

The exceptional industrial growth in Santa Clara County meant rapid population change. Between 1950 and 1970 the population jumped from 290,547 residents to 1,064,714. Around the same time in 1940, the county had 101,666 acres of farmland; by 1973 only 23,511 acres remained. People came to the Silicon Valley for high-paying jobs that were mostly manufacturing and trade positions. There were also many homes available that the federal government made possible to own with low-interest rate loans and tax benefits.

Today, the Silicon Valley continues to see a migration into its region for many of the same reasons it enticed settlers back in the 1800s. Job opportunities, good weather, and quality of life are what probably attracted most of the 35,100 people who relocated to Santa Clara County in 1997. The following chapters will help you to relocate to the Silicon Valley by providing useful information and resources. From finding an apartment to keeping entertained on the weekends, you will soon discover the many diverse people and places that make the area universally appealing. The Silicon Valley has something for everyone, and new residents will soon discover that computers and technology are only one part of the equation.

TRANSPORTATION INFORMATION

Santa Clara Valley Transportation Authority (VTA)
(408) 321-2300
www.vta.org

Local bus service in Santa Clara County. They operate Historic Trolleys in downtown San Jose.

CalTrain
(800) 660-4287
www.caltrain.com

Offers passenger train service between San Francisco, San Jose, and Gilroy

San Jose International Airport
(408) 277-4759
www.sjc.org

CHAPTER THIRTEEN

SILICON VALLEY COMMUNITIES

CAMPBELL

Campbell Chamber of Commerce

1628 West Campbell Avenue
Campbell, CA 95008
(408) 378-6252
www.ci.campbell.ca.us

HISTORY

Benjamin Campbell was the founder of the small farming community of Campbell back in the 1850s. He was a prominent community leader and rancher whose hay and grain fields later became the historical downtown of the city. In 1878, Mr. Campbell donated an acre of his land to the railroad. Nine years later, the drying grounds and canneries of the town made Campbell an important rail center for shipping fruit. In 1903, President Theodore Roosevelt visited Campbell and planted a redwood tree on the grounds of Campbell Union High School, which now serves as a community center.

Before going high tech, Campbell was famous for its prunes. It was known as the home of the world's largest fruit drying plant, giving it the moniker "Prune Capital of the World." During the building boom of the 1950s, prune orchards disappeared to make way for home and business construction. Campbell remembers its agricultural past at its annual Prune Festival and at the Pruneyard Shopping Center, a local attraction.

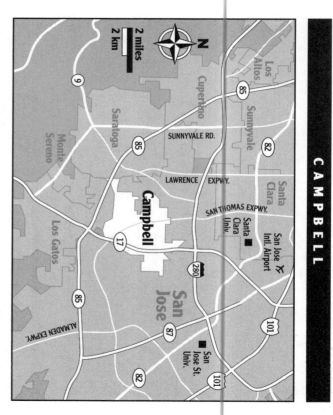

Campbell was officially incorporated as a city in 1952. Today it is a modern, suburban community that still maintains its small-town charm. It is located in the heart of Silicon Valley in the southwest portion of Santa Clara County, adjacent to Los Gatos, Saratoga, and San Jose. The city has a pro-growth development attitude and is working on many projects to redevelop and revitalize its downtown.

DEMOGRAPHICS/ STATISTICS

Average Rent

Studio: $827

One-bedroom: $1,058

Two-bedroom, One-bath: $1,189

Two-bedroom, Two-bath: $1,348

Ethnic/Racial Distribution

White: 79%

African American: 2%

Asian: 9%

Hispanic: 10%

Gender Distribution

Male: 49%

Female: 51%

Population: 38,267

Median Age: 39

Renters: 53%

Crime

Homicide: 0

Rape: 2.6

Robbery: 10.3

Assault: 21.4

Burglary: 52.1

Larceny: 290.1

Auto Theft: 26.7

Local Newspapers

Campbell Express, (408) 374-9700
Campbell Times, (408) 494-7000

TOP TEN EMPLOYERS IN CAMPBELL

1. HAL Computer Systems: 400 employees

2. Burns International Security Services: 350 employees

3. Pana Pacific Corp.: 280 employees

4. Zilog Inc.: 260 employees

5. Meta-Software, Inc.: 125 employees

6. Santa Clara Valley Associates: 125 employees

7. Daley's Drywall & Taping Inc.: 100 employees

8. Draeger Construction Inc.: 100 employees

9. Haig Precision Manufacturing Corp.: 100 employees

10. P-Com Inc.: 100 employees

NUMBERS TO KNOW

Fire Department (non-emergency)

(408) 378-4010

Garbage Collection and Recycling

Green Valley Disposal Company
(408) 354-2100
www.greenvalley.com

Gas and Electric Utilities

Pacific Gas & Electric
(800) 743-5000

Phone Service

Pacific Bell
(800) 310-2355

Police Department (non-emergency)

(408) 866-2101

Television Cable Service

TCI Cablevision
(408) 744-1515

Water Service

San Jose Water Company
(408) 279-7900

CUPERTINO

Cupertino Chamber of Commerce

20455 Silverado Avenue
Cupertino, CA 95014
(408) 252-7054
www.cupertino.org

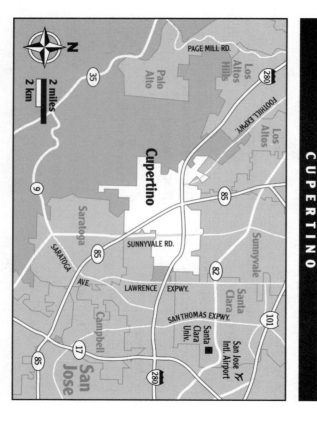

HISTORY

In 1776, the 93rd encampment of Spanish explorer Don Bautista de Anza settled by a creek on the land that is now Cupertino. Christened Arroyo San Joseph Cupertino by Anza's diarist Petrus Font, it was named after the patron saint of Font's hometown, San Guiseppe of Copertino, Italy.

The Spanish and Mexican settlers of this area used the land to raise cattle and harvest wheat. When California became a state in 1848, American and European settlers began to arrive in part for the Gold Rush as well as to escape economic hardships and political turmoil in Europe. These immigrants used the land to plant vineyards for wine-producing grapes. Cupertino became a wine region until 1895, when all the vines were plagued with the phylloxera microbe.

CUPERTINO

The village of Cupertino sprang up at the intersection of Saratoga-Sunnyvale Road and Stevens Creek Boulevard. It was first called "West Side," but because other towns already used the name, it was changed to Cupertino. This crossroad became the center of town, with a post office, blacksmith, hardware store, library, church, and dress shop. The Cali Brothers opened a million-dollar feed store and grain hauling business that is still in operation today.

With the completion of the San Francisco–San Jose railroad line in 1864, Cupertino and its neighboring towns became the weekend destination for wealthy San Franciscans. Visitors on their way to vacation homes or the Saratoga mineral springs passed through the sleepy farming town of Cupertino with its orchards and fruit-drying yards.

In 1912, real estate developer George Hensley saw the potential of the area and began aggressively promoting it. Following World War II, the city experienced a tremendous population growth that became the impetus for its incorporation in 1955. Today Cupertino is a thriving residential and business community, home to famous technology companies like Apple Computer, Tandem Computers, and the founding father, Hewlett-Packard.

DEMOGRAPHICS/STATISTICS

Average Rent

Studio: $1,053

One-bedroom: $1,366

Two-bedroom, One-bath: $1,536

Two-bedroom, Two-bath: $1,849

Ethnic/Racial Distribution

White: 71%

African American: 1%

Asian: 23%

Hispanic: 5%

Gender Distribution

Male: 50%

Female: 50%

Population: 43,627

Median Age: 36

Crime

Homicide: 0

Rape: 2.3

Robbery: 6.2

Assault: 15.7

Burglary: 50.1

Larceny: 228.9

Auto Theft: 13.9

Local Newspaper

Cupertino Courier, (408) 255-7500

TOP TEN EMPLOYERS IN CUPERTINO

1. Hewlett-Packard: 3,600 employees
2. Apple Computer: 3,500 employees
3. Tandem Computers: 3,000 employees
4. Cupertino Union School District: 1,200 employees
5. Foothill/DeAnza Community College District: 1,100 employees
6. Fremont Union High School District: 722 employees
7. Honeywell-Measurex: 500 employees
8. Symantec: 450 employees
9. Rational Software Corp.: 425 employees
10. Sears: 295 employees

NUMBERS TO KNOW

Fire Department (non-emergency)
(408) 378-4010

Garbage Collection and Recycling
Los Altos Garbage
(408) 725-4020

Gas and Electric Utilities
Pacific Gas & Electric
(800) 743-5000

Phone Service
Pacific Bell
(800) 310-2355

Sheriff Department (non-emergency)
(408) 299-2622

Television Cable Service
TCI Cablevision
(408) 744-1515

Water Service
San Jose Water Company
(408) 279-7900

GILROY

Gilroy Chamber of Commerce
7471 Monterey Street
Gilroy, CA 95020
(408) 842-6437
www.gilroy.org

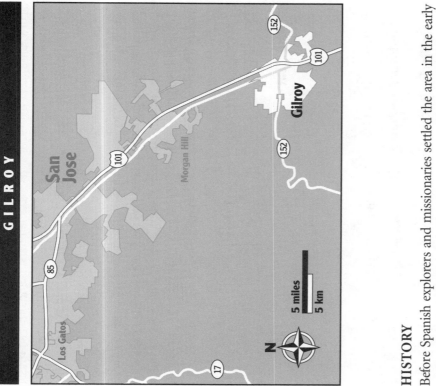

GILROY

HISTORY

Before Spanish explorers and missionaries settled the area in the early 1800s, Gilroy's first inhabitants were the Ohlone Indians. The first new-comers arrived in 1843 and by 1849 the Gold Rush brought pioneers from all over the world to the area first known as Pleasant Valley. Early settlers raised cattle and farmed grain, earning Gilroy the distinction of being named the Hay and Grain Capital of California. When the railroad arrived in Gilroy in 1869, it became the hub of the south Santa Clara Valley. In 1865, the Gilroy Hot Springs were discovered and developed into one of the leading resorts on the West Coast. This spa offered swim-ming, mineral baths, mud baths, and massage. In the 1870s, Gilroy be-came known as the Tobacco Capital of the United States. It had the world's largest cigar factory that produced over one million cigars each month. In the 1880s, with the arrival of Swiss immigrants, dairy and cheesemaking became the leading industry and earned Gilroy the title of Dairy and Cheese Capital of California. In the 1890s, the hay and grain fields were cleared for fruit and nut orchards. Gilroy became known as Prune Capital of California in the 1920s and '30s. Then Italians and other southern Europeans arrived in Gilroy and started growing tomatoes, peppers, onions, and garlic that were canned or dehydrated. World War I and the arrival of the Japanese was a boom for the garlic industry, and today Gilroy is known as the Garlic Capital of the World. Though located only twenty miles from San Jose, technology has not taken over this strong agriculture and farming community. Food and seed processing are big industries, as is wine production. Many visitors come to Gilroy for its outlet shopping and plethora of auto dealerships. Gilroy offers an affordable, country lifestyle with proximity to Silicon Valley.

DEMOGRAPHICS/ STATISTICS

Average Rent

Studio: N/A

One-bedroom: $823

Two-bedroom, One-bath: $931

Two-bedroom, Two-bath: $968

Ethnic/Racial Distribution

White: 49%

African American: 1%

Asian: 3%

Hispanic: 47%

Gender Distribution

Male: 50%

Female: 50%

Population: 36,500

Median Age: 30

Crime

Homicide: .3

Rape: 2.6

Robbery: 28.7

Assault: 100.3

Burglary: 112

Larceny: 356

Auto Theft: 42.2

Local Newspaper

Dispatch, (408) 842-6400

TOP TEN EMPLOYERS IN GILROY

1. Gilroy Foods, Inc.: 1,053 employees

2. A & D Christopher Ranch: 725 employees

3. Lohmar: 375 employees

4. Filice Trucking: 375 employees

5. Headstart Nursery: 210 employees

6. California Door Company: 180 employees

7. Westside Transport: 175 employees

8. Security Packaging Inc.: 175 employees

9. Delta Lithograph Co.: 175 employees

10. Gaylord Container Corp.: 175 employees

NUMBERS TO KNOW

Fire Department (non-emergency)
(408) 848-0350

Garbage Collection and Recycling
South Valley Disposal and Recycling
(408) 842-3358

Gas and Electric Utilities
Pacific Gas & Electric
(800) 743-5000

Phone Service
GTE
(408) 842-7187

Police Department (non-emergency)
(408) 848-0350

Television Cable Service
Falcon Cable Television
(408) 842-5653

Water Service
City of Gilroy
(408) 848-0420

LOS ALTOS/LOS ALTOS HILLS

Los Altos Chamber of Commerce
321 University Avenue
Los Altos, CA 94022
(408) 948-1455
www.losaltosonline.com

HISTORY

This is a prestigious, quiet community that was first inhabited by Ohlone Indians centuries ago. Artifacts, relics, and skeletal remains have been discovered in this area, confirming the past existence of Indian villages and burial grounds. One of the first explorers to the area was Juan Bautista de Anza, who led a Spanish expedition in 1776 on his way to the San Francisco Bay. The area was further explored and settled by the Franciscans, under the leadership of Father Junipero

Serra, who constructed the California missions. When Mexico won its independence from Spain in 1821, land grants to California were given to Catholic natives or naturalized citizens of Mexico. California was ceded to the United States in 1848 and admitted to the union in 1850.

Los Altos was initially developed by Southern Pacific Railroad executive Paul Shoup and his colleagues. They linked Palo Alto and Los Gatos by making Los Altos a commuter town. Nearby San Jose was the county seat at that time, and Stanford University was a cultural attraction. Los Altos developed into a charming small town until World War II, when there was a boom in housing construction and new schools. Los Altos was incorporated as Santa Clara's eleventh city in 1952. Los Altos Hills followed suit in 1956.

Bordered by Palo Alto, Mountain View, Sunnyvale, and Cupertino, today Los Altos and Los Altos Hills have developed with small businesses, schools, churches, apartments, and homes. There are seven commercial centers that service these two areas: Rancho Shopping Center, Loyola Corners, Woodland Plaza, El Camino Real Corridor, Village Court, Foothill Plaza, and Downtown. School rankings are among the highest in California, and crime ranks lowest in the state.

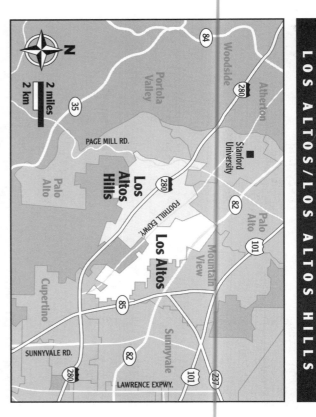

DEMOGRAPHICS/ STATISTICS

Average Rent

Studio: N/A

One-bedroom: $1,337

Two-bedroom, One-bath: $1,537

Two-bedroom, Two-bath: $1,737

Gender Distribution

Male: 49%

Female: 51%

Ethnic/Racial Distribution

White: 87%

African American: 1%

Asian: 10%

Hispanic: 2%

Population: 27,988

Median Age: 42

Crime

Homicide: 0

Rape: 1.1

Robbery: 4.9

Assault: 9.4

Burglary: 42

Larceny: 122.4

Auto Theft: 3.2

Local Newspaper

Los Altos Town Crier
(650) 948-9000

NUMBERS TO KNOW

Fire Department (non-emergency)

(408) 378-4010

Garbage Collection and Recycling

Los Altos Garbage Company
(650) 961-8040

Gas and Electric Utilities

Pacific Gas & Electric
(800) 743-5000

Phone Service

Pacific Bell
(800) 310-2355

Police Department (non-emergency)

(650) 948-8223

Television Cable Service

TCI Cablevision
(650) 940-1090

Water Service

California Water Service
(Los Altos residents)
(650) 917-0152

Purissima Hills Water District
(Los Altos Hills residents)
(650) 948-1217

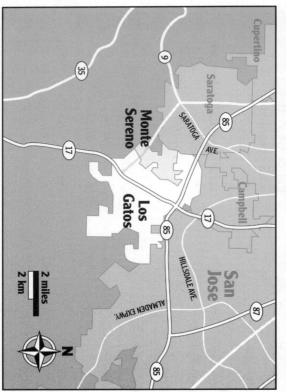

LOS GATOS/MONTE SERENO

Los Gatos Chamber of Commerce

333 North Santa Cruz Avenue
Los Gatos, CA 95030
(408) 354-9300
www.losgatosweb.com

HISTORY

Though only ten square miles in size and with a population of less than 30,000 residents, Los Gatos can boast about once being home to writer John Steinbeck, ice-skater Peggy Fleming, and violinist Yehudi Menuhin. It is located on the eastern slopes of the Santa Cruz mountains, where the weather is mild, trees are abundant, and the commute around Silicon Valley is bearable.

The Costanoan Indians were the first inhabitants of the vast oak forests that carpeted the Los Gatos area. The Spanish arrived in the late 1700s and started clearing the land for farming, disrupting the natural habitat of the Indians and leading to their decline. California ceded from Mexico in 1846, and the area started being settled by European immigrants. The first building in the original 100-acre town was Forbes Mill, and for a while the town was called by that name. It was later renamed Los Gatos for the numerous wildcats that lived in the hills and caused destruction to many properties.

When Forbes Mill, a flour mill, opened in 1854, it formed the economic foundation of Los Gatos at that time. Later, because of their profitability, fruit orchards replaced grain fields, and this led to the development of canning and fruit drying industries. Los Gatos became an agricultural fruit basket with prunes, apricots, and grapes being the biggest crops. The most prosperous time for Los Gatos started in 1877 when South Pacific Coast Railroad came to town. In 1887, the town had grown so much that it decided to incorporate.

Far from its agricultural peak in the 1920s, today only a handful of farms remain in the area. The town of Los Gatos has become a quiet, safe, residential community mixed with some technology and health care businesses. There is a thriving downtown area that includes a historic district with boutiques, restaurants, coffee shops, and antique stores.

DEMOGRAPHICS/STATISTICS

Average Rent

Studio: N/A

One-bedroom: $1,267

Two-bedroom, One-bath: $1,421

Two-bedroom, Two-bath: $1,628

Ethnic/Racial Distribution

White: 89%

African American: 1%

Asian: 5%

Hispanic: 5%

Gender Distribution

Male: 48%

Female: 52 %

Population: 28,951

Median Age: 39

Crime

Homicide: 0

Rape: 0.7

Robbery: 3.7

Assault: 13.5

Burglary: 63.4

Larceny: 187.2

Auto Theft: 12.5

NUMBERS TO KNOW

Fire Department (non-emergency)
(408) 378-4010

Garbage Collection and Recycling
Green Valley Disposal Company
(408) 354-2100
www.greenvalley.com

Gas and Electric Utilities
Pacific Gas & Electric
(800) 743-5000

Phone Service
GTE
(408) 842-7187

Police Department (non-emergency)
(409) 354-8600

Television Cable Service
TCI Cablevision
(408) 744-1515

Water Service
San Jose Water Company
(408) 279-7900

Local Newspaper
Los Gatos Weekly Times,
(408) 354-3110

TOP TEN EMPLOYERS IN LOS GATOS

1. Community Hospital: 800 employees
2. Caere Corporation: 250 employees
3. Metricom Inc.: 150 employees
4. Maxxim Medical Inc.: 130 employees
5. Red Brick Systems: 170 employees
6. Compuware Corporation: 100 employees
7. Rhetorex Technology Inc.: 100 employees
8. ICTV Inc.: 85 employees
9. America's Funding Source: 75 employees
10. CMS Properties: 70 employees

MILPITAS

Milpitas Chamber of Commerce
138 North Milpitas Boulevard
Milpitas, CA 95035
(408) 262-2613
www.milpitas-chamber.com

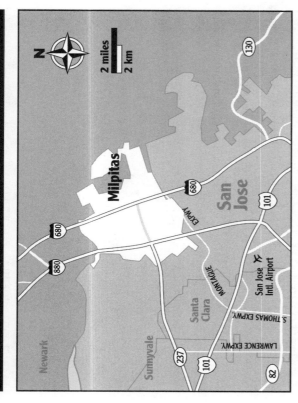

HISTORY

For three thousand years, Milpitas was the land of Ohlone Indians until the Spanish settled the area in the early 1800s. The land grew into a settlement of ranchos, with the largest one, measuring almost 4,458 acres, called Rancho Milpitas, which is how the area got its name. The town of Milpitas, which is Spanish for "little corn fields," came into existence in 1856 when Frederick Creighton erected the first building and opened a store. The Southern Pacific Railroad came through town in 1869.

In the 1870s, Milpitas became an agricultural region with vegetable crops, vineyards, and fruit orchards. The huge old oak forests were cut for firewood, and the mustard stalks that filled the valley were cleared for hay and grain fields. In the 1880s, strawberries and asparagus became major crops, making Milpitas an important supply and shipping center.

For years, settlement into the area was slow, and the town remained unaffected by the changes the rest of the county was experiencing. In 1954, after World War II, the city incorporated and began to evolve from a small agricultural community into an industrial center. It became home to a Ford auto assembly plant, which has since been turned into the Great Mall of the Bay Area, a local attraction. In the early

1980s, it started attracting high-tech companies and employees who liked the affordable housing, decent schools, and low crime rate. Today Milpitas is an economically and culturally rich community. Compared to other cities and towns in Santa Clara County, much of Milpitas is new and still growing. It is a family community with 27 percent of the population under eighteen years of age.

DEMOGRAPHICS/ STATISTICS

Average Rent

Studio: N/A

One-bedroom: $1,052

Two-bedroom, One-bath: $1,129

Two-bedroom, Two-bath: $1,409

Ethnic/Racial Distribution

White: 42%

African American: 6%

Asian: 34%

Hispanic: 18%

Gender Distribution

Male: 53%

Female: 47%

Population: 59,725

Median Age: 31

Crime

Homicide: .35

Rape: 4.1

Robbery: 11.6

Assault: 24.5

Burglary: 61.7

Larceny: 283.1

Auto Theft: 44.8

Local Newspaper

Milpitas Post, (408) 262-2454

TOP TEN EMPLOYERS IN MILPITAS

1. Solectron California: 6,400 employees

2. LSI Logic: 4,000 employees

3. Quantum: 2,700 employees

4. Great Mall of Bay Area: 2,300 employees

5. Sun Microsystems: 2,250 employees

6. Read-Rite: 2,000 employees

7. Lifescan, Inc.: 1,700 employees

8. KOMAG: 1,700 employees

9. Octel Communications Corp.: 1,600 employees

10. Adaptec, Inc.: 1,145 employees

NUMBERS TO KNOW

Fire Department (non-emergency)
(408) 942-2383

Garbage Collection and Recycling
Browning Ferris Industries (BFI)
(408) 432-1234

Gas and Electric Utilities
Pacific Gas & Electric
(800) 743-5000

Phone Service
Pacific Bell
(800) 310-2355

Police Department (non-emergency)
(408) 942-2400

Television Cable Service
TCI Cablevision
(408) 744-1515

Water Service
City of Milpitas Water Department
(408) 942-2333

MORGAN HILL

Morgan Hill Chamber of Commerce
25 West First Street
Morgan Hill, CA 95037
(408) 779-9444
www.morganhill.org/mhcc

HISTORY

At the time of its incorporation in 1906, early settlers felt Morgan Hill should have been named Murphysboro, after its original founder, Martin Murphy, Sr. Murphy was a prominent name, not only in the Bay Area, but nationwide, since he was the richest landowner in America. His grand-daughter, Diana, married Hiram Morgan Hill and went on to inherit the land holdings that became Morgan Hill.

Located at the southern end of the county near Gilroy, about twenty miles from San Jose, the oak tree–covered land of Morgan Hill was first inhabited by Ohlone Indians. Then Spanish expeditions arrived in the area from Mexico in the early 1800s. In 1821, when Mexico declared its independence from Spain, Murphy took advantage of land grants that became available and purchased them for his sons.

In 1898, a Southern Pacific Railroad station was built and named Huntington, but since there was another stop by that name, it was changed to Morgan Hill. The city has been known as Morgan Hill ever since. After the death of Daniel Murphy, who was Diana's father, Hiram began managing the Murphy land by reducing the size of the original land grants and opening it up to new settlers. The town attracted many newcomers because of its low land prices and the potential success of fruit orchard businesses. Also, the fact that there were no saloons in town at the time, as well as the convenience of the railroad, made it an appealing, wholesome place to live.

Today Morgan Hill continues to change from a small agricultural community to a business city, mixing high-tech industry with conventional manufacturing firms. It still has plenty of open space and a country feel. It is considered a good place to work, live, and raise a family.

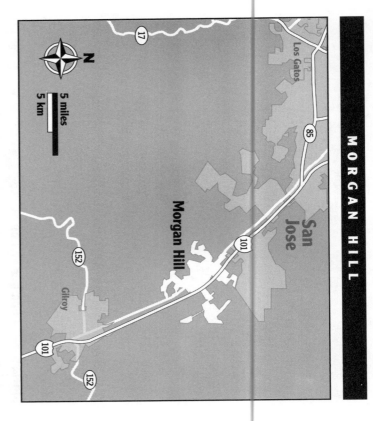

MORGAN HILL

DEMOGRAPHICS/ STATISTICS

Average Rent

Studio: N/A

One-bedroom: $1,150

Two-bedroom, One-bath: N/A

Two-bedroom, Two-bath: $1,463

Ethnic/Racial Distribution

White: 70%

African American: 2%

Asian: 5%

Hispanic: 23%

Gender Distribution

Male: 50%

Female: 50%

Population: 33,800

Median Age: 32

Crime

Homicide: 0

Rape: 3.3

Robbery: 5.2

Assault: 10

Burglary: 82.9

Larceny: 309

Auto Theft: 24

Local Newspaper

Morgan Hill Times, (408) 779-4106

TOP TEN EMPLOYERS OF MORGAN HILL

1. Morgan Hill Unified School District: 950 employees

2. CIDCO Corporation: 550 employees

3. Wiltron Co.: 520 employees

4. A.M.P.: 300 employees

5. B.A.S. Sheet Metal: 300 employees

6. Saint Louise Hospital: 250 employees

7. Specialized Bicycle: 230 employees

8. Ra-Tek Inc.: 200 employees

9. Custom Chrome: 180 employees

10. Target: 165 employees

NUMBERS TO KNOW

Fire Department (non-emergency)
(800) 800-1793

Garbage Collection and Recycling
Morgan Hill Water & Garbage Service
(408) 779-7221

Gas and Electric Utilities

Pacific Gas & Electric
(800) 743-5000

Phone Service

GTE

(408) 842-7187

Police Department (non-emergency)

(408) 779-7211

Television Cable Service

Falcon Cable TV
(408) 842-5653

Water Service

Morgan Hill Water & Garbage Service
(408) 779-7221

MOUNTAIN VIEW

Mountain View Chamber of Commerce

580 Castro Street
Mountain View, CA 94041
(650) 968-8378
www.mountainviewchamber.org

HISTORY

Mountain View is located eight miles north of San Jose and gets its name from the hilly views in the area. It was originally occupied by Ohlone Indians until the late 1700s when Spanish explorers arrived, taking over the land to build missions and establish settlements. In 1821, Mexico declared its independence from Spain, and California became a part of Mexico. Land grants were issued and the Mountain View title went to Mariano Castro. The land was first used for ranching and cattle raising. With the end of the Mexican-American War in 1848, California became part of the United States territory and American pioneers began moving west to stake their claim on the new territory.

The development of Mountain View came about because of its location as a pass-through between San Francisco and San Jose, two main cities in the state at that time. Mountain View started out as a stagecoach stop in 1850, and its first store was opened to serve passengers. Soon other stores, hotels, saloons, and a post office were established that helped build up the area.

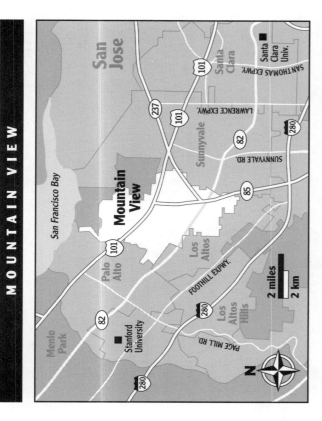

MOUNTAIN VIEW

In 1849, Mariano Castro sold about half of his land holdings in small parcels to new settlers who were flooding in for the Gold Rush. In 1864, the railroad came through Mountain View, and the rest of the country started hearing about the fertile lands and temperate climate of the area. By the late 1800s, Mountain View had become a rich agricultural region and the original oak forests were turned into fields of hay and grain and then into orchard groves and vineyards that were more profitable.

The 1900s brought more industrial and commercial growth to the area. Population increased because of agricultural and related job opportunities and then the war effort. The need for more homes resulted in farmlands being developed into tract housing. Between 1950 and 1965, an average of 250 people relocated to Mountain View each month.

Today Mountain View is home to top computer and electronics firms and attracts many single professionals to the area. According to the 1990 Census, over half of Mountain View residents are single. It is also the only city in Santa Clara County where apartments outnumber single family homes by a two-to-one ratio. The downtown has recently been renovated to include new bookstores, cafés, and restaurants.

DEMOGRAPHICS/ STATISTICS

Average Rent

Studio: $932

One-bedroom: $1,158

Two-bedroom, One-bath: $1,329

Two-bedroom, Two-bath: $1,553

Ethnic/Racial Distribution

White: 65%

African American: 5%

Asian: 14%

Hispanic: 16%

Gender Distribution

Male: 51%

Female: 49%

Population: 72,453

Median Age: 35

Renters: 52%

Crime

Homicide: 0

Rape: 1.9

Robbery: 15.3

Assault: 45.8

Burglary: 48.8

Larceny: 325.7

Auto Theft: 28.8

Local Newspaper

Mountain View Voice,
(650) 964-6300

TOP TEN EMPLOYERS IN MOUNTAIN VIEW

1. Silicon Graphics, Inc.: 4,014 employees

2. Hewlett-Packard Co.: 2,950 employees

3. Camino Health Care: 2,601 employees

4. Synopsys, Inc.: 1,800 employees

5. Acuson Corp.: 1,700 employees

6. Netscape Communications: 1,600 employees

7. Sun Microsystems: 1,340 employees

8. GTE Corp.: 700 employees

9. ALZA Corp.: 550 employees

10. Knight-Ridder Information, Inc.: 550 employees

NUMBERS TO KNOW

Fire Department (non-emergency)
(650) 903-6365

Garbage Collection and Recycling

Foothill Disposal Company
(650) 967-3034

Gas and Electric Utilities

Pacific Gas & Electric
(800) 743-5000

Phone Service

Pacific Bell
(800) 310-2355

Police Department (non-emergency)

(650) 903-6395

Television Cable Service

TCI Cablevision
(650) 968-1313

Water Service

City of Mountain View
(650) 903-6317

PALO ALTO/STANFORD

Palo Alto Chamber of Commerce

325 Forest Avenue
Palo Alto, CA 94301
(650) 324-3121
www.city.palo-alto.ca.us/palo/chamber

HISTORY

Palo Alto, which means "tall tree," got its name from the landmark redwood under which Don Gaspar de Portola and his Spanish explorers camped during their search for the Monterey Bay. Much of what became Palo Alto was part of a Spanish land grant dating back to the early 1800s. The area developed into a ranching community that gradually gave way to country estates of wealthy San Franciscans. In 1891, U.S. Senator Leland Stanford and his wife founded Leland Stanford, Junior, University in memory of their son, who died at the age of sixteen. Palo Alto was officially named in 1892, and in 1893 it was established as a Southern Pacific railway stop. The city was incorporated in 1894, and the city charter was adopted in 1950.

Palo Alto/Stanford is comprised of fifteen main neighborhoods in its jurisdiction: Downtown, Professorville, Community Center, Crescent Park, Green Gables, Old Palo Alto, College, Ventura, Barron Park, Green Acres, West Charleston, East Charleston, Midtown, South Palo

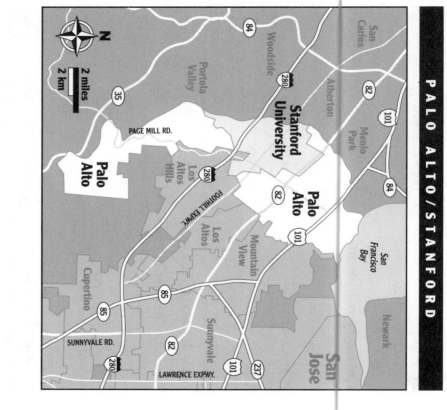

Alto, and Palo Alto Hills. Each neighborhood landscape and personality is different, ranging from formal old moneyed estates to the eclectic college communities.

After World War II, Palo Alto became a key industrial area due to developments in radio technology by Stanford University Professor Frederick Emmons Terman. He encouraged his electrical engineering students to create job opportunities locally and even brought together two former students who became the founders of Hewlett-Packard. Palo Alto/Stanford, the birthplace of the Silicon Valley, is an interesting and dynamic community that successfully integrates business and residential life. It is recognized internationally for its education, medical advancements, and technology opportunities.

DEMOGRAPHICS/ STATISTICS

Average Rent

Studio: $1,158

One-bedroom: $1,432

Two-bedroom, One-bath: $1,442

Two-bedroom, Two-bath: $2,044

Ethnic/Racial Distribution

White: 82%

African American: 3%

Asian: 10%

Hispanic: 5%

Gender Distribution

Male: 49%

Female: 51%

Population: 55,971

Median Age: 40

Renters: 43%

Crime

Homicide: 0.2

Rape: 1.0

Robbery: 11.3

Assault: 11.4

Burglary: 59.9

Larceny: 462.1

Auto Theft: 26.2

Local Newspapers

Palo Alto Weekly, (650) 326-8210, www.service.com/PAW

Palo Alto Daily News, (650) 327-NEWS

TOP TEN EMPLOYERS IN PALO ALTO

1. Stanford University Medical Center: 5,141 employees

2. Stanford University: 5,005 employees

3. Hewlett-Packard: 5,000 employees

4. Space Systems/LORAL: 1,979 employees

5. El Camino Hospital: 1,900 employees

6. Varian Associates: 1,850 employees

7. Roche Bioscience: 1,600 employees

8. Lockheed Martin: 1,480 employees

9. Sun Microsystems: 1,180 employees

10. Palo Alto Unified School District: 1,070 employees

Fire Department (non-emergency)

(650) 329-2184

Garbage Collection Service

Palo Alto Sanitation Company

(650) 493-4894

Gas and Electric Utilities

City of Palo Alto Utilities

(650) 329-2161

Phone Service

Pacific Bell

(800) 310-2355

Police Department (non-emergency)

(650) 329-2413

Recycling Program

City of Palo Alto Recycling

(650) 496-5910

Television Cable Service

Cable Co-Op of Palo Alto

(650) 856-8181

Water Service

City of Palo Alto Utilities

(650) 329-2161

SAN JOSE

San Jose Silicon Valley Chamber of Commerce

180 South Market Street

San Jose, CA 95113

(408) 291-5250

www.sjchamber.com

HISTORY

This is the third largest city in California and eleventh largest in the nation. San Jose was the first civil settlement in the state, established in 1777, and the first state capital. Originally called Pueblo de San Jose de Guadalupe, it was a farming and cattle community whose products supported the military garrisons in San Francisco and Monterey. San Jose then became a forerunner in the food processing industry until World War II. During the war it was home to military personnel and those supporting the war effort. After the war ended, many people stayed in San Jose and became part of its technology revolution. The area became known as the Silicon Valley, named after the main material used to produce semiconductors, the first big technology industry. Today it is the nation's top high-tech growth center.

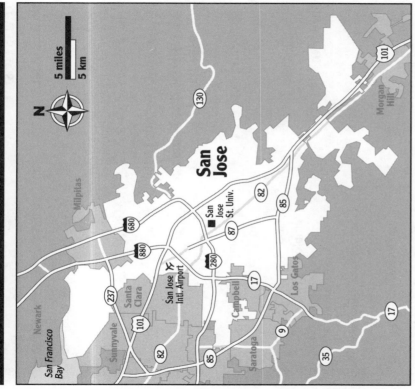

San Jose and its metropolitan area are home to over 4,100 high-tech companies that employ more than 214,000 people. Forty percent of Silicon Valley's workforce live in San Jose, a city ranked eighth in *Money* magazine's 1997 survey of best places to live in the United States. For such a large metropolitan city, San Jose has the lowest crime rate of any major U.S. city with a population of 300,000 or more, according to a 1995 FBI study.

What began as a community of eighty-two settlers back in the early 1800s has grown into a 175-square mile city with twelve different neighborhoods. These various neighborhoods are Almaden Valley, Alviso, Blossom Valley, Cambrian, Central San Jose, East San Jose, East Valley, Evergreen, North Valley, Santa Teresa, South San Jose, and Willow Glen.

DEMOGRAPHICS/ STATISTICS

Average Rent

Studio: $818

One-bedroom: $1,042

Two-bedroom, One-bath: $1,119

Two-bedroom, Two-bath: $1,388

Ethnic/Racial Distribution

White: 59%

African American: 3%

Asian: 16%

Hispanic: 22%

Gender Distribution

Male: 51%

Female: 49%

Population: 894,000

Median Age: 32

Crime

Homicide: .48

Rape: 4.1

Robbery: 13.2

Assault: 55.3

Burglary: 56.6

Larceny: 238.4

Auto Theft: 44.8

Local Newspapers

San Jose Mercury News, (408) 920-5000 or www.sjmercury.com

San Jose City Times, (408) 298-8000

San Jose Post Record, (408) 287-4866

Metro, (408) 298-8000

Business Journal, (408) 295-3800

TOP TEN EMPLOYERS IN SAN JOSE

1. County of Santa Clara: 12,446 employees

2. Cisco Systems: 10,200 employees

3. IBM Corp.: 7,200 employees

4. Santa Clara Valley Health & Hospital System: 5,400 employees

5. City of San Jose: 5,387 employees

6. U.S. Postal Service: 3,430 employees

7. Cadence Design Systems, Inc.: 3,200 employees

8. San Jose State University: 3,030 employees

9. San Jose Unified School District: 2,840 employees

10. Pacific Bell 2,407 employees

NUMBERS TO KNOW

Fire Department (non-emergency)
See the San Jose Pacific Bell White Pages under City Government for individual stations.

Garbage Collection and Recycling
City of San Jose Environmental Services
(408) 277-2700

Gas and Electric Utilities
Pacific Gas & Electric
(800) 743-5000

Phone Service
Pacific Bell
(800) 310-2355

Police Department (non-emergency)
(408) 277-5300

Television Cable Service
TCI Cablevision
(408) 744-1515

Water Service
San Jose Water Company
(408) 279-7900

Great Oaks Water Company
(408) 227-9540

SANTA CLARA

Santa Clara Chamber of Commerce
1850 Warburton Avenue
Santa Clara, CA 95052
(408) 244-8244
www.santaclara.org

HISTORY

Santa Clara was first inhabited by Ohlone Indians until the Spanish explorer, Jose Francisco Ortega, visited the valley in 1769. Shortly after, Franciscan missionaries began establishing twenty-one missions from San Diego to Sonoma. The eighth mission to be founded, Mission Santa Clara, was established in 1777 in the city of Santa Clara. Ohlone Indians were brought to this mission for their required conversion to Christianity. When Mexico achieved independence from Spain, it began issuing land grants of the area to selected people. On these lands, ranches were built and cattle was raised, making hides and tallow the first industries and commercial export products of the

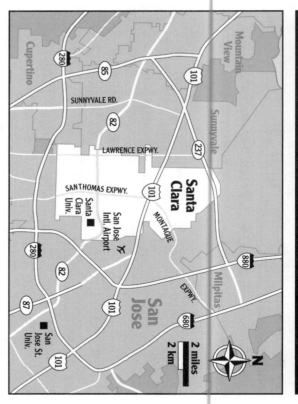

area. After the Gold Rush of 1849, unsuccessful prospectors moved to the area to farm its fertile lands. Santa Clara grew in size, and its main industries became manufacturing, seed, and fruit. At the time, the Pacific Manufacturing Company became the largest wood products supplier on the Pacific Coast, and J. M. Kimberlin & Co. was the largest seed grower on the Pacific Coast. Fruit was also a big business since orchards proliferated in the region. Cherries, peaches, and plums were shipped fresh, dried, or canned and sent to all parts of the United States, England, and the Orient.

Santa Clara was incorporated as a town in 1852 and became a state-chartered city in 1862. The mild climate and good job prospects continued to attract newcomers to the area, and the orchards and farmlands gave way to homes to accommodate this population growth. In the 1950s, with the development of the semiconductor chip, high-tech industry was born, and it eventually replaced agriculture. Today, good climate and job prospects, as well as top schools and clean neighborhoods, continue to attract newcomers to the city of Santa Clara, making it the third largest city in the county.

DEMOGRAPHICS/ STATISTICS

Average Rent

Studio: $835

One-bedroom: $1,225

Two-bedroom, One-bath: $1,331

Two-bedroom, Two-bath: $1,585

Ethnic/Racial Distribution

White: 64%

African American: 2%

Asian: 18%

Hispanic: 16%

Gender Distribution

Male: 51%

Female: 49%

Population: 100,300

Median Age: 35

Crime

Homicide: 0

Rape: 2.0

Robbery: 8.0

Assault: 35.1

Burglary: 57.9

Larceny: 326.9

Auto Theft: 37.2

Local Newspapers

Santa Clara Weekly, (408) 243-2000

Santa Clara Silicon Valley Visitors Guide, (408) 244-8244

TOP TEN EMPLOYERS IN SANTA CLARA

1. 3COM Corp.

2. Applied Materials

3. Hewlett-Packard

4. Intel

5. National Semiconductor

6. United Defense

7. NORTEL

8. Siemens Rolm Communications

9. Analog Devices & Long Devices, Inc.

10. Guidant

NUMBERS TO KNOW

Fire Department (non-emergency)

(408) 984-3059

Garbage Collection Service

Mission Trail Waste Systems

(408) 727-5365

Gas and Electric Utilities

Pacific Gas & Electric

(800) 743-5000

Phone Service

Pacific Bell

(800) 310-2355

Police Department (non-emergency)

(408) 984-3191

Recycling Program

Stevens Creek Disposal and Recycling

(408) 970-5100

Television Cable Service

TCI Cablevision

(408) 744-1515

Water Service

Santa Clara Water and Sewer Dept.

(408) 948-5111

SARATOGA

Saratoga Chamber of Commerce

20460 Saratoga–Los Gatos Road

Saratoga, CA 95070

(408) 867-0753

www.saratoga-ca.com

HISTORY

Saratoga got its name from the nearby mineral springs that resembled those of Saratoga Springs, New York. Besides popular mineral springs, it was also known for its lumber industry, given its location by the redwood-covered Santa Cruz Mountains. Once inhabited by the Ohlone Indians, Saratoga later became a prosperous agricultural community with apricots, prunes, and cherries as its main crops. During the 1800s, the 680-acre Glen Una Ranch was the world's largest producer of prunes and the equally well-known Sorosis Farm shipped dried fruit worldwide. During the late 1880s, the sunny hillsides were found to be ideal for growing grapes, and soon wineries were established, including the world-renowned Paul Masson Winery. Another claim to fame in Saratoga is Olivia de Havilland and her sister Joan Fontaine, who grew up there and launched their careers at the now-defunct Theatre-in-the-Glade.

Because of its mild climate, attractive surroundings and mineral springs, Saratoga became a haven for wealthy San Franciscans who built retreats in the hills overlooking the valley. Villa Montalvo, a

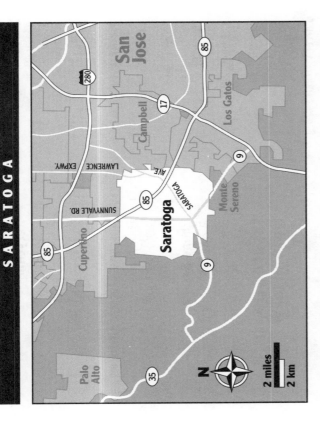

SARATOGA

Mediterranean-style home built by U.S. Senator James Phelan, is now a Historic Estate for the Arts.

After World War II, Saratoga's fields and orchards were replaced by charming, woodsy neighborhoods for residents who worked in the space, defense, and electronics industries of nearby communities. The city of Saratoga was incorporated in 1956 to protect it from industrial development. Though it is considered to be part of Silicon Valley, Saratoga is not home to any major computer companies or large corporations. Instead the town has five small business districts.

DEMOGRAPHICS/ STATISTICS

Average Rent

Studio: $800 to $1,000

One-bedroom: $1,025 to $1,500

Two-bedroom: $1,700 to $2,700

Ethnic/Racial Distribution

White: 82%

African American: 1%

Asian: 15%

Hispanic: 2%

Gender Distribution

Male: 49%

Female: 51%

Population: 28,061

Median Age: 40

Crime

Homicide: 0

Rape: .66

Robbery: 2.0

Assault: 11.8

Burglary: 37

Larceny: 103.0

Auto Theft: 4.0

Local Newspaper

Saratoga News, (408) 867-6397

NUMBERS TO KNOW

Fire Department (non-emergency)

(408) 867-9001

Gas and Electric Utilities

Pacific Gas & Electric

(800) 743-5000

Phone Service

Pacific Bell

(800) 310-2355

Sheriff Department (non-emergency)

(408) 867-9715

Television Cable Service

TCI Cablevision

(408) 727-3900

Water Service

Santa Clara Valley Water District

(408) 265-2600

San Jose Water Company

(408) 279-7900

Garbage Collection and Recycling

Green Valley Disposal Company

(408) 354-2100

www.greenvalley.com

SUNNYVALE

Sunnyvale Chamber of Commerce

499 South Murphy Avenue

Sunnyvale, CA 94086

(408) 736-4971

www.ci.sunnyvale.ca.us

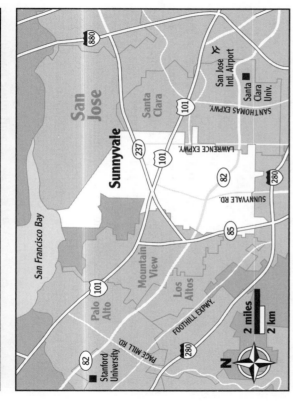

HISTORY

The first family associated with Sunnyvale is Mariano Castro, who received a land grant from the Mexican government in the early 1800s. Martin Murphy, an Irish immigrant who crossed the Sierra Nevada by covered wagon, bought 4,800 acres from Castro. Murphy is credited with planting the first orchards, introducing American cattle, and bringing the first farm machinery to the region. In 1864, the Central Railroad wanted to connect San Francisco and San Jose. Murphy agreed to let the railroad pass through his land and built "Murphy Station" in what is now Sunnyvale. For many years Sunnyvale was known as the town of Murphy. It was then called Encinal, after its first post office, from a Spanish word meaning "place where the live oak grows." Because Murphy and Encinal were names already being used by other towns, Sunnyvale was its new christening.

In 1897, Walter Crossman became the first developer of Sunnyvale, laying out the streets of the town and dubbing it the "City of Destiny." He had the vision of a factory town and marketed it to manufacturers, inviting them to open up factories and bring jobs to the area. Some familiar companies that relocated there were Westinghouse, producer of industrial electrical products, and Libby's, which opened a successful fruit and produce cannery and became the largest employer in Sunnyvale at the time.

Sunnyvale was incorporated in 1912 and chartered in 1949. In 1956, after World War II, Lockheed Missiles and Space Company was first to lead the effort to bring tech jobs to the area to replace those jobs that had been supported by the war. Today Lockheed is the largest employer in town. There are also hundreds of other high-tech, biotech, software, and telecommunications companies as well. In 1980, Sunnyvale was identified by the press as the heart of Silicon Valley because it was home to more high-tech companies than any other city in the world. Though sprawling and developed, Sunnyvale has many housing choices, several shopping centers, and good commutes.

DEMOGRAPHICS/ STATISTICS

Average Rent

Studio: $883

One-bedroom: $1,170

Two-bedroom, One-bath: $1,354

Two-bedroom, Two-bath: $1,568

Ethnic/Racial Distribution

White: 65%

African American: 3%

Asian: 19%

Hispanic: 13%

Gender Distribution

Male: 51%

Female: 49%

Population: 129,300

Median Age: 36

Crime

Homicide: 0

Rape: 1.9

Robbery: 6.6

Assault: 10.1

Burglary: 34.6

Larceny: 208.0

Auto Theft: 26.0

Local Newspaper

Sun, (408) 481-0176

TOP TEN EMPLOYERS IN SUNNYVALE

1. Lockheed Martin: 12,433 employees

2. Advanced Micro Devices: 2,298 employees

3. Amdahl: 1,751 employees

4. National Semiconductor: 1,600 employees

5. Maxim Integrated: 1,400 employees

6. TRW/Electronic Magnetic Systems Division: 1,200 employees

7. Northrop Grumman Marine Systems: 910 employees

8. Cupertino Electric: 800 employees

9. Hewlett-Packard: 700 employees

10. Spectrian Corporation: 690 employees

NUMBERS TO KNOW

Fire Department (non-emergency)
(408) 730-7110

Garbage Collection and Recycling
Specialty Solid Waste & Recycling
(408) 565-9900

Gas and Electric Utilities
Pacific Gas & Electric
(800) 743-5000

Phone Service
Pacific Bell
(800) 310-2355

Police Department (non-emergency)
(408) 730-7110

Television Cable Service
TCI Cablevision
(408) 744-1515

Water Service
City of Sunnyvale
(408) 730-7400

EDUCATION

Santa Clara County boasts more distinguished schools than any other county in the state. The county school system also has a lower than average dropout rate and a higher than average percentage of students qualifying for advanced placement in the University of California system. More Santa Clara County school system students attend college (61 percent) than the rest of the state (49 percent). The decrease in statewide public school funding has brought about strong support from the corporate community, and over a hundred businesses participate in the school district's Adopt-A-School program.

The Santa Clara County Office of Education has information on all thirty-three elementary, high school, and unified school districts in Santa Clara County. You can contact them as follows:

Santa Clara County Office of Education
1290 Ridder Park
San Jose, CA 95131
(408) 453-6500
www.sccoe.k12.ca.us

ELEMENTARY/HIGH SCHOOL DISTRICTS

Alum Rock Union School District
2930 Gay Avenue
San Jose, CA 95127
(408) 258-4923

Berryessa Union School District
1376 Piedmont Road
San Jose, CA 95132
(408) 923-1800
www.berryessa.k12.ca.us

Cambrian School District
4115 Jacksol Drive
San Jose, CA 95124
(408) 377-2103
www.cambrian.k12.ca.us

Campbell Union High School District
3235 Union Avenue
San Jose, CA 95124
(408) 371-0960
http://206.213.157.3/

Campbell Union School District (Elementary and Middle Schools)
155 North Third Street
Campbell, CA 95008
(408) 341-7200
www.campbellusd.k12.ca.us

Cupertino Union Elementary School District
10301 Vista Drive
Cupertino, CA 95014
(408) 252-3000

East Side Union High School District
830 North Capitol Avenue
San Jose, CA 95133
(408) 272-6400

Evergreen Elementary School District
3188 Quimby Road
San Jose, CA 95148
(408) 270-6800

Franklin-McKinley School District
645 Wool Creek Drive
San Jose, CA 95112
(408) 283-6000
www.fmsd.k12.ca.us

Fremont Union High School District
589 West Fremont Avenue
Sunnyvale, CA 94087
(408) 522-2200
www.fuhsd.org

**Gilroy Unified
School District**
7810 Arroyo Circle
Gilroy, CA 95020
(408) 847-2700
www.gusd.k12.ca.us

**Lakeside Joint
School District**
19621 Black Road
Los Gatos, CA 95030
(408) 354-2372

**Loma Prieta Joint Union
School District**
23800 Summit Road
Los Gatos, CA 95030
(408) 353-1101
www.loma.k12.ca.us

**Los Altos Elementary
School District**
201 Covington Road
Los Altos, CA 94024
(408) 941-4010

**Los Gatos Union Elementary
School District**
15766 Poppy Lane
Los Gatos, CA 95030
(408) 395-5570

**Los Gatos-Saratoga Joint
Union High School District**
17421 Farley Road West
Los Gatos, CA 95030
(408) 354-2520

**Luther Burbank Elementary
School District**
4 Wabash Avenue
San Jose, CA 95128
(408) 295-2450

**Milpitas Unified
School District**
1331 East Calaveras Boulevard
Milpitas, CA 95035
(408) 945-2300
www.milpitas.k12.ca.us

**Montebello Elementary
School District**
15101 Montebello Road
Cupertino, CA 95014
(408) 867-3618

**Moreland Elementary
School District**
4710 Campbell Avenue
San Jose, CA 95130
(408) 379-1370

**Morgan Hill Unified
School District**
15600 Concord Circle
Morgan Hill, CA 95037
(408) 779-5272
www.mhu.k12.ca.us

**Mountain View
School District**
220 View Street
Mountain View, CA 94041
(415) 526-3500

Mountain View–Los Altos Union High School District
1299 Bryant Avenue
Mountain View, CA 94040
(415) 940-4650

Mount Pleasant Elementary School District
3434 Marten Avenue
San Jose, CA 95148
(408) 223-3700

Oak Grove Elementary School District
6578 Santa Teresa Boulevard
San Jose, CA 95119
(408) 227-8300

Orchard School District
711 East Gish Road
San Jose, CA 95112
(408) 998-2889

Palo Alto Unified School District
25 Churchill Avenue
Palo Alto, CA 94306
(650) 329-3700

San Jose Unified School District
855 Lenzen Avenue
San Jose, CA 95126
(408) 535-6000
www.sjusd.k12.ca.us

Santa Clara County Office of Education (San Jose)
1290 Ridder Park Drive
(408) 453-6500
www.sccoe.k12.ca.us

Santa Clara Unified School District
1889 Lawrence Road
Santa Clara, CA 95052
(408) 983-2000
www.scu.k12.ca.us

Saratoga Union School District
20460 Forest Hills Drive
Saratoga, CA 95070
(408) 867-3424
www.susd.k12.ca.us

Sunnyvale Elementary School District
819 West Iowa Avenue
Sunnyvale, CA 94088
(408) 522-8200

Union Elementary School District
5175 Union Avenue
San Jose, CA 95124
(408) 377-8010

Whisman School District
750-A San Pierre Way
Mountain View, CA 94043
(415) 903-6900

COMMUNITY COLLEGES

Evergreen Valley College
3095 Yerba Buena Road
San Jose, California 95135
(408) 274-7900
www.evc.edu

San Jose City College
2100 Moorpark Avenue
San Jose, CA 95128
(408) 298-2181
www.sjcc.cc.ca.us

Mission College
3000 Mission College Boulevard
Santa Clara, CA 95054
(408) 988-2200
www.wvmccd.cc.ca.us/mc

**University of California
Extension-Santa Cruz**
1180 Bordeaux Drive
Sunnyvale, CA 94089
(800) 660-8639
www.ucsc-extension.edu

**West Valley
Community College**
14000 Fruitvale Avenue
Saratoga, CA 95070
(408) 741-2001
www.westvalley.edu

TRADE SCHOOLS

Heald Business College
2665 North First Street, Suite 110
San Jose, CA 95134
(408) 955-9555
www.heald.edu

**Institute for Business and
Technology**
2550 Scott Boulevard
Santa Clara, CA 95050
(408) 727-1060
www.ibtedu.com

**Institute of Computer
Technology**
589 West Fremont Avenue
Sunnyvale, CA 94087
(408) 736-4291
www.ict.org

**International Technological
University**
1650 Warburton Avenue
Santa Clara, CA 95050
(408) 556-9010
www.itu.edu/main/htm

UNIVERSITIES AND
COLLEGES

City University
675 North First Street
San Jose, CA 95112
(408) 289-1270
www.cityu.edu

**Cogswell Polytechnical
College**
1175 Bordeaux Drive
Sunnyvale, CA 94089
(408) 541-0100
www.cogswell.edu

DeAnza College

21250 Stevens Creek Boulevard
Cupertino, CA 95014
(408) 864-8969
www.deanza.fhda.edu

Foothill College

12345 El Monte Road
Los Altos, CA 94022
(650) 949-7777
www.fh.fhda.edu

John F. Kennedy University

One West Campbell Avenue
Campbell, CA 95008
(408) 874-7700
www.jfku.edu

National University

5300 Stevens Creek Boulevard,
Suite 250
San Jose, CA 95129
(408) 236-1100
www.nu.edu

San Jose State University Continuing Education

Professional Development
3031 Tisch Way,
Suite 200 Plaza East
San Jose, CA 95128
(408) 985-SJSU
www.profdev.sjsu.edu

Santa Clara University

500 El Camino Real
Santa Clara, CA 95053
(408) 554-4000
www.scu.edu

Stanford University Continuing Education

Building 590, Room 103
Stanford, CA 94305
(650) 725-2650
www.stanford.edu

University of Phoenix-San Jose

3590 North First Street
San Jose, CA 95134
(408) 435-8500
www.uophx.edu/northcal

HEALTH

The Santa Clara County health care system has one of the highest doctor-to-patient ratios in the state. Many of its hospitals are recognized as being front-runners in medical care. For over a decade, San Jose Medical Center Trauma Center has been a leader among trauma centers in the county. Columbia Good Samaritan Hospital has a top Neonatal Intensive Care Unit as well as a Cancer Center that offers the latest advancements in diagnosis and treatment. Stanford University Medical Center is world-renowned for medical treatment and research as well as having a prominent medical school. The following are hospitals in Silicon Valley:

Alexian Brothers Hospital

225 North Jackson Avenue

San Jose, CA 95116

(408) 259-5000

Columbia Good Samaritan Hospital

2425 Samaritan Drive

San Jose, CA 94124

(408) 559-2011

Columbia San Jose Medical Center

675 East Santa Clara Street

San Jose, CA 95112

(408) 998-3212

Columbia South Valley Community Hospital

9400 No Name Uno

Gilroy, CA 95020

(408) 848-2000

www.columbia.net

Community Hospital of Los Gatos

815 Pollard Road

Los Gatos, CA 95030

(408) 378-6131

El Camino Hospital

2500 Grant Road

Mountain View, CA 94040

(650) 940-7000

Good Samaritan Hospital

2425 Samaritan Drive

San Jose, CA 95124

(408) 559-2011

Kaiser Permanente Mountain View Medical Center

555 Castro Street

Mountain View, CA 94041

(650) 903-3000

Kaiser Santa Teresa Community Medical Center

250 Hospital Parkway

San Jose, CA 95119

(408) 972-7000

www.kaiserpermanente.org

Kaiser Santa Clara Medical Center

900 Kiely Boulevard

Santa Clara, CA 95050

(408) 236-6400

www.kaiserpermanente.org

Lucile Salter Packard Children's Hospital at Stanford

725 Welch Road

Palo Alto, CA 94304

(650) 497-8000

wwwmed.stanford.edu/lpch/

Mission Oaks Hospital

15891 Los Gatos-Almaden Road

Los Gatos, CA 95032

(408) 559-2011

O'Connor Hospital

2105 Forest Avenue

San Jose, CA 95128

(408) 947-2500

Saint Louise Hospital

18500 Saint Louise Drive

Morgan Hill, CA 95037

(408) 779-1500

Santa Clara Valley Medical Center

751 South Bascom Avenue
San Jose, CA 95128
(408) 885-5000

Saratoga Family Health Center

12961 Village Drive, Suite Q
Saratoga, CA 95070
(408) 255-6477

Saratoga Walk-In Clinic

12224 Saratoga-Sunnyvale Road
Saratoga, CA 95070
(408) 446-4774

Stanford University Hospital

300 Pasteur Drive
Stanford, CA 94305
(650) 723-4000
www-med.stanford.edu

LOCAL GOVERNMENT

Santa Clara County is the fifth-largest county in California and is governed by a local charter. A five-member board of supervisors sets policies as the governing body for county government. The board of supervisors appoints a county executive to direct day-to-day government operations.

Local city government in Santa Clara County operates under a council-manager system. Under this system, cities are managed by professional administrators who are appointed by city councils that are elected by voters. The city council provides political leadership and sets the policies, while the full-time professional manager directs city departments in carrying out those policies. Local mayors are either selected from among council members or elected by voters, depending on the city charter.

The League of Women Voters (**www.lwv.org**) has publications about local politics and government. Another good resource for local government information is the Web site for the Association of Bay Area Governments (ABAG). ABAG, established in 1961, is one of more than 560 regional planning agencies across the nation working to help solve problems in areas such as land use, housing, environmental quality, and economic development. It is owned and operated by the cities and counties of the San Francisco Bay Area.

ABAG

101 Eighth Street
Oakland, CA 94607
(510) 464-7900
www.abag.org

CITY HALLS

Campbell City Hall

70 North First Street
Campbell, CA 95008
(408) 866-2100
www.ci.campbell.ca.us

Structure of Government: The city council is the legislative and policy-making branch of Campbell's municipal government. Local voters elect the city council, and the mayor is selected from among the five council members for a one-year term. Elections are held every two years, and council members serve four-year overlapping terms. Also elected by Campbell voters is a city clerk and city treasurer. The council appoints the city manager and city attorney, as well as members of the city's advisory boards and commissions.

Cupertino City Hall

10300 Torre Avenue
Cupertino, CA 95014
(408) 777-3200
www.cupertino.org

Structure of Government: Cupertino voters elect five council members to serve four-year, overlapping terms with elections held every two years. Several advisory boards and commissions assist the city council. Council members select a mayor among themselves.

Gilroy City Hall

7351 Rosanna Street
Gilroy, CA 95020
(408) 848-0400
www.ci.gilroy.ca.us

Structure of Government: Six council members and one mayor are elected by voters and serve four-year overlapping terms. Elections are held every two years. The council appoints the city administrator.

Los Altos City Hall

One North San Antonio Road
Los Altos, CA 94022
(650) 948-1491
www.ci.los-altos.ca.us

Structure of Government: Los Altos voters elect five council members who serve four-year overlapping terms. Elections are held every two years in odd-numbered years during November. The mayor is selected from among city council members based on seniority. Appointed commissions and committees assist the council in an advisory capacity. The council appoints the city manager and city attorney.

Los Altos Hills Town Hall

26379 Fremont Road
Los Altos Hills, CA 94022
(650) 941-7222
www.losaltosonline.com/lah

Structure of Government: Los Altos Hills voters elect a five-member council to serve four-year overlapping terms. Elections are held every two years in even-numbered years during November. A mayor is selected among city council members. City council also appoints a city manager and local residents to serve on various commissions.

Los Gatos Town Hall

110 East Main Street
Los Gatos, CA 95030
(408) 354-6834
www.losgatosweb.com

Structure of Government: Los Gatos voters elect five council members on a four-year rotation. Elections are held every two years, and there are no term limits. A mayor is selected by council members among themselves. A town manager is appointed by council members.

Milpitas City Hall

455 East Calaveras Boulevard
Milpitas, CA 95035
(408) 942-2310
www.ci.milpitas.ca.gov

Structure of Government: Every two years a mayor and two council members are elected. A total of four council members and one mayor govern the city, with council members serving four-year-terms on a rotating basis. The city manager and city attorney are appointed by the city council.

Monte Sereno City Hall

18041 Saratoga-Los Gatos Road
Monte Sereno, CA 95030
(408) 354-7635
www.montesereno.org

Structure of Government: Monte Sereno is governed by a five-member city council. A mayor and vice mayor are selected among council members. City council members serve four-year, overlapping terms with elections held every two, even-numbered years in November. The council appoints a city manager and city attorney.

Morgan Hill City Hall

17555 Peak Avenue
Morgan Hill, CA 95037
(408) 779-7271
www.morgan-hill.ca.gov

Structure of Government: Morgan Hill voters elect four city council members and a mayor. Council members serve four-year overlapping terms and the mayor serves for two years. Elections are held every two years. The city council and mayor establish city policies and appoint a city manager and city attorney. All department heads report to the city manager.

Mountain View City Hall

500 Castro Street
Mountain View, CA 94041
(650) 903-6300
www.ci.mtnview.ca.us

Structure of Government: The seven Mountain View city council members are elected at-large to serve a maximum of two consecutive four-year terms. Elections are held every two years during even-numbered years. Each year the council selects one of its members as mayor and another as vice mayor. The council appoints the city manager and city attorney.

Palo Alto City Hall

250 Hamilton Avenue
Palo Alto, CA 94301
(650) 329-2311
www.city.palo-alto.ca.us

Structure of Government: Palo Alto voters elect nine council members, one of whom serves as mayor and another as vice mayor. Council members are elected at large every two years for overlapping four-year terms. They appoint a city manager.

San Jose City Hall

801 North First Street
San Jose, CA 95110
(408) 277-4000
www.ci.san-jose.ca.us

Structure of Government: The city council of San Jose consists of eleven members including the mayor. San Jose is divided into ten geographical districts, each represented on the city council. Voters elect the mayor and city council members for four-year terms. Council members serve on overlapping terms. Elections are held every two years with odd- and even-numbered districts taking turns. The council appoints the city manager.

Santa Clara City Hall

1500 Warburton Avenue
Santa Clara, CA 95050
(408) 984-3000
www.ci.santa-clara.ca.us

Structure of Government: Santa Clara voters elect the six-member city council as well as the mayor. The mayor serves a four-year term, and city council members are elected for numbered seats and serve staggered four-year terms. The city charter limits the mayor and all council members to serving two consecutive terms. Elections are held every two years. The council appoints a city manager.

Saratoga City Hall

13777 Fruitvale Avenue
Saratoga, CA 95070
(408) 868-1200
www.saratoga-ca.com/chamber/gov/htm

Structure of Government: Saratoga voters elect a five-member, nonpartisan council that functions as the policy-making governmental body. Council members are elected every two years and serve staggered four-year terms. The mayor is selected among members of the city council each year. The council appoints the city manager.

Sunnyvale City Hall

456 West Olive Avenue
Sunnyvale, CA 94088
(408) 730-7500
www.ci.sunnyvale.ca.us

Structure of Government: Sunnyvale has seven council members elected to four-year overlapping terms. Elections are held every two years in odd-numbered years. A council member is selected annually to serve as mayor. The city council appoints the city manager and city attorney. The administrative staff of the city is appointed through a competitive civil service process under the general direction of the city manager.

PARKS AND RECREATION

Silicon Valley/Santa Clara County communities have many well-maintained parks and open spaces for recreation and exploration. In 1924, Santa Clara County purchased its first parkland of four hundred acres near Cupertino that became Stevens Creek County Park. Today, the Department of Parks and Recreation has expanded to twenty-seven park units encompassing nearly 45,000 acres. Visit their Web site for more information and local park activities at **http://claraweb.co.santa-clara.us/parks.**

The following are phone numbers for the Recreation and Parks departments in the various cities in Santa Clara County:

POST OFFICES

Individual phone numbers for local post offices listed below are no longer available. The post office has a toll-free number for any questions you might have, like directions and hours. Call 800-275-8777. For general postal information, visit the United States Postal Service Web site at www.usps.gov.

Campbell
500 West Hamilton Avenue

Cupertino
21701 Stevens Creek Boulevard

Gilroy
100 4th Street

Los Altos/Los Altos Hills
100 First Street

Los Gatos/Monte Sereno
101 South Santa Cruz Avenue

Milpitas
450 South Abel Street

Monte Sereno
18041 Saratoga-Los Gatos Road

Morgan Hill
16000 South Monterey Road

Mountain View
211 Hope Street

Palo Alto/Stanford
Cambridge Station, 265 Cambridge Avenue

Main, 2085 East Bayshore Road

Hamilton Station, 380 Hamilton Avenue

San Jose
Almaden Valley, 6525 Crown Boulevard

Bayside, 2731 Junction Avenue

Berryessa, 1315 Piedmont Road

Blossom Hill, 5706 Cahalan Avenue

Cambrian Park, 1769 Hillsdale Avenue

Campbell, (408) 866-2105

Cupertino, (408) 777-3110

Gilroy, (408) 848-0460

Los Altos, (650) 941-0950

Los Gatos, (408) 354-6809

Milpitas, (408) 942-2470

Morgan Hill, (408) 779-7271

Mountain View, (650) 903-6331

Palo Alto, (650) 329-2261

San Jose, (408) 277-4661

Santa Clara, (408) 984-3223

Saratoga, (408) 868-1200

Sunnyvale, (408) 730-7517

Colonnade, 200 South 3rd Street

Coyote, 8220 Monterey Road

Eastridge, 1 Eastridge Center

Garden Station, 1165 Lincoln Avenue

Hillview, 2450 Alvin Avenue

Parkmoor, 1545 Parkmoor Avenue

Robertsville, 1175 Branham Lane

Seven Trees, 80 Lewis Road

St. James Park, 105 North First Street

Station D, 70 South Jackson Avenue

Westgate, 4285 Payne Avenue

Willow Glen, 1750 Meridian Avenue

Santa Clara

Main, 1200 Franklin Mall

Agnew Station, 4601 Lafayette Street

Mission Station, 1050 Kiely Boulevard

Saratoga

19630 Allendale Avenue

Sunnyvale

580 North Mary Avenue

CHAPTER FOURTEEN

FINDING A PLACE TO LIVE

LIFE IN THE Silicon Valley rates high with good weather, clean communities, low crime rates, high-ranked schools, many cultural and social activities, and plenty of well-paying jobs. Unfortunately, it is not all utopian. The housing market is tight, with low rental vacancy rates and home purchase prices the highest in the country. Since 1995, average apartment-rental costs have increased 29 percent, compared to an 8 percent increase in median income. At the same time, demand for rental units is on the rise due to the flourishing job market, placing the vacancy rate at 3.1 percent.

But there are ways to approach your apartment search, whether it is using an apartment- or roommate-finding agency, settling into short-term corporate housing, checking out an apartment complex community, or trying a budget-conscious alternative. Though rental prices are high, rent usually includes many amenities, especially in apartment communities, like parking, security, and swimming pools. You could even find yourself renting a single-family house with a yard, since they outnumber apartments two to one in the county.

The following is a list of corporate housing, apartment-finding agencies, budget options, and the largest apartment communities in the county. All prices and fees are subject to change and should be used only as guidelines. Also, check out the Sunday edition of the *San Jose Mercury News* for classified listings of rooms for rent, shared housing, room and board situations, and short-term rentals.

Given the difficult Silicon Valley rental housing market, why not let apartment- and roommate-finding agencies do the work for you. For a fee, agencies will match your profile and needs with apartments and homes that are available for rent. This can leave you with more time to find work or get to know the area better.

Bay Rentals

3396 Stevens Creek Boulevard

San Jose, CA 95117

(408) 244-4900

www.bayarearentals.com

Services

Provides listings with detailed information on apartments, condominiums, cottages, houses, duplexes, multiplexes, and townhouses.

Will organize your search by your criteria and desired area.

An average of 50 to 100 new rentals are received every day, and new listings are sent out Monday, Wednesday, and Friday via e-mail or fax.

Fees

$98 for ninety days with unlimited access to new rental information via the Internet.

CAL Rentals

3911 Stevens Creek Boulevard

Santa Clara, CA 95051

(408) 244-2300

www.calrentals.com

Services

A profile is taken of the client to find out desired areas to live and other specifics.

98 percent placement rate.

New listings come in every day and are faxed or e-mailed to the client.

Sign up by phone or in person.

Fees

$108 for ninety days or unlimited listings in office.

$20 for Zip Service which is e-mail or fax of new listings daily.

Satisfaction guaranteed with a full refund less $20.

Client placement rate is about 95 percent, with most people typically finding something in the first few weeks.

Clients can update or change their criteria at any time.

Sign up over the Internet or by phone.

Metro Rent

2050 South Bascom Avenue
Campbell, CA 95008
(408) 369-9700
www.metrorent.com

Services

Apartment listings in the South Bay that match your criteria.

New vacancies are listed every day, and all information is kept current.

Descriptions of vacancies are matched to your personal search, complete with contact information.

Searches available via fax, e-mail, or Web site as soon as they are entered into the database.

Join by using their Web site.

Credit report service and cell phone rental available.

Free phone access on the premises to call for appointments.

Fees

Fax, e-mail, or Web site search: $95 for sixty days with a $40 money-back guarantee.

In-office search: $60 for forty days with a $40 money-back guarantee.

$25 credit report service.

Rental Experts

249 South Mathilda Avenue
Sunnyvale, CA 94086
(408) 732-8777

Services

They work closely with the client to let them know of a good match as soon as it is available.

Will set up appointments with landlords and negotiate deposits and pets.

Over 140 new listings are received daily and faxed, phoned, or e-mailed to the client.

Fees

$85 one-time fee for as long as it takes to find a place.

$35 refund if you are not successful.

Rental Solutions

437 Cambridge Street
Palo Alto, CA 94306
(650) 473-3000
www.bayrentals.com

Services

Full-service rental search company.

Agent works with you to meet your needs and specifications.

When you find a place you like, the agent will negotiate the rent and deposits with the landlord.

You can transfer your paperwork to their other offices at no charge if you decide to look in a different area.

Fees

5 percent of one year's rent or 60 percent of one month's rent.

Additional charge if you are a pet owner.

$30 for interview and prescreening.

Roommate Express

4546 El Camino Real, Suite 218
Los Altos, CA 94022
(800) 487-8050 or (650) 948-4300
www.e-roommate.com

Services

Computer matches prospective roommates on nine variables: city, rent, sex, age, smoking, children, pets, sexual preference, and personality compatibility.

MatchLine service available to check for new matches twenty-four hours a day over the phone. Phone listings are updated twice a day.

Offers a free reference check or will do a credit check for $20 on your potential roommate.

More than 70 percent of clients find a roommate while over 90 percent are satisfied with the service.

They have thirty-three locations in the South Bay and San Francisco Bay areas. Call to find the location nearest you to sign up or do it over the Internet.

It takes about one to three weeks to find a roommate using this service, but there are no guarantees.

Fees

If you have an apartment and need a roommate, the fee is $129 for sixty days of service and an additional $10 for optional phone updates on their MatchLine.

If you do not have an apartment and are looking for a roommate situation, the fee is $69 for sixty days, which includes the MatchLine phone service.

CORPORATE HOUSING

Corporate housing is temporary housing that has all the comforts of home. It offers fully furnished apartments with the necessary amenities like sheets, towels, and kitchen supplies. In many cases, housing agents will customize the apartment to your needs, say if you have kids or pets. Though convenient and readily available, corporate housing can be pricey, but not as much as staying at a hotel. A $2,000 a month one-bedroom apartment is about $67 a day, and you will be getting more space and privacy than with a hotel room as well as saving money by preparing your meals at home. The only drawback is most corporate housing requires a one-month stay. If you can afford it or if your company is paying, corporate housing is a very convenient way to relocate. The list below is a few of the many corporate housing and relocation services available. You can also visit your public library and look in the phone book of the city you plan on moving to or try the Internet for more options.

ExecuStay

(800) 500-5110

www.execustay.com

ExecuStay has hundreds of locations throughout the country. They offer fully furnished apartments with housewares, linens, and accessories. They can accommodate children and pets. Monthly rents start at $1,500 for a studio and $2,200 for a one-bedroom apartment.

Gracious Corporate Lodging

2906 Lafayette Street
Santa Clara, CA 95054
(800) 944-7966

They have a range of short-term rentals from efficient studios to posh condos. All apartments are furnished and include housewares and linens. Junior one-bedroom rentals start at $2,290 per month with a thirty-day minimum stay.

K & M Relocation Network, Inc.

747-E Camden Avenue
Campbell, CA 95008
(800) 381-0907
www.kmrelo.com

Offers corporate housing apartments with modern, comfortable furnishings and all amenities. One-bedroom apartments start at $91 a day and include weekly maid service. Monthly rentals start at $2,600.

Key Housing Connections, Inc.

(800) 989-0410
www.keyhousing.net

They offer standard packages from Economy to Premier or they can customize a program to meet your requirements. A bare-bones one-bedroom apartment starts at $1,800 a month and does not include housewares and linens. An all-inclusive one-bedroom will start at about $2,250 per month.

Oakwood Corporate Housing

(800) 888-0808

www.oakwood.com

Oakwood Apartments can be found all over Silicon Valley from Palo Alto to San Jose. They own the buildings they lease, and rentals are fully furnished with amenities like bed and bath linens, kitchen supplies, television, and phone. The agent can customize an apartment to your needs. Minimum stay is thirty days and prices range from $80 to $120 per day.

Relocation Services

(800) 990-9292

www.execustay.com

Let them know your needs and they will search for a short-term rental that meets them. Furnished one-bedroom apartments start at $3,000 per month.

BUDGET OPTIONS

The following are a few low-cost, temporary options for those who are watching their budgets. The accommodations may be worn down or even rustic, but the savings will be put to good use when that hefty security deposit is due for a permanent rental.

Hidden Villa Hostel

26870 Moody Road

Los Altos Hills, CA 94022

(650) 949-8648

www.hostelweb.com/sanfrancisco

This facility has heated cabins, a kitchen, linen rental, and on-site parking. The downside is it's closed from June through August. Reservations are required and there is no curfew. Price is about $10 per night.

Mother Olson's Inn

72 North Fifth Street

San Jose, CA

(408) 998-0223

This is a residence hotel that rents private rooms with shared baths on a weekly basis. Rates are between $165 to $190 per week and include housekeeping. Rooms are furnished with a bed, linens, dresser, and television. There are community bathrooms and a kitchen with a microwave, stove, and refrigerator but no pots or utensils. An application needs to be completed and a credit check is run. There are twenty-three different inns between Fifth and Eleventh Streets. A one-week minimum stay is required, and they accept cash and money orders only.

Sanborn Park Hostel

15808 Sanborn Road
Saratoga, CA 95070
(408) 741-0166
www.hiayh.org/ushostel/pnwreg/
sanjos.htm

This is a quiet, safe hostel with dormitory-style rooms and shared baths. The atmosphere is informal and friendly with recreation activities like volleyball and barbecues. Parking is available, laundry is on the premises, and there is use of a communal kitchen. Rates for non-

members is about $10.50 per night; members' cost is $8.50 per night.

Santa Clara University Student Resource Center

500 El Camino Real
Benson Center, Room 203
Santa Clara, CA
(408) 554-4109

They have binders of listings of rooms for rent in homes, apartments for rent, and subleasing situations. This service is available for free to students and non-students.

APARTMENT COMMUNITIES

Apartment communities are large rental complexes that offer many amenities like health clubs, tennis courts, swimming pool, security, on-site management, and more. Depending on the complex, it can come close to resort living. The rents are high, but the busy professional will appreciate a clean, well-managed community full of conveniences. Following are the largest apartment communities in the Santa Clara County Silicon Valley, according to the *San Jose Business Journal 1998 Book of Lists*. You will find more listings in the *San Jose Mercury News* newspaper and the *Apartments for Rent* magazine (www.aptsforrent.com or call 800-452-0845).

Bella Vista Luxury Apartments

1500 Vista Club Circle
Santa Clara, CA 95054
(408) 496-6300 or (800) 216-1932

Average Rent:

One-bedroom: $1,475 to $1,625

Two-bedroom: $1,735 to 2,155

Minimum Lease: Six Months

Pets: Yes

Corporate Housing Available: Yes

Amenities: Clubhouse, parking, exercise room, full-time manager, full-time maintenance, laundry, security, swimming pool

Cherrywood Apartments

4951 Cherry Avenue
San Jose, CA 95118
(408) 266-8070

Average Rent:

One-bedroom: N/A

Two-bedroom: N/A

Minimum Lease: Six Months

Pets: No

Corporate Housing Available: No

Amenities: Clubhouse, parking, exercise room, full-time manager, full-time maintenance, laundry, swimming pool

E'Lan

345 Village Center Drive
San Jose, CA 95134
(408) 428-9200

Average Rent:

One-bedroom: $1,075 to $1,575

Two-bedroom: $1,730 to $2,195

Minimum Lease: Six Months

Pets: Yes (cats only)

Corporate Housing Available: Yes

Amenities: Clubhouse, parking, exercise room, full-time manager, full-time maintenance, laundry, security, swimming pool, tennis courts

El Rancho Verde

303 Checkers Drive
San Jose, CA 95133
(408) 272-0356

Average Rent:

One-bedroom: N/A

Two-bedroom: N/A

Minimum Lease: One Month

Pets: No

Corporate Housing Available: No

Amenities: Parking, exercise room, full-time manager, full-time maintenance, laundry

Fair Oaks West Apartments

655 South Fair Oaks Avenue
Sunnyvale, CA 94086
(408) 735-9780

Average Rent:

One-bedroom: $1,095 to 1,280

Two-bedroom: $1,440 to $1,645

Minimum Lease: Six Months

Pets: No

Corporate Housing Available: Yes

Amenities: Clubhouse, parking, exercise room, full-time manager, full-time maintenance, laundry, security, swimming pool, tennis courts

Glenbrook Apartments

10100 Mary Avenue
Cupertino, CA 95014
(408) 253-2323

Average Rent:

One-bedroom: $1,115 to $1,530

Two-bedroom: $1,755 to $2,085

Minimum Lease: Three Months

Pets: No

Corporate Housing Available: Yes

Amenities: Clubhouse, parking, exercise room, full-time manager, full-time maintenance, laundry, security, swimming pool, tennis courts

Heritage Park Apartments

155 East Washington Avenue
Sunnyvale, CA 94086
(408) 738-3553

Average Rent:

One-bedroom: $1,150 to $1,200

Two-bedroom: $1,450 to $1,500

Minimum Lease: One Month

Pets: No

Corporate Housing Available: Yes

Amenities: Clubhouse, parking, exercise room, full-time manager, full-time maintenance, laundry, swimming pool

Mansion Grove

502 Mansion Park Drive
Santa Clara, CA 95054
(408) 980-0502

Average Rent:

One-bedroom: $1,245 to $1,310

Two-bedroom: $1,470 to 1,580

Minimum Lease: Three Months

Pets: Yes (cat only)

Corporate Housing Available: Yes

Amenities: Clubhouse, parking, exercise room, full-time manager, full-time maintenance, laundry, security, swimming pool, tennis courts

Oak Pointe

450 North Mathilda Avenue
Sunnyvale, CA 94086
(408) 245-3030

Average Rent:

One-bedroom: $1,135 to $1,210

Two-bedroom: $1,235 to $1,410

Minimum Lease: One Month

Pets: Yes (cat only)

Corporate Housing Available: No

Amenities: Clubhouse, parking, exercise room, full-time manager, full-time maintenance, laundry, swimming pool

Oakwood Apartments South

700 South Saratoga Avenue
San Jose, CA 95129
(408) 551-6900
www.oakwood.com

Average Rent:

One-bedroom: $1,200 to $1,350

Two-bedroom: $1,420 to $1,550

Minimum Lease: One Month

Pets: Yes

Corporate Housing Available: Yes

Amenities: Clubhouse, parking, exercise room, full-time manager, full-time maintenance, laundry, swimming pool

Olive West Apartments

1229 Vincente Drive
Sunnyvale, CA 94086
(650) 961-0141

Average Rent:

One-bedroom: $960 to $1,035

Two-bedroom: $1,250 to $1,310

Minimum Lease: Six Months

Pets: No

Corporate Housing Available: No

Amenities: Clubhouse, parking, exercise room, full-time manager, full-time maintenance, laundry, swimming pool, tennis courts

Summerwood Apartments

444 Saratoga Avenue
Santa Clara, CA 95054
(408) 241-1445

Average Rent:

One-bedroom: $1,000 to $1,140

Two-bedroom: $905 to $1,245

Minimum Lease: One Month

Pets: No

Corporate Housing Available: Yes

Amenities: Parking, exercise room, full-time manager, full-time maintenance, laundry, security, swimming pool

The Arches

1235 Wildwood Avenue
Sunnyvale, CA 94089
(408) 735-1300

Average Rent:

One-bedroom: $925 to $995

Two-bedroom: $1,150 to $1,260

Minimum Lease: One Month

Pets: No

Corporate Housing Available: No

Amenities: Clubhouse, parking, exercise room, full-time manager, full-time maintenance, laundry, swimming pool

The Woods Apartments

4300 The Woods Drive
San Jose, CA 95136
(408) 227-3700

Average Rent:

One-bedroom: $765 to $1,095

Two-bedroom: $905 to $1,245

Minimum Lease: Six Months

Pets: No

Corporate Housing Available: No

Amenities: Clubhouse, parking, exercise room, full-time manager, full-time maintenance, laundry, swimming pool

Valley Green Apartments

20875 Valley Green Drive
Cupertino, CA 95014
(408) 253-0200

Average Rent:

One-bedroom: $1,215 to $1,380

Two-bedroom: $1,510 to $1,740

Minimum Lease: Three Months

Pets: No

Corporate Housing Available: Yes

Amenities: Clubhouse, parking, exercise room, full-time manager, full-time maintenance, laundry, security, swimming pool, tennis courts

Willow Lake at North Park

1331 Lakeshore Circle
San Jose, CA 95131
(408) 453-7272

Average Rent:

One-bedroom: $1,250 to $1,450

Two-bedroom: $1,495 to $1,895

Minimum Lease: Six Months

Pets: No

Corporate Housing Available: Yes

Amenities: Clubhouse, parking, exercise room, full-time manager, laundry, swimming pool, tennis courts

FINAL TIPS

Here are a few tips to gain the advantage in a challenging rental market:

- Make a list of your housing criteria, including nonnegotiable items (maybe laundry or parking) and those things you are willing to compromise on (maybe you don't need that swimming pool).

- Prepare a tenants résumé. Like a job résumé, it should highlight your rental and job history, proving you will be an ideal tenant who pays the rent on time.

- Buy the Sunday *San Jose Mercury News* and study the rental listings.

- Make a list of possible places to visit, map them out, and hit the road early Sunday morning.

- Wear dressy casual clothing or even go for the professional look.

- Bring your checkbook, tenants résumé, and all the information you would need to complete an application like financial, landlord, and job contact information.

- Timing is key. Try to be one of the first people to look at a place and be ready to write a check if you like it.

Project Sentinel is a no-charge service agency funded in part by the City of Sunnyvale for Sunnyvale residents. Project Sentinel specializes in landlord/tenant disputes and can offer mediation services if needed. They can also help in resolving disputes within local neighborhoods. For more information about their services or for general landlord/tenant information, contact Project Sentinel at (408) 720-9888.

CHAPTER FIFTEEN

FINDING A JOB

Silicon Valley has one of the healthiest job markets in the nation. An estimated 53,000 jobs were added in 1997, bringing the total number of jobs in the region to more than 1.2 million. In fact, since 1994, employment has grown faster than local labor supply. It should be no surprise that the biggest job gains were in software and computer industries.

When the demand for skilled workers is high and the supply is low, salaries continue to grow. Wages for Silicon Valley employees continue to outpace the national average, as they have since 1994. In fact, Silicon Valley has the second-highest average wage of all metro regions in the United States (New York ranks first and San Francisco ranks third). The average salaries for someone working in the computer or semiconductor industry are about $85,000 and $75,000, respectively.

With statistics like these, you may find that the most difficult part of getting a job is deciding which offer to take. This chapter lists some of the major companies, personnel agencies, and executive search firms in Silicon Valley. You will also find information on career development organizations and job fairs to help broaden your search.

MAJOR COMPANIES

Following is a list of some top technology companies in the area. Visit their Web sites for more information on employment opportunities.

3Com Corp.
5400 Bayfront Plaza
Santa Clara, CA 95052
(408) 764-5000
www.3com.com

Industry: Local computer networks manufacturer

Adobe Systems, Inc.
345 Park Avenue
San Jose, CA 95110
(408) 536-6000
www.adobe.com

Industry: Computer software

Amdahl Corp.
1250 East Arques Avenue
Sunnyvale, CA 94088
(408) 746-6000
www.amdahl.com

Industry: Mainframe computers

Apple Computers, Inc.
1 Infinite Loop
Cupertino, CA 95014
(408) 996-1010
www.apple.com

Industry: Computer manufacturer

Applied Materials, Inc.
3050 Bowers Avenue
Santa Clara, CA 95054
(408) 727-5555
www.appliedmaterials.com

Industry: Semiconductor equipment manufacturer

Cirrus Logic, Inc.
3100 West Warren Avenue
Fremont, CA 94538
(510) 623-8300
www.cirrus.com

Industry: Semiconductor manufacturer

Cisco Systems, Inc.
170 West Tasman Drive
San Jose, CA 95134
(408) 526-4000
www.cisco.com

Industry: Computer network equipment

Hewlett-Packard
3000 Hanover Street
Palo Alto, CA 94304
(650) 857-1501
www.hp.com

Industry: Computers and related products

Intel Corp.
2200 Mission College Boulevard
Santa Clara, CA 95052
(408) 765-8080
www.intel.com

Industry: Semiconductor manufacturer

National Semiconductor Corp.
2900 Semiconductor Drive
Santa Clara, CA 95051
(408) 721-5000
www.national.com

Industry: Semiconductor manufacturer

Industry: Semiconductor manufacturer

Netscape Communications Corp.

501 East Middlefield Road
Mountain View, CA 94043
(650) 962-5000
www.netscape.com

Industry: Computer software

Oracle Corp.

500 Oracle Parkway
Redwood City, CA 94065
(650) 506-7000
www.oracle.com

Industry: Database software

Quantum Corp.

500 McCarthy Boulevard
Milpitas, CA 95035
(408) 894-4000
www.quantum.com

Industry: Computer memory devices

Seagate Technology, Inc.

920 Disc Drive
Scotts Valley, CA 95066
(408) 438-6550
www.seagate.com

Industry: Computer memory devices

Silicon Graphics, Inc.

2011 North Shoreline Boulevard
Mountain View, CA 94043
(650) 960-1980
www.sgi.com

Industry: Computer workstations

Stanford University

Stanford, CA 94305
(650) 723-2300
www.stanford.edu

Industry: Education

Sun Microsystems, Inc.

2550 Garcia Avenue
Mountain View, CA 94043
(650) 960-1300
www.sun.com

Industry: Computer workstations

Symantec Corp.

10201 Torre Avenue
Cupertino, CA 95014
(408) 596-9000
www.symantec.com

Industry: Computer software

Syquest Technology, Inc.

47071 Bayside Parkway
Fremont, CA 94538
(510) 226-4000
www.syquest.com

Industry: Computer memory devices

Tandem Computers, Inc.

19333 Vallco Parkway
Cupertino, CA 95014
(408) 285-6000
www.tandem.com

Industry: Computers

WebTV Networks, Inc.

305 Lytton Avenue

Palo Alto, CA 94301

(650) 326-3240

www.webtv.net

Industry: Television Internet access

Yahoo! Inc.

3420 Central Expressway

Santa Clara, CA 95051

(408) 731-3300

www.yahoo.com

Industry: Internet media

PERSONNEL AGENCIES

Finding a temporary or permanent job through a personnel agency is a good bet when you are new to the area and unsure of the market. The following is a list of the largest temporary agencies in Silicon Valley according to the *San Jose Business Journal 1998 Book of Lists*. You can find out about other agencies in the local phone book Yellow Pages or by looking at the *San Jose Mercury News* job classified ads.

Accounting Partners Inc.

2041 Mission College Boulevard, Suite 200

Santa Clara, CA 95054

(408) 986-1990

www.apartner.com

Industries: Accounting, finance

Benefits and training: Benefits only

Accustaff Inc.

2901 Tasman Drive, Suite 100

Santa Clara, CA 95054

(408) 727-1782

www.accustaff.com

Industries: Accounting, administration, clerical, data processing, engineering, finance, hospitality, marketing, sales, technical/systems, executives

Benefits and training: Both

Adecco International

Nontechnical:

111 West Evelyn Avenue, Suite 104

Sunnyvale, CA 94086

(408) 727-6460

Technical:

2900 Gordon Avenue, Suite 207

Santa Clara, CA 95051

(408) 328-0760

www.adecco.com

Industries: Accounting, administration, clerical, data processing, engineering, finance, hospitality, marketing, sales, technical/systems, executives

Benefits and training: Both

Advanced Technical Resources

1230 Oakmead Parkway, Suite 110
Sunnyvale, CA 94086
(408) 328-8000
www.atr1.com

Industries: Accounting, administration, clerical, data processing, engineering, finance, marketing, sales, technical/systems, executives

Benefits and training: Both

American Technical

4701 Patrick Henry Drive,
Suite 2501
Santa Clara, CA 95054
(408) 727-4653

Industries: Accounting, administration, clerical, data processing, engineering, finance, technical/systems

Benefits and training: Both

Barrett Business Services

2930 Patrick Henry Drive
Santa Clara, CA 95054
(408) 980-9555
www.barrettbusiness.com

Industries: Accounting, administration, clerical, data processing, engineering, finance, hospitality, marketing, sales, technical/systems, executives

Benefits and training: Both

Coast Personnel Services, Inc.

2295 De La Cruz Boulevard
Santa Clara, CA 95050
(408) 653-2100

Industries: Accounting, administration, clerical, data processing, engineering, finance, technical, executives

Benefits and training: Benefits only

Crossroads Staffing Services

4300 Stevens Creek Boulevard,
Suite 117
San Jose, CA 95129
(408) 246-6351

Industries: Accounting, administration, clerical, data processing, engineering, finance, hospitality, marketing, sales, technical/systems, executives

Benefits and training: Both

Echo Design and Temporary Personnel

1605 Remuda Lane
San Jose, CA 95112
(408) 436-1294
www.echotemp.com

Industries: Accounting, administration, clerical, data processing, engineering, finance, hospitality, marketing, sales, technical/systems, executives

Benefits and training: Both

Hall Kinion

19925 Stevens Creek Boulevard,
Suite 180
Cupertino, CA 95014
(408) 863-5647
www.hallkinion.com

Industries: Administration, engineering, marketing, technical/systems

Benefits and training: Both

Josephine's Personnel Services, Inc.

2680 North First Street, Suite 110
San Jose, CA 95134
(408) 943-0111
www.jps-inc.com

Industries: Accounting, administration, clerical, data processing, finance, marketing, technical, executives

Benefits and training: Both

Management Solutions, Inc.

99 Almaden Boulevard, Suite 600
San Jose, CA 95113
(408) 292-6600
www.mgmtsolutions.com

Industries: Accounting, data processing, engineering, finance, technical/systems, executives

Benefits and training: Benefits only

Midcom Corp.

888 Villa Street, Suite 430
Mountain View, CA 94041
(650) 938-1000
www.midcom.com

Industries: Data processing, engineering, technical/systems

Benefits and training: Benefits only

Nelson Staffing Solutions

4010 Moorpark Avenue, Suite 210
San Jose, CA 95117
(408) 241-8450
www.nelsonjobs.com

Industries: Accounting, administration, clerical, data processing, engineering, finance, hospitality, technical/systems

Benefits and training: Both

Palo Alto Staffing Services

2471 East Bayshore Road,
Suite 525
Palo Alto, CA 94303
(650) 493-0223
www.wehire.com

Industries: Accounting, administration, clerical, finance, hospitality, marketing, sales

Benefits and training: Benefits only

Remedy Personnel

4300 Stevens Creek Boulevard,
Suite 190
San Jose, CA 95129
(408) 554-8174
www.remedystaff.com

Industries: Accounting, administration, clerical, data processing, finance, hospitality, marketing, sales

Benefits and training: Both

Robert Half International, Inc.

333 West Santa Clara Street,
Suite 950
San Jose, CA 95113
(408) 293-9040
www.accountemps.com

Industries: Accounting, administration, clerical, data processing, finance

Benefits and training: Both

Technical Aid Corp.

1733 North First Street
San Jose, CA 95134
(408) 434-9800
www.onetech.com

Industries: Accounting, administration, clerical, data processing, engineering, finance, hospitality, technical/systems

Benefits and training: Benefits only

Trendtec Inc.

1620 Zanker Road
San Jose, CA 95112
(408) 436-1200
www.trendtec.com

Industries: Accounting, administration, clerical, data processing, engineering, finance, technical/systems

Benefits and training: Both

Western Staff Services, Inc.

97 Metro Drive
San Jose, CA 95110
(408) 441-1141
www.westaff.com

Industries: Accounting, administration, clerical, data processing, engineering, finance, marketing, technical/systems

Benefits and training: Both

RECRUITMENT/EXECUTIVE SEARCH FIRMS

Recruitment and executive search firms focus on permanent placement of executives and those with specialized industry experience. The following is a partial list of executive recruiting firms in Silicon Valley:

Advanced Technology Consultants, Inc.

536 Weddell Drive, Suite 7
Sunnyvale, CA 94089
(408) 734-5833

Areas of specialization: Software development, marketing, technical support

Bryson Myers Co.

2083 Old Middlefield Way,
Suite 806
Mountain View, CA 94043
(650) 964-7600

Areas of specialization: Computer hardware and software, engineering, health/medical, technical

Complimate Technical Staffing

150 West Iowa Avenue, Suite 203
Sunnyvale, CA 94086
(408) 773-8994
www.complimate.com

Areas of specialization: Network, operations, and programming

Corporate Search

6457 Edgemoor Way
San Jose, CA 95129
(408) 996-3000

Areas of specialization: Engineering, computer programming, systems analysis, technical writing

Culver Personnel Services

226 Airport Parkway, Suite 530
San Jose, CA 95110
(408) 441-7878

Areas of specialization: Sales and management

Essential Solutions, Inc.

2542 South Bascom Avenue,
Suite 225
Campbell, CA 95008
(408) 369-9500
www.esiweb.com

Areas of specialization: Wireless communications, systems, semiconductors, networking, multimedia

Fell & Nicholson Technology Resources

1731 Embarcadero Road, Suite 210
Palo Alto, CA 94303
(650) 856-9200

Areas of specialization: Technical, including network communications, multimedia, software, Internet, information services, and capital equipment systems

General Employment Enterprises, Inc.

2540 North First Street, Suite 110
San Jose, CA 95131
(408) 954-9000
www.genp.com

Areas of specialization: Technical, engineering, accounting

Heuristics Search Inc.

160 West Santa Clara Street,
Suite 1200
San Jose, CA 95113
(408) 748-1500
www.heuristicsearch.com

Areas of specialization: Software engineers

J. A. Cox & Associates

1305 Mildred Avenue
San Jose, CA 95125
(800) 362-9822

Area of specialization: Insurance

Management Recruiters International of Silicon Valley

2055 Gateway Place, Suite 420

San Jose, CA 95110

(408) 453-9999

www.mrisanjose.com

Areas of specialization: Semiconductor, systems integration, medical electronics, health care, software, hardware, client server

Online Staffing

111 West St. John Street, 12th Floor

San Jose, CA 95113

(408) 998-4100

www.olstaffing.com

Areas of specialization: Technical including Internet, software engineering, and information technology

Parker & Lynch

1250 Aviation Avenue, Suite 240

San Jose, CA 95110

(408) 298-6700

www.parkerlynch.com

Areas of specialization: Accounting, finance, human resources, MIS

Rusher, Loscavio & LoPresto

2479 East Bayshore Road,

Suite 700

Palo Alto, CA 94303

(650) 494-0883

www.rll.com

Area of specialization: Technical

Sources Services

1290 Oakmead Parkway, Suite 318

Sunnyvale, CA 94086

(408) 738-8440

www.romac-source.com

Areas of specialization: Accounting, information systems, software engineering, legal

Techniquest

2005 De La Cruz Boulevard,

Suite 121

Santa Clara, CA 95050

(408) 748-1122

Areas of specialization: Biotechnology, electronics, medical devices

OTHER JOB FINDING IDEAS

There are other ways to find a job in the Silicon Valley besides direct contact with the company or using a search firm. The following is a list of career development centers that can provide a different approach to your job search.

CAREER DEVELOPMENT ORGANIZATIONS

Career Action Center

10420 Bubb Road, Suite 100
Cupertino, CA 95014
(408) 253-3200
(408) 257-6400 (fax)
www.careeraction.org

Description: The Career Action Center is a nonprofit organization nationally recognized for its leadership and expertise in the development and delivery of career management services. Clients range from recent graduates and those looking for entry-level positions to technical specialists and managers with many years of experience. Currently there are about two hundred corporate partners.

Fee: $75 for a three-month membership or $100 for an annual membership.

What You Get: Your membership includes the newsletter *Member Connections*, mailed twice a year; the *Career Action Center Resource Guide*, published quarterly; and access to programs, resources, counseling, and workshops. Programs include Career Action Network, Career Management Forums, Employer Forums, and Friday Forums. There are also more than 13,000 job listings monthly from over 1,400 local employers.

Note: Attend a free introduction to the programs and services of the center. Also, you can try the Resource Center for a day for a $15 fee.

Employment Development Department Job Service Office

2450 South Bascom Avenue
Campbell, CA 95008
(408) 369-3611
www.jobs1.cahwnet.gov
www.ajb.dni.us

190 Leavesley Road
Gilroy, CA 95020
(408) 842-2164

1901 Zanker Road
San Jose, CA 95112
(408) 436-5600

Description: Career counseling, job search skills workshops, job listings and placement.

Fee: None

Mission College Santa Clara Career Center

3000 Mission College Boulevard
Room C1-117
Santa Clara, CA 95054
(408) 748-2729

Description: Services include a résumé center, career exploration library, workshops, seminars, job listings, interview coaching, and career fairs. They are not open during summer break.

Fee: None

Pro Match

505 West Olive Street, Suite 200
Sunnyvale, CA 94086
(408) 736-2391
www.promatch.org

Description: This is a career development center for professionals sponsored by the California State Employment Development Department. They offer career counseling, networking groups, professional development workshops, job listings, and other resources. Prospective members must attend an orientation session held every Wednesday. Members are required to complete necessary enrollment workshops, attend weekly meetings, and volunteer at the center.

Fee: None

San Jose State University Career Planning and Placement Center

Business Classroom Building,
Room 13
One Washington Square
San Jose, CA 95192
(408) 924-6033

Description: For nonstudents this is a self-help service that includes access to the career resource library and job listings.

Fee: $95 for three months

YWCA Career Center of San Jose

375 South Third Street
San Jose, CA 95112
(408) 295-4011
www.ywca-scv.org

Description: There are job listings, information on educational and training opportunities, and computer and Internet access for a small fee.

Fee: Free except for small computer usage fee.

JOB FAIRS

Career or Job Fairs are a good way to learn about local companies, including their employment opportunities and benefits. The following organizations host regular job fairs in the Silicon Valley. Check out their Web sites for location and date information.

Career Expo

(510) 436-3976
www.logop.com/expo/

Produces quarterly job fairs in January, April, August, and October in the San Jose and San Francisco areas. Focus is on technology, sales, and business jobs.

Job America
(408) 748-7600
www.jobsamerica.com/

Produces about three career fairs
a year in the San Jose and Santa
Clara area. The focus is on service
industry positions from the high-
tech to food.

Westech Career Expo
(408) 970-4970
www.vjf.com

Produces six high-tech job fairs a
year in Silicon Valley and the Bay
Area that are geared to the technical professional.

INTERNET RESOURCES

Career Mosaic
(www.careermosaic.com)
Under Silicon Valley you can find job openings that meet your search criteria.

Career Path
(www.careerpath.com)
You can search employment ads from the nations leading newspapers and job postings from leading employer Web sites.

Career Source Magazine
(www.careersource-magazine.com)
The online version of the magazine on Bay Area employment and career training.

Career.Com
(www.career.com)
Connecting employers and candidates around the world or around the corner. Provides free job-seeker assistance and offers employers an effective recruiting tool.

Digital Stations
(www.digitalstation.com)
This site is a guide to computer and Internet jobs, news, and life in the San Francisco Bay Area and Silicon Valley.

Job Web
(www.jobweb.com)
This site is sponsored by the National Association of Colleges and Employers, which serves as a bridge between higher education and the world of work. It has employment, job fair, and other career develop-ment information.

Monster Board
(www.monster.com)
Offers a worldwide jobs database, a job search agent that searches the database for jobs that match your experience, online recruitment seminars, and other career support.

Online Career Center
(www.occ.com)
Allows you to browse job listings by city and state. It has other employment and relocation resources as well.

Silicon Valley Job Source
(www.valleyjobs.com)
This site lists jobs specifically in the Silicon Valley and Bay Area.

Talent Scout
(www.talentscout.com)
This is the Silicon Valley job source with access to the *San Jose Mercury News* job database, employment-related articles, résumé postings, company profiles, advice columnists, and more.

The Business Journal
(www.amcity.com/sanjose)
Read about local business news and industry developments.

CHAPTER SIXTEEN

GETTING INVOLVED

COMPUTERS AND TECHNOLOGY are only one aspect of the Silicon Valley. There is also a recreational, playful side for exercising, meeting people, and getting involved in the community. This chapter lists some of the many health and sports clubs, cultural and social organizations, singles activities, and volunteer opportunities that help keep Santa Clara County residents busy and active in their leisure time.

HEALTH AND SPORTS CLUBS

HEALTH CLUBS

Silicon Valley has many health clubs and gyms, and finding the right one is a matter of personal choice. Maybe location is important to you or an outdoor swimming pool or an active social scene. Besides membership gyms, many Silicon Valley companies provide employees with health club facilities that are well-equipped and convenient. The following is a list of Silicon Valley health clubs with the most mem-

bers according to the 1998 San Jose Business Journal Book of Lists.

21st Point Fitness Center

199 East Middlefield Road
Mountain View, CA 94030

(650) 969-1783

24 Hour Fitness

P.O. Box 9071
Pleasanton, CA 94566
(800) 204-2400 call for locations nearest you
www.24hourfitness.com

309

Albert L. Schultz Jewish Community Center

655 Arastradero Road

Palo Alto, CA 94306

(650) 493-9400

www.paloaltojcc.org

Almaden Valley Athletic Club

5400 Camden Avenue

San Jose, CA 95124

(408) 267-3700

Bayhill Athletic Club

1000 Jacklin Road

Milpitas, CA 95035

(408) 946-2151

California Athletic Club

1211 East Arques Avenue

Sunnyvale, CA 94086

(408) 749-0300

Courtside Tennis Club

14675 Winchester Road

Los Gatos, CA 95030

(408) 395-7111

Decathlon Club

3250 Central Expressway

Santa Clara, CA 95051

(408) 738-8743

First Lady Spas

P.O. Box 5034

Livermore, CA 94550

(800) 696-0396

www.athleticclubs.com/
firstladyspas

Fitness 101

355 West San Fernando Street

San Jose, CA 95110

(408) 287-3101

George Brown Fitness

15445 Los Gatos Boulevard

Los Gatos, CA 95032

(408) 358-3551

www.businessquest.com/
gbfitness.htm

Los Gatos Athletic Club

285 East Main Street

Los Gatos, CA 95032

(408) 354-5808

www.lgac.com

Los Gatos Swim & Racquet Club

14700 Oka Road

Los Gatos, CA 95030

(408) 356-2136

Main Street Athletic Clubs

1902 South Bascom Avenue,

Suite 1440

Campbell, CA 95008

(408) 371-7144

Royal Courts Club Fitness

400 Saratoga Avenue

San Jose, CA 95129

(408) 296-1676

Schoeber's Athletic Club

7012 Realm Drive

San Jose, CA 95119

(408) 629-3333

enthusiasts like yourself. Getting involved in a sports club is a good way to meet people with whom you share a common interest. I have listed some of the sports clubs in Silicon Valley. For other resources, look into athletic departments at local colleges and universities (see chapter 13, "Silicon Valley Communities") or check out the *San Jose Mercury News* Adventure section published on Thursdays. Sporting goods stores in the area, like Any Mountain or Big 5, are also good resources for local clubs. Look in the local phone book for their locations.

Silicon Valley Athletic Club
801 Martin Avenue
Santa Clara, CA 95050
(408) 980-1392

South Bay Athletic Club
271 Houret Drive
Milpitas, CA 95035
(408) 946-0600

Supreme Court Racquet & Health Club
415 North Mathilda Avenue
Sunnyvale, CA 94086
(408) 739-1250

The Right Stuff Health Club
1730 West Campbell Avenue
Campbell, CA 95008
(408) 866-8855
www.bacnet.com/rightstuff/club_info.htm

YMCA of Santa Clara Valley
1190 Emory Street
San Jose, CA 95126
(408) 298-3888
www.sanjoseymca.org

YMCA of the Mid-Peninsula
4151 Middlefield Road, Suite 211
Palo Alto, CA 94303
(650) 856-3955
www.ymcamidpen.org

SPORTS CLUBS

If there is a particular sport you do, say, running or mountain biking, there may be a club out there of other

Bicycling

Almaden Cycle Touring Club
P.O. Box 7286
San Jose, CA 95150
www.actc.org

The Almaden Cycle Touring Club is a group of bicycling enthusiasts of all levels. There are an average of eighty rides per month that emphasize group fun and safety. There is also social time for food, drink, and mingling.

Apple/Velox Cycling Team
http://veloxs.apple.com/

Formed by a group of Apple employees, the team now has twenty-five bicycle athletes from inside and outside the company. You don't have to be an employee of Apple to join, but you must be sponsored.

Los Gatos Bicycle Racing Club

E-mail: lgbrc@cycling.org

Training, races, meetings, and social time for bicycling enthusiasts.

R.O.M.P. (Responsible Organized Mountain Pedalers)

P.O. Box 1723
Campbell, CA 95009

www.stanford.edu/~scoop/romp

This is a mountain cycling advocacy and social group for San Mateo and Santa Clara counties. They hold several rides a week that are open to members and nonmembers. Some themes are Fat Wednesday rides and Friday Hookey rides.

San Jose Bicycling Club

(408) 287-SJBC Hotline

This club has been around since 1939. They are committed to developing beginning and junior cyclists through club racing and competition. The club provides its members with coaching and organized racing events aimed at increasing the skill, ability, and enjoyment of each member.

Hiking/Walking

Midpeninsula Regional Open Space District

330 Distel Circle
Los Altos, CA 94022

(650) 691-1200

www.openspace.org

Their purpose is to create a regional greenbelt of open space lands, linking district preserves with other public parklands in order to preserve open space in the area. In the summer they have guided hikes and walks in the area.

Sierra Club

Loma Prieta Chapter
3921 East Bayshore Road, Suite 204
Palo Alto, CA 94303
(650) 390-8411
www.sierraclub.org/chapters/lomaprieta

Outdoor activities for all interests like hiking, backpacking, nature photography, singles events, skiing, and more.

Running

The *Runner's Schedule* is a free newspaper published monthly and found at sporting goods stores, cafés, and other locations. It is the complete guide to running and racing in California. Check out their Web site at **www.theschedule.com**

for resources that include local running groups in Silicon Valley. Some groups mentioned are:

BADRunners (Bay Area Dead Runners): An Internet-based running, chat, and social group that holds weekend trail runs throughout the Bay Area.

Galloway Marathon Training: Weekly runs and personalized training for marathons along with social events.

Los Gatos Running Club: Weekly runs at various high-school tracks.

Silicon Valley Triathlon Club: Triathlon training with group rides, runs, and swims. They host monthly meetings and forums.

South Valley Tri-Sport Club: A competitive racing club for all levels and ages. They host monthly meetings and social events.

Stevens Creek Striders: Running for all levels and ages plus monthly meetings and social events.

West Valley Joggers and Striders (www.accesscom.com/~jwhalen/wvjs.html): Recreational and competitive running with socials and potlucks thrown in.

Skiing

Apres Ski Club
(888) 277-3746
www.apres.org

This is a ski club for singles that offers many other social activities and sports.

Snowdrifters Ski Club
P.O. Box 396
Mountain View, CA 94042
(800) SUN-OR-SKI or
(800-786-6775)
www.snowdrifters.org

This is a winter ski and snowboard club composed of singles over twenty-one. Besides winter skiing, there are a number of other outdoor activities like hiking and biking. There are also non-sports related social activities like going to the theater and dining out.

Tennis

Mountain View Tennis Club
P.O. Box 336
Mountain View, CA 94042
http://shell3.ba.best.com/~jbh/

The club is open to all residents of Mountain View. Activities include tournaments, ladder programs, interclub competitions, social events, and USTA league play.

Palo Alto Tennis Club

www.nanospace.com/~patc/

They are a public club, with over five hundred members, making use of public courts. Most tournaments are held at the Rinconada Courts in Palo Alto.

Sunnyvale Tennis Club

http://u2.netgate.net/~cruzspray/stc/

The club promotes year-round tennis activities in Sunnyvale. There are recreational and competitive tennis, tournaments, ladders, and social events.

CULTURAL AND SOCIAL ORGANIZATIONS

Churchill Club

2323 South Bascom Avenue
Campbell, CA 95008
(408) 371-4460
www.churchillclub.com

This is Silicon Valley's public affairs forum, similar to the Commonwealth Club in San Francisco. The purpose of the Churchill Club is to provide Silicon Valley with a nonpartisan forum for the exchange of ideas on timely issues, particularly those in which business and politics converge. Their lectures are geared toward Silicon Valley and have a technology bent. Past speakers include Bill Gates of Microsoft and Larry Ellison of Oracle. Annual membership is $75.

Commonwealth Club Silicon Valley Forum

306 South Third Street
San Jose, CA 95112
(408) 298-8342
www.commonwealthclub.org

Offers a high-quality speakers program that has been the hallmark of the Commonwealth Club for nearly a century. The Silicon Valley Forum is actively engaged in developing events that address issues pertinent to the Silicon Valley community.

Opus 21

(408) 985-7204

Rod Diridon is the founder of this young professional's group that supports local museums and performing arts in the Silicon Valley through activities and fund-raising. Past events have been affiliated with the San Jose Museum of Art and San Jose Repertory Theater.

The following arts organizations are in the process of or interested in forming young professional groups for social and fundraising activities. If you are interested in getting involved, give them a call. What better way to meet people when you are new in town.

San Jose Museum of Art, (408) 271-6840

Museum of Tech Innovation, (408) 279-7101

Opera San Jose, (408) 437-4450

San Jose Symphony, (408) 288-2828

San Jose Cleveland Ballet, (408) 288-2820

San Jose Repertory Theater, (408) 291-2255

SINGLES ACTIVITIES

Diocese of San Jose

900 Lafayette Street, Suite 301
Santa Clara, CA 95050
(408) 983-0100
www.dsj.org

Contact the Catholic Archdiocese to find a young adults group in your area for socializing and fellowship.

Menlo Park Presbyterian Church

950 Santa Cruz Avenue
Menlo Park, CA 94025
(650) 328-2340
www.mppc.org

This is a very active church with many different ministries for all interests. Their singles ministry has gatherings for those in their twenties, thirties, and forties, and for single parents. Visit their Web site for details of other social and outreach activities.

Singles Supper Club

P. O. Box 60518
Palo Alto, CA 94306
(650) 327-4645
www.best.com/~ssc/

This is a dining club of single professionals who range in age from 28 to 55. Though there are separate events specifically for those in their late twenties to early forties, most events are open to all members. There are three to six dinners, social, or cultural events held each month for its more than five hundred members. Events include tennis, dancing, and dinners at fine restaurants mostly in Santa Clara County. Membership is about $125 a year and event and dinner costs are extra.

Young Jewish Community

26790 Arastradero Road
Los Altos, CA 94022
(650) 493-4661
www.best.com/~dbloom/yjc.html

Young Jewish Community (YJC) is a social, cultural, and community group dedicated to promoting a stronger sense of community among Jewish adults aged 21 to 35. They are affiliated with Congregation Beth Am in Los Altos Hills. They have social activities like rollerblading, concerts, dinners, and volunteer events.

VOLUNTEER OPPORTUNITIES

Many cities in Santa Clara County have community service programs that can match interested people with city departments or outside agencies in need of volunteers. You may work with seniors, assist at the local library, or help with a homeless program. Contact the center in your community for more details.

Campbell Volunteer Services

(408) 866-2198

Cupertino Community Services

(408) 255-8033

Gilroy Community Services

(408) 848-0460

Los Altos/Mountain View Community Services

(650) 968-0836

Another excellent resource for information about volunteer opportunities is the Volunteer Exchange. Their mission is to promote, support, and facilitate volunteerism in Santa Clara County. It is the only agency of its kind in the county to provide information on the many volunteer opportunities available. They have relationships with major companies in the Silicon Valley to promote employee volunteerism. They will match interested volunteers with one-time or continuing projects as well as offer tools and training.

Volunteer Exchange
1922 The Alameda, Suite 211
San Jose, CA 95126
(408) 247-1126
www.volunteerexchange.org

Milpitas Volunteer Services
(408) 942-5141

Morgan Hill Volunteer Services
(408) 779-7271

City of San Jose Volunteer Hotline
(408) 277-2468

City of Santa Clara Volunteer Department
(408) 984-3110

City of Saratoga Volunteer Department
(408) 868-1252

Sunnyvale Volunteer Services Program
(408) 730-7533

CHAPTER SEVENTEEN

THINGS TO DO
ON THE WEEKENDS

S ILICON VALLEY HAS many cultural activities and attractions to entertain its residents and visitors alike. There are museums, performing arts, amusement parks, and professional sports teams. This chapter lists many unique ways to spend your free time in Santa Clara County.

**San Jose Convention &
Visitors Bureau**
333 West San Carlos Street, Suite 1000
San Jose, CA 95110
(408) 295-9600
www.sanjose.org

**Santa Clara Convention &
Visitors Bureau**
1850 Warburton Avenue
Santa Clara, CA 95050
(408) 244-9660
www.santaclara.org

MUSEUMS

**Campbell Historical Museum
and Ainsley House**
51 North Central Avenue
(Historical Museum)
300 Grant Street
(Ainsley House)
Campbell, CA 95008
(408) 866-2119
web.nvcom.com/chm/

Free Day: None

The Campbell Historical Museum is located in the historic Ainsley House, an English Tudor-style home built in the 1920s. The museum showcases life in the Santa Clara Valley during the 1920s and '30s as well as an exhibit on the history of Campbell. There are also beautiful formal gardens that have been recreated based on the original 1926 landscape design.

Center for Beethoven Studies and Museum
San Jose State University
615 Wahlquist North
San Jose, CA 95116
(408) 924-4590

Free Day: Always

This is the only research archive in North America devoted entirely to the life and work of Ludwig van Beethoven. The library and museum houses first and early editions of his music, a Viennese forte piano, and even a lock of his hair.

Free Day: None

Children's Discovery Museum of San Jose
180 Woz Way
San Jose, CA 95110
(408) 298-5437
www.cdm.org

Free Day: None

This is the largest children's museum in the West, impressively ranked among the top five in the United States since its opening in 1990. There are many interactive exhibits and programs in the arts, science, and technology for children up to thirteen years of age.

Cupertino History Museum
10185 North Stelling Road
Cupertino, CA 95014
(408) 973-1495

Free Day: Always

Changing exhibits of the history of business, community, and people in Cupertino and the Santa Clara Valley.

de Saisset Museum
Santa Clara University
500 El Camino Real
Santa Clara, CA 95053
(408) 554-4528

Free Day: Always

The de Saisset Museum is the caretaker of Santa Clara University's California History Collection, which includes historic and ethnographic artifacts from the pre-contact Native American period, through the founding of the Franciscan Mission in 1777, to the early days of the university. The museum's permanent collection includes a wide range of art from Africa, the Americas, Asia, and Europe. There is also a strong collection of contemporary prints and photographs. The museum presents changing art exhibitions, lectures, readings, concerts, films, and tours throughout the year.

Hiller Aviation Museum
San Carlos Airport
601 Skyway Road
San Carlos, CA
(650) 654-0200
www.hiller.org

Free Day: None

This 53,000-square-foot museum is the largest indoor aviation museum in California. There are interactive exhibits, over fifty aircraft on display, and other items of interest covering 128 years in the history of flight. There are also previews to the future of aviation with robotic aircraft, hypersonic aircraft, and more.

Intel Museum

2200 Mission College Boulevard
Santa Clara, CA 95952
(408) 765-0503
www.intel.com/intel/intelis/museum

Free Day: Always

The Intel Museum, located, where else, but at the Intel Corporation headquarters, introduces visitors to the microminiature world of computer chips. Featured exhibits include a giant microprocessor and a demonstration of how chips are made.

Japanese American Museum

565 North Fifth Street
San Jose, CA 95112
(408) 294-3138

Free Day: Donations requested

This museum exhibits artifacts and historical documents on the history of Japanese Americans, with emphasis in the Santa Clara Valley.

Rodin Sculpture Garden

Stanford University Museum of Art
B. Gerald Cantor Rodin
Sculpture Garden
Stanford, CA 94305-5060
(650) 723-4177

This is the world's largest public collection of bronze sculptures by Rodin.

Rosicrucian Egyptian Museum and Planetarium

1342 Naglee Avenue
San Jose, CA 95191
(408) 947-3636
www.rosicrucian.org

Free Day: None

This museum exhibits the largest collection of Egyptian artifacts in the western United States. More than five thousand objects are housed in an Egyptian-style building inspired by the Temple of Amon at Karnak. Located in the gardens of Rosicrucian Park, the museum grounds are landscaped with elaborate fountains and colossal statues of Egyptian gods. There are weekly lectures on Egyptian topics and free hieroglyphics workshops every weekend. There is also a planetarium in the park.

San Jose Historical Museum

1650 Senter Road
San Jose, CA 95112
(408) 287-2290
www.serve.com/sjhistory

This museum consists of twenty-one restored and reconstructed homes and businesses from 1870 to 1910. Located in Kelley Park, these buildings document the history of San Jose, providing a unique glance of life at that time.

Free Day: None

San Jose Institute of Contemporary Art
451 South First Street
San Jose, CA 95113
(408) 283-8155

Free Day: First Thursday of the month

Features contemporary art with an emphasis on local Bay Area artists.

San Jose Museum of Art
110 South Market Street
San Jose, CA 95113
(408) 294-2787
www.sjmusart.org

Free Day: First Thursday of each month

Originally built as a post office in 1892, the museum is now home to a permanent collection of nearly one thousand works of art from twentieth-century artists. It also hosts changing exhibits of photography, painting, sculpture, and other art forms. The museum is engaged in a six-year collaboration with the Whitney Museum of American Art in a presentation of the Whitney's permanent collection. Besides exhibits, the museum also has activities like Wednesday night concerts and free public art walks in downtown San Jose.

San Jose Museum of Quilts and Textiles
60 South Market Street
San Jose, CA 95108
(408) 971-0323

Free Day: First Thursday of the month

The mission of the museum is to promote the art, craft, and history of quilts. The museum exhibits quilts and textiles from around the world and has programs on the appreciation of quilts and textiles as art and understanding their role in cultural traditions.

The Tech Museum of Innovation
145 West San Carlos Street
San Jose, CA 95113
(408) 279-7150
www.thetech.org

Free Day: None

Silicon Valley, the birthplace of technology, is a logical place for a museum that focuses on the development and advances of technology.

nology. Its mission is to engage people of all ages and backgrounds in exploring and experiencing technologies affecting their lives, and to inspire the young to become innovators in the technologies of the future.

Triton Museum of Art

1505 Warburton Avenue
Santa Clara, CA 95050
(408) 247-9340
www.tritonmuseum.org

Free Day: Always except for special exhibits

The Triton Museum of Art collects and exhibits contemporary and historical works of art with an emphasis on local and California artists. The museum also offers art classes and education programs.

Villa Montalvo Historic Estate for the Arts

15400 Montalvo Road
Saratoga, CA 95071
(408) 961-5800
www.villamontalvo.org

This is a 175-acre estate that is a center for the arts in Saratoga. It features the works of regional artists, an arboretum, formal gardens, bird sanctuary, and trails for nature walks.

Wings of History Air Museum

12777 Murphy Avenue
San Martin, CA 95046
(408) 683-2290

Free Day: Always

There are more than twenty antique aircraft on display at this museum along with photographs and exhibits.

PARKS AND GARDENS

Filoli

Canada Road
Woodside, CA 94062
(650) 364-8300
www.filoli.org

Visitors will recognize the Roth Estate from the opening shot on TV's *Dynasty* series. There are tours of the house and exquisite gardens.

Hakone Gardens

21000 Big Basin Way
Saratoga, CA 95070
(408) 741-4994

This is the only authentic Japanese-style garden in North America designed as a traditional seventeenth-century Zen garden. It has gazebos, ponds, waterfalls, stone lanterns, and a moon bridge. The 15-acre garden was created in 1918 by the former gardener to the Emperor of Japan.

Happy Hollow Park & Zoo

1300 Senter Road

San Jose, CA 95112

(408) 295-8383

This is a children's park and zoo that offers hands-on contact with animals, a petting zoo, and endangered species conservation and education. The park has play areas, rides, and a puppet theater.

Lake Cunningham Regional Park

2305 South White Road

San Jose, CA 95148

(408) 277-4319

This fifty-acre lake is surrounded by parklands, picnic areas, playground, and golf course. The lake has sailboat, pedal boat, canoe, and rowboat rentals and there is plenty of fishing.

Overfelt Gardens

2145 McKee Road

San Jose, CA 95133

(408) 251-3323

This thirty-three-acre community park has formal botanical gardens, a wildlife sanctuary, fragrance garden for the visually impaired, and a Chinese cultural garden.

Prusch Farm Park

647 South Kind Road

San Jose, CA 95116

(408) 926-5555

Learn about San Jose's agricultural past in this forty-seven-acre park which features San Jose's largest barn. There are community gardens, farm animals, fruit orchards, old farm equipment displays, and picnic areas. Classes are offered in landscaping and gardening.

San Jose Municipal Rose Garden

Corner of Dana and Naglee
Avenues

San Jose, CA 95126

(408) 277-5422

Stroll through five acres of roses with more than 189 varieties represented. It is also home to newly hybridized roses and new rose varieties.

OTHER ATTRACTIONS

Billy Jones Wildcat Railroad & W. E. Mason Carousel

P.O. Box 234
Oak Meadow Park
Los Gatos, CA 95031
(408) 395-RIDE

Take a ride on a 1905 miniature locomotive steam engine around Oak Meadow Park. Another attraction is a restored carousel originally manufactured for the 1915 Panama-Pacific Exposition in San Francisco.

Burlingame Museum of Pez Memorabilia

214 California Drive
Burlingame, CA 94010
(650) 347-2301
www.spectrumnet.com/pez

This one-note museum is devoted to Pez candy dispenser memorabilia.

Lick Observatory

Mt. Hamilton Road
Santa Cruz, CA 95140
(408) 274-5061
www.ucolick.org

Visitors can enjoy a guided tour of the Great Lick Refractor. Highlights are the 120-degree viewing gallery and the Shane Reflector.

Mission Santa Clara de Asis

500 El Camino Real at the
University of Santa Clara
Santa Clara, CA 95053
(408) 554-4023

Located on the campus of Santa Clara University, this mission was founded by Franciscan missionaries in 1777.

Monterey Bay Aquarium

886 Cannery Row
Monterey, CA 93940
(408) 648-4888
www.mbayaq.org

This is a famous aquarium that showcases California marine life and special aquatic exhibits.

Paramount's Great America

Great America Parkway
Santa Clara, CA 95052
(408) 988-1776
www.pgathrills.com

This is the Disneyland of Silicon Valley. It is a 100-acre family theme park with thrill rides, shows, fireworks, Nickelodeon characters, restaurants, and shops.

Peralta Adobe & Fallon House Historic Site

175 West St. John Street
San Jose, CA 95110
(408) 993-8182
www.serve.com/sjhistory

The Peralta Adobe House was built in 1797 and is San José's oldest building and last remaining structure from the Spanish pueblo of San José de Guadalupe.

The Fallon House is a restored Italianate Victorian that housed the area's most popular restaurant, which was frequented by celebrities of the time like John Steinbeck and Charlie Chaplin.

Raging Waters

2333 South White Road
Lake Cunningham Regional Park
San Jose, CA 95151
(408) 238-9111
www.raging-waters.com

This is a fourteen-acre water theme park with more than twenty waterslides, rides, and attractions.

Roaring Camp & Big Trees Railroad

P.O. Box G-1, Graham Hill Road
Felton, CA 95018
(408) 335-4484

Located in the redwood forests of the Santa Cruz mountains, this is America's last steam-powered passenger railroad. Visitors can ride old-fashioned steam passenger trains through some of the most beautiful and primitive scenery in the American West.

San Jose Pavilion Farmers Market

150 South First Street
San Jose, CA 95113
(408) 279-1775

This is a downtown farmers market that takes place every Thursday from May through November.

San Jose Flea Market

1590 Berryessa Road
San Jose, CA 95133
(408) 453-1110
www.sjfm.com

This is the largest flea market in California with some six thousand vendors covering 120 acres. Besides being a bargain hunter's paradise, there is food and entertainment to keep the eighty thousand weekly visitors busy.

Santa Cruz Beach Boardwalk

400 Beach Street
Santa Cruz, CA 95060
(408) 423-5590
www.beachboardwalk.com

This is a seaside amusement park that features rides, miniature golf, arcades, shops, and restaurants along a one-mile stretch of beach.

Winchester Mystery House

525 South Winchester Boulevard
San Jose, California 95128
(408) 247-2000
www.winchestermysteryhouse.com

This house was built by the eccentric widow of the manufacturer of the famous Winchester Repeating Rifle. After the death of her infant daughter and husband, Mrs. Winchester consulted a spiritualistic medium who told her that the spirits who had been killed by the rifles her family manufactured had sought their revenge by taking the lives of her loved ones. Furthermore, these spirits had placed a curse on her and would haunt her forever. The only escape from this curse was to move west, buy a house, and continually build on it as the spirits directed. And build she did, twenty-four hours a day for thirty-eight years until her death. Today visitors get to roam this unusual mansion and hear about the legend.

MUSIC

Cupertino Symphonic Band

P.O. Box 2692
Cupertino, CA 95015
(408) 262-0471
www.netview.com/csb

This is a local symphony band that started back in 1989 by a group of Cupertino High School Band alumni. The band has been giving performances to the Silicon Valley community for over seven years.

Opera San Jose

2149 Paragon Drive
San Jose, CA 95131
(408) 437-4450
www.operasj.org

This regional opera company showcases the nation's top young performers in the intimate 500-seat Montgomery Theater.

Palo Alto Chamber Orchestra

723 Matadero Avenue
Palo Alto, CA 94306
(650) 856-3848

Founded in 1966, this chamber orchestra is composed of some of the Bay Area's most talented young musicians.

Palo Alto Philharmonic

3790 El Camino Real, Suite 215
Palo Alto, CA 94306
Check Web site for phone numbers.
www.paphil.ai.sri.com

Founded in 1988, this is a community orchestra that gives six performances annually at the Cubberley Theatre in Palo Alto. One of the goals of this orchestra is to make classical music more widely accessible for all, including the seniors and youths of the

San Jose Symphony Orchestra

495 Almaden Boulevard
San Jose, CA 95110
(408) 288-2828
www.sanjosesymphony.org

The San Jose Symphony was founded 110 years ago making it the oldest symphony west of the Mississippi. It offers a full season of classical music including a signature series, familiar classics series, and SuperPops.

Peninsula, by keeping ticket prices down and offering programs of a wide variety, including an annual free youth concert.

Stanford Symphony Orchestra

Braun Music Center
Stanford, CA 94305
(650) 723-3811
www.leland.stanford.edu/group/sso

The first Stanford Orchestra was organized in 1891, after Stanford University opened its doors. This century-old, on-campus student organization presents at least five programs at the university each season.

THEATER/DANCE

City Lights Theater Company

529 South Second Street
San Jose, CA 95112
(408) 295-4200
www.cltc.org

Palo Alto Players

Lucie Stern Theater
1305 Middlefield Road
Palo Alto, CA 94301
(650) 329-0891
www.paplayers.org

San Jose Cleveland Ballet

40 North First Street
San Jose, CA 95113
(408) 288-2820
www.csjballet.org

San Jose Repertory Theatre

101 Paseo de San Antonio
San Jose, CA 95113
(408) 291-2255
www.sjrep.com

San Jose Stage Company

490 South First Street
San Jose, CA 95109
(408) 283-7142
www.sanjose-stage.com

SPORTS

San Jose Clash
Major League Soccer

San Jose Municipal Stadium at
10th and Alma Streets
(408) 985-GOAL (4625)
www.clash.com

San Jose Giants
Minor League Baseball

San Jose Municipal Stadium at
10th and Alma Streets
(408) 297-1435
www.sjgiants.com

San Jose Lasers
Women's Basketball

Events Center at 7th and San
Carlos Streets or
San Jose Arena at 525 West Santa
Clara Street
(408) 271-1500
www.sjlasers.com

San Jose SaberCats
Arena Football

San Jose Arena at 525 West Santa
Clara Street
(408) 573-5577
www.sanjosesabercats.com

San Jose Sharks
Hockey League

San Jose Arena at 525 West Santa
Clara Street
(408) 287-7070
www.sj-sharks.com

San Jose Spitfires
Ladies Professional
Baseball

San Jose Municipal Stadium at
10th and Alma Streets
(408) 729-8700

TOURS

NASA/Ames Research
Center

Moffet Field in Mountain View
(650) 604-6274 or 6497
www.arc.nasa.gov

This is the tour of the NASA Research Center in Mountain View,
including the world-famous wind
tunnel.

Past Heritage Walking Tours
of Palo Alto

(650) 299-8878
www.pastheritage.org

They offer two different historic
walking tours that begin at the
downtown library (270 Forest Avenue). One travels through the
downtown historical districts, and

another is a walk through the Professorville historical district, home to many Stanford University professors since the 1890s.

Stanford University Tours

www.stanford.edu

Tour the campus of beautiful Stanford University and visit the various arts, science, and educational centers it's known for.

Campus Tour: (650) 723-2560

Hoover Institute: (650) 723-1754

Jasper Ridge Biological Reserve: (650) 327-2277

Stanford Art Gallery: (650) 723-2842

Stanford Linear Accelerator Center: (650) 926-2204

Stanford University Museum of Art: (650) 723-477

U.S. Geological Survey

345 Middlefield Road in Palo Alto
(650) 853-8300
www.usgs.net

Individual and docent-led tours for larger groups. Both types of tours include earthquake information and a visit to the map center.

OTHER RESOURCES

Discover Silicon Valley
(650) 366-6099: This is a free monthly publication about events, nightlife, dining, and other points of interest in Silicon Valley.

Eye (**www.justgo.com/bayarea**): This is a weekly entertainment guide published each Friday by the *San Jose Mercury News*.

WORLD WIDE WEB RESOURCES

San Jose Living
(**www.sjliving.com**)
Arts, tourism, and entertainment in San Jose.

San Jose
(**www.sanjose.org**)
General visitor information and calendar of events for San Jose.

YEAR-ROUND
CALENDAR OF EVENTS

There is so much going on in San Francisco that a weekend rarely goes by without a sporting event, convention, conference, festival, show, and more. The following calendar lists some annual city events that have become almost tradition. The San Francisco Convention and Visitors Bureau Web site (**www.sfvisitor.org**) has more information about city happenings. If you are interested in events outside of the city, check with each town's visitor and convention bureaus.

JANUARY

First Run New Year's Eve Run: (415) 668-2243

MacWorld Expo: (415) 974-4000

FEBRUARY

Chinese New Year Celebration: (415) 982-3000

San Francisco Ballet Season begins: (415) 865-2000

TulipMania: (415) 705-5500

MARCH

Bay Area Music Awards (BAMMIES): (415) 388-4000

St. Patrick's Day Parade: (415) 661-2700

APRIL

American Conservatory Theater (ACT) Opening Season: (415) 749-2228

Cherry Blossom Festival: (415) 563-2313

Opening Day on the Bay: (510) 523-2098

San Francisco Giants Baseball Season begins: (415) 467-8000

San Francisco International Film Festival: (415) 929-5000

MAY

Bay to Breakers Race:
(415) 777-7000

Carnival Celebration and Parade:
(415) 826-1401

Cinco de Mayo celebration and
parade: (415) 826-1401

JUNE

Black and White Ball
(odd numbered years only):
(415) 864-6000

Haight Street Fair:
(415) 661-8025

KQED International Beer and
Food Festival: (510) 762-BASS

North Beach Fair: (415) 989-6426

San Francisco Lesbian/Gay/
Bisexual/Transgender Pride
Celebration Parade:
(415) 864-3733

Stern Grove Concerts:
(415) 252-6252

Union Street Fair: (415) 346-4446

JULY

Cable Car Bell Ringing Champi-
onships: (415) 474-1887

Chronicle Fourth of July Waterfront Festival: (415) 777-8498

Jazz and All That Art on Fillmore
Street Festival: (415) 346-9162

Jewish Film Festival:
(415) 621-0556

Peach Festival: (415) 771-3112

San Francisco Marathon:
(415) 296-7111

AUGUST

San Francisco 49ers football
season begins: (415) 656-4900

SEPTEMBER

Blues and Art Festival:
(415) 346-9162

Chocolate Festival:
(415) 775-5500

Festival of the Sea: (415) 561-6662

Folsom Street Fair:
(415) 861-3247

Opera in the Park:
(415) 864-3330

San Francisco Blues Festival:
(415) 979-5588

San Francisco Hillstride:
(415) 759-2690

San Francisco Opera season
begins: (415) 864-3330

San Francisco Shakespeare
Festival: (415) 422-2222

San Francisco Symphony season begins: (415) 431-5400

Sausalito Arts Festival: (415) 332-3555

OCTOBER

American Conservatory Theater season begins: (415) 749-2ACT

Autumn Moon Festival Street Fair in Chinatown: (415) 982-6306

Bridge to Bridge Run: (415) 974-6800

Castro Street Fair: (415) 467-3354

Columbus Day Celebration and Parade: (415) 434-1492

Exotic Erotic Halloween Ball: (415) 864-1500

Fleet Week: (415) 434-1492

Great Halloween and Pumpkin Festival: (415) 346-9162

Halloween Festival: (415) 771-3112

Reggae in the Park: (415) 458-1988

San Francisco Fall Antiques Show: (415) 546-6661

San Francisco Jazz Festival: (415) 398-5655

San Francisco Open Studios: (415) 861-9838

NOVEMBER

Run to the Far Side: (415) 564-0532

San Francisco Bay Area Book Festival: (415) 908-2833

DECEMBER

Ice skating rink at Justin Herman Plaza

San Francisco Ballet Nutcracker: (415) 865-2000

Santa Claus Parade

Union Square Christmas Tree Lighting

BAY AREA NUMBERS TO KNOW

The phone book is always the best reference for phone numbers. But if you need an emergency number or important city number for, say, the phone company, then this quick reference guide will help.

SERVICES

Pacific Bell Telephone
800-310-2355 (To order service)
800-848-8000 (To order directories)
www.pacbell.com

Pacific Gas and Electric (PG&E)
800-743-5000 (Customer service and 24-hour emergency assistance)
www.pge.com

San Francisco Water Department
(415) 923-2400

TCI Cable
800-945-2288 (To order service and for billing questions)
www.tci.com

GARBAGE AND SANITATION IN SAN FRANCISCO

Golden Gate Disposal
(415) 626-4000
www.norcalwaste.com/ goldengate.htm

Sunset Scavengers
(415) 330-1300

RECYCLING AND ENVIRONMENTAL INFORMATION

Recycling Program Hotline
(415) 554-6193

NEWSPAPERS

Bay Guardian
(weekly free city paper)
www.bayguardian.com
(510) 208-6300
www.newschoice.com

San Francisco Chronicle
(morning daily newspaper)
(415) 777-1111
www.sfgate.com

San Francisco Examiner
(afternoon daily
newspaper)
(415) 777-2424
www.examiner.com

Oakland Tribune

For other newspapers online, visit the News Choice Web site (www. newschoice.com) which lists Northern California newspapers as well as other U.S. newspapers.

EMERGENCY/SECURITY

POLICE IN SAN FRANCISCO

Emergency: 911

Non-emergency dispatch:
(415) 553-0123

Bayview Station
201 Williams Avenue
(415) 671-2300

Central Station
766 Vallejo Street
(415) 553-1532

Ingleside Station
Balboa Park
(415) 553-1603

Mission Station
630 Valencia Street
(415) 553-5400

Northern Station
1125 Fillmore Street
(415) 553-1563

Park Station
Kezar Drive and Waller Street
(415) 753-7280

Richmond Station
461 6th Street
(415) 553-1385

Southern Station
850 Bryant Street
(415) 553-1373

Taraval Station
2345 24th Avenue
(415) 553-1612

Tenderloin Task Force
1 Jones Street
(415) 557-6700

FIRE DEPARTMENT IN SAN FRANCISCO

Emergency: 911

Non-emergency: (415) 558-3268

HOSPITALS IN SAN FRANCISCO

California Pacific Medical Center

3700 California Street
(415) 387-8700
(415) 923-3333 *(Emergency)* or
2333 Buchanan Street
(415) 563-4321
www.cpmc.org

Davies Medical Center

Castro and Duboce Streets
(415) 565-6000
www.daviesmed.org

San Francisco General Hospital

1001 Potrero Avenue
(415) 206-8000
(415) 206-8111 *(Emergency)*

St. Francis Memorial Hospital

900 Hyde Street
(415) 353-6000

St. Luke's Hospital

3555 Cesar Chavez Street
(415) 647-8600

St. Mary's Medical Center

450 Stanyan Street
(415) 668-1000

UCSF Medical Center

505 Parnassus Avenue
(415) 476-1000
(415) 476-1037 *(Emergency)*

UCSF Mount Zion Medical Center

1600 Divisadero Street
(415) 567-6600
(415) 885-7520 *(Emergency)*

MISCELLANEOUS EMERGENCY INFORMATION

American Red Cross:
(415) 427-8000

Poison Control (twenty-four-hour service): (800) 876-4766

San Francisco Health Department:
(415) 554-2500

TRANSPORTATION INFORMATION

The Bay Area Transit Information Project Web site (**www.transitinfo.org**) provides instant online access to transit information for the nine-county San Francisco Bay Area.

PARKING AND TRAFFIC DEPARTMENT IN SAN FRANCISCO

General parking information:
(415) 554-7275

Residential parking permits:
(415) 554-5000

Bicycle information:
(415) 554-2351

Department of Motor Vehicles in San Francisco

1377 Fell Street
(415) 557-1179 (General information and appointments)
www.dmv.ca.gov

PUBLIC TRANSPORTATION

AC Transit

(510) 817-1717
www.actransit.dst.ca.us

Bus service for Alameda and Contra Costa Counties.

Alameda-Oakland Ferry

(510) 522-3300
www.transitinfo.org/alaoakferry

Daily commuter and excursion service between Alameda, Oakland, and San Francisco.

BART
(Bay Area Rapid Transit)

(650) 992-2278
www.bart.org

Rapid train service for San Francisco, Daly City, Alameda, and Contra Costa counties.

CalTrain

(800) 660-4287
www.transitinfo.org/caltrain

Train service runs between San Francisco and San Jose.

Golden Gate Transit

(415) 923-2000
www.goldengate.org

Provides bus and ferry service from Marin and Sonoma counties to San Francisco.

Red & White Fleet

(415) 447-0597
www.redandwhite.com

Ferry service between Sausalito, Tiburon, and San Francisco.

SamTrans

(800) 660-4287
www.samtrans.com

Bus service to Daly City and Hayward BART stations, San Francisco International Airport, Southern Pacific Cal-Train stations, San Francisco Greyhound Depot, Stonestown Mall, and Santa Clara County Transit.

San Francisco MUNI Bus Lines

MUNI Bus Information (routes, schedules, and Fast Pass outlets): (415) 673-6864

MUNI Complaints: (415) 923-6164

www.ci.sf.ca.us/muni

TAXI SERVICE IN SAN FRANCISCO

De Soto: (415) 673-1414

Luxor: (415) 282-4141

Veterans: (415) 552-1300

Yellow Cab: (415) 626-2345

CAR RENTAL COMPANIES

Avis: (415) 885-5011 or www.avis.com

Budget: (415) 775-5800 or www.budgetrentacar.com

Hertz: (800) 654-3131 or www.hertz.com

National: (415) 474-5300 or www.nationalcar.com

AIRPORT SHUTTLES

Share-A-Ride to SFO (800-SFO-2008) can help find transportation options to San Francisco International Airport. Airport shuttle options include:

Bay Shuttle: (415) 564-3400

Marin Airporter: (415) 461-4222

M&M Shuttle: (800) 286-0303

Quake City: (415) 255-4899

SFO Airporter: (415) 641-3100

SuperShuttle: (415) 558-0469 or www.supershuttle.com

AIRPORTS

Oakland International Airport: (510) 577-4000 or www.flyoakland.com

San Francisco International Airport: (650) 876-2377

San Jose International Airport: (408) 277-4759 or www.sjc.org

CHAMBERS OF COMMERCE

These are good sources for relocation packets and information about communities. Another good resource is the California Chamber of Commerce Web site (www.calchamber.com) that lists all Chambers of Commerce in California.

MARIN COUNTY/
NORTH BAY

Corte Madera Chamber of Commerce
121 Corte Madera Town Center
Corte Madera, CA 94925
(415) 924-0441

Fairfax Chamber of Commerce
P.O. Box 1111
Fairfax, CA 94978
(415) 453-5928

Larkspur Chamber of Commerce
P.O. Box 315
Larkspur, CA 94977
(415) 453-8225

Mill Valley Chamber of Commerce
85 Throckmorton Avenue
Mill Valley, CA 94942
(415) 388-9700
www.milvalley.org

Novato Chamber of Commerce
807 De Long Avenue
Novato, CA 94945
(415) 897-1164
www.novato.org

San Anselmo Chamber of Commerce
P.O. Box 2844
San Anselmo, CA 94979
(415) 454-2510

San Rafael Chamber of Commerce
817 Mission Avenue
San Rafael, CA 94901
(415) 454-4163
www.sanrafael.org

Sausalito Chamber of Commerce
333 Caledonia Street
Sausalito, CA 94965
(415) 331-7262
www.sbt.com/sausalito/

Tiburon Chamber of Commerce
96B Main Street
Tiburon, CA 94920
(415) 435-5633

West Marin Chamber of Commerce
P.O. Box 1045
Point Reyes Station, CA 94956
(415) 663-9232
www.pointreyes.org

ALAMEDA COUNTY/
EAST BAY

Alameda Chamber of Commerce
2447 Santa Clara Avenue, Suite 302
Alameda, CA 94501
(510) 521-8677

Albany Chamber of Commerce
1108 Solano Avenue
Albany, CA 94706
(510) 525-1771

Berkeley Chamber of Commerce
1834 University Avenue
Berkeley, CA 94703
(510) 549-7000
www.berkeleychamber.com

Castro Valley Chamber of Commerce
3467 Castro Valley Boulevard
Castro Valley, CA 94546
(510) 537-5300
www.autoexecinc.com/cvcc/

Dublin Chamber of Commerce
7080 Donlon Way, Suite 110
Dublin, CA 94568
(925) 828-6200

Emeryville Chamber of Commerce
1900 Powell Street, Suite 1126
Emeryville, CA 94608
(510) 652-5223

Fremont Chamber of Commerce
39488 Stevenson Place, Suite 100
Fremont, CA 94539
(510) 795-2244
www.fremontbusiness.com

Hayward Chamber of Commerce
22561 Main Street
Hayward, CA 94541
(510) 537-2424
www.hayward.org

Livermore Chamber of Commerce
2157 First Street
Livermore, CA 94550
(510) 447-1606
www.livermorechamber.com

Newark Chamber of Commerce
6066 Civic Terrace Avenue, Suite 8
Newark, CA 94560
(510) 744-1000
www.newark-chamber.com

Oakland Chamber of Commerce
475 14th Street
Oakland, CA 94612
(510) 874-4800
www.oaklandchamber.com

Pleasanton Chamber of Commerce
777 Peters Avenue
Pleasanton, CA 94566
(925) 846-5858
www.pleasanton.org

San Leandro Chamber of Commerce

262 Davis Street

San Leandro, CA 94577

(510) 351-1481

www.sanleandro.com

Union City Chamber of Commerce

33428 Alvarado-Niles Road

Union City, CA 94587

(510) 471-3115

www.unioncity.com

CONTRA COSTA COUNTY/ EAST BAY

Antioch Chamber of Commerce

301 West 10th Street, Suite 1

Antioch, CA 94509

(510) 757-1800

www.antioch-coc.org

Brentwood Chamber of Commerce

P.O. Box 773

Brentwood, CA 94513

(510) 634-3344

Concord Chamber of Commerce

2151A Salvio Street

Concord, CA 94520

(925) 685-1181

www.ci.concord.ca.us

Danville Chamber of Commerce

117-E Town & Country Drive

Danville, CA 94526

(925) 837-4400

www.danvilleca.com

El Cerrito Chamber of Commerce

10848 San Pablo Avenue

El Cerrito, CA 94530

(510) 233-7040

Hercules Chamber of Commerce

P.O. Box 5283

Hercules, CA 94547

(510) 799-0282

www.herculescc.com

Lafayette Chamber of Commerce

100 Lafayette Circle, #103

Lafayette, CA 94549

(925) 284-7404

www.lafayettechamber.org

Martinez Chamber of Commerce

620 Las Juntas Street

Martinez, CA 94553

(925) 228-2345

Moraga Chamber of Commerce

440 Center Street

Moraga, CA 94556

(510) 376-0150

Orinda Chamber of Commerce

2 Theatre Square, Suite 137

Orinda, CA 94563

(925) 254-3909

Pinole Chamber of Commerce

1249 Pinole Valley Road

Pinole, CA 94564

(510) 724-3600

Pittsburg Chamber of Commerce

2010 Railroad Avenue

Pittsburg, CA 94565

(925) 432-7301

www.pittsburg.org

Pleasant Hill Chamber of Commerce

91 Gregory Lane, Suite 11

Pleasant Hill, CA 94523

(925) 687-0700

Richmond Chamber of Commerce

3925 MacDonald Avenue

Richmond, CA 94805

(510) 234-3512

www.rcoc.com

San Pablo Chamber of Commerce

P.O. Box 6204

San Pablo, CA 94806

(510) 234-2067

San Ramon Chamber of Commerce

2355 San Ramon Valley Boulevard, Suite 101

San Ramon, CA 94583

(925) 831-9500

www.sanramon.org

Walnut Creek Chamber of Commerce

1501 North Broadway Street, Suite 110

Walnut Creek, CA 94596

(925) 934-2007

www.walnut-creek.com

SAN MATEO COUNTY/ PENINSULA

Belmont Chamber of Commerce

1070 Sixth Street, Suite 102

Belmont, CA 94002

(650) 595-8696

Brisbane Chamber of Commerce

50 Park Lane

Brisbane, CA 94005

(650) 467-7283

Burlingame Chamber of Commerce

290 California Drive

Burlingame, CA 94010

(650) 344-1735

www.spectrumnet.com/ burlingame.html

Daly City/Colma Chamber of Commerce

355 Gellert Boulevard, Suite 230

Daly City, CA 94015

(650) 991-5101

www.dalycity-colmachamber.org

Foster City Chamber of Commerce

1125 East Hillsdale Boulevard,

Suite 114

Foster City, CA 94404

(650) 573-7600

www.fostercitychamber.com

Half Moon Bay Chamber of Commerce

520 Kelly Avenue

Half Moon Bay, CA 94019

(650) 726-8380

www.halfmoonbaychamber.org

Menlo Park Chamber of Commerce

1100 Merrill Street

Menlo Park, CA 94025

(650) 325-2818

www.mpchamber.com

Millbrae Chamber of Commerce

50 Victoria Avenue,

Suite 103

Millbrae, CA 94030

(650) 697-7324

www.millbrae.com

Pacifica Chamber of Commerce

225 Rockaway Beach Avenue,

Suite 1

Pacifica, CA 94044

(650) 355-4122

Redwood City Chamber of Commerce

1675 Broadway Street

Redwood City, CA 94063

(650) 364-1722

www.ci.redwood-city.ca.us/city/chamber

San Bruno Chamber of Commerce

618 San Mateo Avenue

San Bruno, CA 94066

(650) 588-0180

www.sanbruno.com

San Carlos Chamber of Commerce

1560 Laurel Street

San Carlos, CA 94070

(650) 593-1068

www.scchamber.com

San Mateo Chamber of Commerce

1021 South El Camino Real,

2nd Floor

San Mateo, CA 94402

(650) 341-5679

www.netonline.com/smchamber

South San Francisco Chamber of Commerce

213 Linden Avenue
South San Francisco, CA 94083
(650) 588-1911

MISCELLANEOUS

Lawyer Referral Service sponsored by the San Francisco Bar Association

(415) 989-1616

San Francisco Convention and Visitors Bureau

900 Market Street
San Francisco, CA 94102

GENERAL INFORMATION

Time: (415) 767-8900

Weather: (415) 936-1212

Highway road conditions: (415) 557-3755

SAN FRANCISCO COUNTY

San Francisco Chamber of Commerce

465 California Street
San Francisco, CA 94104
(415) 392-4520
www.sfchamber.com

(415) 391-2000
Twenty-four-hour events recording:
(415) 391-2001

San Francisco Library

General information:
(415) 557-4400
sfpl.lib.ca.us

LOCAL GOVERNMENT

San Francisco is the only city in California that is also a county. It is a charter city, meaning it can legislate itself without permission from the California legislature. Voters elect an eleven-member board of supervisors as well as a mayor, city assessor, treasurer, public defender, city attorney, district attorney, and sheriff every four years. The mayor appoints the city administrator and controller.

LOCAL GOVERNMENT CONTACT INFORMATION

San Francisco Mayor's Office
(415) 554-6141

San Francisco City Hall General Information
(415) 554-4000

San Francisco Board of Supervisors
(415) 554-5184
www.ci.sf.ca.us/bdsupvrs/

Registrar of Voters (register to vote)
(415) 554-4398

ELECTED OFFICIALS

All San Francisco city and county officials are elected to four-year terms. These elected officials are:

- Mayor
- Board of Supervisors
- Assessor
- Treasurer
- Sheriff
- City Attorney
- Public Defender
- District Attorney
- Trial Courts

To get an overall picture of what San Francisco city government looks like, the organization chart on pages 348–349 shows the different elected officials and departments they oversee.

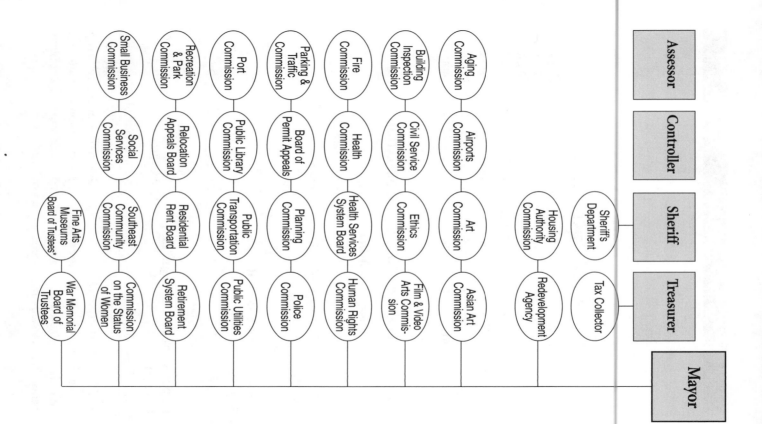

Small Business Commission
Recreation & Park Commission
Port Commission
Parking & Traffic Commission
Fire Commission
Building Inspection Commission
Aging Commission

Social Services Commission
Relocation Appeals Board
Public Library Commission
Board of Permit Appeals
Health Commission
Civil Service Commission
Airports Commission

Fine Arts Museums Board of Trustees*
Southeast Community Commission
Residential Rent Board
Public Transportation Commission
Planning Commission
Health Services System Board
Ethics Commission
Art Commission
Housing Authority Commission
Sheriff's Department

War Memorial Board of Trustees
Commission on the Status of Women
Retirement System Board
Public Utilities Commission
Police Commission
Human Rights Commission
Film & Video Arts Commission
Asian Art Commission
Redevelopment Agency
Tax Collector

Assessor
Controller
Sheriff
Treasurer
Mayor

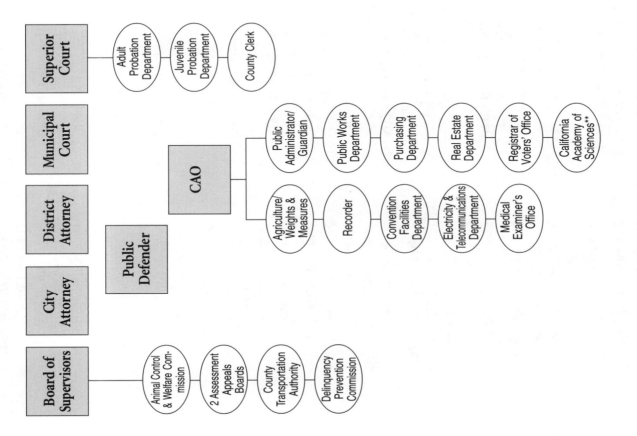

Board of Supervisors
- Animal Control & Welfare Commission
- 2 Assessment Appeals Boards
- County Transportation Authority
- Delinquency Prevention Commission

City Attorney

District Attorney

Municipal Court

Superior Court
- Adult Probation Department
- Juvenile Probation Department
- County Clerk

Public Defender

CAO
- Public Administrator/Guardian
- Public Works Department
- Purchasing Department
- Real Estate Department
- Registrar of Voters' Office
- California Academy of Sciences**
- Agriculture/Weights & Measures
- Recorder
- Convention Facilities Department
- Electricity & Telecommunications Department
- Medical Examiner's Office

* The mayor is an ex-officio member of the Fine Arts Museums Board of Trustees. Board members are elected through a process of trustee nomination and election.

** The California Academy of Sciences is a private institution. The CAO has jurisdiction only over city-related functions of the Academy.

Alameda City Hall
2263 Santa Clara Avenue
Alameda, CA 94501
(510) 748-4505
www.ci.alameda.ca.us

Berkeley City Hall
2180 Milvia Street
Berkeley, CA 94704
(510) 644-6480
www.ci.berkeley.ca.us

Concord City Hall
1950 Parkside Drive
Concord, CA 94519
(925) 671-3000
www.ci.concord.ca.us

Corte Madera City Hall
300 Tamalpais Drive
Corte Madera, CA 94926
(415) 927-5050

Daly City City Hall
333 90th Street
Daly City, CA 94015
(650) 991-8000
www.ci.daly-city.ca.us

Foster City City Hall
610 Foster City Boulevard
Foster City, CA 94404
(650) 349-1200
www.fostercity.org

Menlo Park City Hall
701 Laurel Street
Menlo Park, CA 94025
(650) 858-3380
www.ci.menlo-park.ca.us

Mill Valley City Hall
26 Corte Madera Avenue
Mill Valley, CA 94941
(415) 388-4033
www.milvalley.org

Oakland City Hall
1 Frank Ogawa Plaza
Oakland, CA 94612
(510) 444-CITY
www.oaklandnet.com

Palo Alto City Hall
250 Hamilton Avenue
Palo Alto, CA 94301
(650) 329-2571
www.city.palo-alto.ca.us

Redwood City City Hall
1017 Middlefield Road
Redwood City, CA 94063
(650) 780-7000
www.ci.redwood-city.ca.us

San Anselmo City Hall
525 San Anselmo Avenue
San Anselmo, CA 94960
(415) 258-4600
www.sananselmo.com

San Bruno City Hall
567 El Camino Real
San Bruno, CA 94066
(650) 877-8858

San Carlos City Hall

666 Elm Street
San Carlos, CA 94070
(650) 802-4210
www.ci.san-carlos.ca.us

San Francisco City Hall

400 Van Ness Avenue
San Francisco, CA 94102
(415) 554-4000
www.ci.sf.ca.us

San Leandro City Hall

835 East 14th Street
San Leandro, CA 94577
(510) 577-3351
www.ci.san-leandro.ca.us

San Mateo City Hall

330 West 20th Avenue
San Mateo, CA 94403
(650) 377-4789
www.ci.sanmateo.ca.us

San Rafael City Hall

1400 Fifth Avenue
San Rafael, CA 94901
(415) 485-3074

Sausalito City Hall

420 Litho Street
Sausalito, CA 94965
(415) 289-4100
www.ci.sausalito.ca.us

Tiburon Town Hall

1505 Tiburon Boulevard
Tiburon, CA 94920
(415) 435-0956
www.tiburon.org

Walnut Creek City Hall

1666 North Main Street
Walnut Creek, CA 94596
(925) 943-5800
www.ci.walnut-creek.ca.us

WORLD WIDE WEB RESOURCES

Association of Bay Area Governments (ABAG)
(www.abag.ca.gov)
This is a public information service for government information.

San Francisco CitySpan
(www.ci.sf.ca.us)
This is the official Web site of the city and county of San Francisco.

SCHOOLS

There are approximately 105 K–12 public schools in San Francisco along with thirty-six private and parochial schools. Bay Area counties also have their share of elementary, middle, and high schools. The following is a listing of school resources for those new to the area.

PUBLIC SCHOOLS

ALAMEDA COUNTY

Alameda Unified School District
2200 Central Avenue
Alameda, CA 94501
(510) 748-4000 or 337-7000
www.alameda.k12.ca.us

Albany Unified School District
904 Talbot Avenue
Albany, CA 94706
(510) 559-6500

Berkeley Unified School District
2134 Martin Luther King Jr. Way
Berkeley, CA 94704
(510) 644-6147
www.berkeley.k12.ca.us

Castro Valley Unified School District
4400 Alma Avenue
Castro Valley, CA 94546
(510) 537-3000

Dublin Unified School District
7471 Larkdale Avenue
Dublin, CA 94568
(510) 828-2551

Emeryville Unified School District
4727 San Pablo Avenue
Emeryville, CA 94608
(510) 655-6936

Fremont Unified School District
4210 Technology Drive
Fremont, CA 94538
(510) 657-2350
www.fremont.k12.ca.us

Hayward Unified School District
24411 Amador Street
Hayward, CA 94544
(510) 784-2600

Livermore Valley Joint Unified School District
685 East Jack London Boulevard
Livermore, CA 94550
(510) 606-3200
www.lvjusd.k12.ca.us

New Haven Unified School District
34200 Alvarado-Niles Road
Union City, CA 94587
(510) 471-1100
www.nhusd.k12.ca.us

Newark Unified School District
5715 Musick Avenue
Newark, CA 94560
(510) 794-2141
www.nusd.k12.ca.us

Oakland Unified School District
1025 Second Avenue
Oakland, CA 94606
(510) 879-8100
www.ousd.k12.ca.us

Piedmont Unified School District
760 Magnolia Avenue
Piedmont, CA 94611
(510) 594-2600

Pleasanton Unified School District
4665 Bernal Avenue
Pleasanton, CA 94566
(510) 462-5500
www.pleasanton.k12.ca.us

San Leandro Unified School District
14735 Juniper Street
San Leandro, CA 94579
(510) 667-3500

San Lorenzo Unified School District
15510 Usher Street
San Lorenzo, CA 94580
(510) 317-4600
www.sanlorenzousd.k12.ca.us

CONTRA COSTA COUNTRY

Acalanes Union High School District
1212 Pleasant Hill Road
Lafayette, CA 94549
(925) 935-2800
www.acalenes.k12.ca.us

Antioch Unified School District
510 G Street
Antioch, CA 94509
(925) 706-4100
www.antioch.k12.ca.us

Brentwood Union School District
255 Guthrie Lane
Brentwood, CA 94513
(925) 634-1168

Lafayette School District
3477 School Street
Lafayette, CA 94549
(925) 284-7011
www.lafsd.k12.ca.us

Liberty Union High School District
20 Oak Street
Brentwood, CA 94513
(925) 634-2166
www.libertyuhsd.k12.ca.us

Martinez Unified School District
921 Suzanna Street
Martinez, CA 94553
(925) 313-0480

Moraga School District
1540 School Street
Moraga, CA 94556
(925) 376-5943

Mt. Diablo Unified School District
1936 Carlotta Drive
Concord, CA 94519
(925) 682-8000

Orinda School District
8 Altarinda Road
Orinda, CA 94563
(925) 254-4901

Pittsburg Unified School District
2000 Railroad Avenue
Pittsburg, CA 94565
(925) 473-4000
www.pittsburg.k12.ca.us

San Ramon Valley Unified School District
699 Old Orchard Drive
Danville, CA 94526
(925) 552-5500
www.srvusd.k12.ca.us

Walnut Creek School District
960 Ygnacio Valley Road
Walnut Creek, CA 94596
(925) 944-6850
www.wcsd.k12.ca.us

West Contra Costa Unified School District
1108 Bissell Avenue
Richmond, CA 94802
(925) 234-3825
www.wccusd.k12.ca.us

MARIN COUNTY

Bolinas-Stinson School District
Star Route
Bolinas, CA 94924
(415) 868-1603

Dixie School District
380 Nova Albion Way
San Rafael, CA 94903
(415) 492-3700

Kentfield School District

699 Sir Francis Drake Boulevard

Kentfield, CA 94904

(415) 925-2230

**Lagunitas Elementary
School District**

Sir Francis Drake Boulevard

P.O. Box 308

San Geronimo, CA 94963

(415) 488-4118

Larkspur School District

230 Doherty Drive

Larkspur, CA 94939

(415) 927-6960

**Mill Valley Elementary
School District**

411 Sycamore Avenue

Mill Valley, CA 94941

(415) 389-7700

**Novato Unified
School District**

1015 Seventh Street

Novato, CA 94945

(415) 897-4201

Reed Union School District

105-A Avenida Miraflores

Tiburon, CA 94920

(415) 435-7848

Ross School District

P.O. Box 1058

Ross, CA 94957

(415) 457-2705

Ross Valley School District

46 Green Valley Court

San Anselmo, CA 94960

(415) 454-2162

**San Rafael Elementary and
High School Districts**

310 Noval Albion Way

San Rafael, CA 94903

(415) 492-3200 (elementary)

(415) 492-3233 (high school)

**San Rafael High
School District**

225 Woodland Avenue

San Rafael, CA 94901

(415) 485-2300

Sausalito School District

630 Nevada Street

Sausalito, CA 94965

(415) 332-3190

**Tamalpais Union High
School District**

395 Doherty Drive

Larkspur, CA 94939

(415) 945-3737

SAN FRANCISCO COUNTY

**San Francisco Unified
School District**

135 Van Ness Avenue

San Francisco, CA 94102

(415) 241-6000

nisus.sfusd.k12.ca.us

SAN MATEO COUNTY

Bayshore School District

1 Martin Street
Daly City, CA 94014
(650) 467-5444

Belmont-Redwood Shores School District

2960 Hallmark Drive
Belmont, CA 94002
(650) 637-4800
www.belmont.gov

Brisbane School District

1 Solano Street
Brisbane, CA 94005
(650) 467-0550
www.ci.brisbane.ca.us

Burlingame School District

1825 Trousdale Drive
Burlingame, CA 94010
(650) 259-3800

Cabrillo Unified School District

498 Kelly Avenue
Half Moon Bay, CA 94019
(650) 712-7100
www.coastside.net/cusd

Hillsborough School District

300 El Cerrito Avenue
Hillsborough, CA 94010
(650) 342-5193
hillsborough.net/hcsd

Jefferson Elementary School District

101 Lincoln Avenue
Daly City, CA 94015
(650) 991-1000

Jefferson Union High School District

699 Serramonte Boulevard
Daly City, CA 94015
(650) 756-0300
www.juhsd.k12.ca.us

La Honda-Pescadero Unified School District

620 North Street
Pescadero, CA 94060
(650) 879-0286
lhpusd.k12.ca.us

La Lomitas School District

1011 Altschul Avenue
Menlo Park, CA 94025
(650) 854-6311

Menlo Park City School District

181 Encinal Avenue
Atherton, CA 94027
(650) 321-7140

Millbrae School District

555 Richmond Drive
Millbrae, CA 94030
(650) 697-5694

**Portola Valley
School District**

4575 Alpine Road
Portola Valley, CA 94028

(650) 851-1777

**Ravenswood City
School District**

2160 Euclid Avenue
East Palo Alto, CA 94303

(650) 329-2800

**Redwood City
School District**

2317 Broadway Street
Redwood City, CA 94063

(650) 365-1550

www.rcsd.k12.ca.us

**San Bruno Park
School District**

500 Acacia Avenue
San Bruno, CA 94066

(650) 244-0133

San Carlos School District

826 Chestnut Street
San Carlos, CA 94070

(650) 508-7333

www.sancarlos.k12.ca.us

**San Mateo/Foster City
School District**

51 West 41st Avenue
San Mateo, CA 94403

(650) 312-7700

www.smfc.k12.ca.us

**San Mateo Union High
School District**

650 North Delaware Street
San Mateo, CA 94401

(650) 348-8834

www.smuhsd.k12.ca.us

**Sequoia Union High
School District**

480 James Avenue
Redwood City, CA 94062

(650) 369-1411

www.seq.org

**South San Francisco Unified
School District**

398 B Street
South San Francisco, CA 94080

(650) 877-8700

Woodside School District

3195 Woodside Road
Woodside, CA 94062

(650) 851-1571

NONPUBLIC SCHOOLS

The following is resource information for those interested in private and Catholic schools:

California Department of Education

P.O. Box 271

Sacramento, CA, 95812

(800) 995-4099

goldmine.cde.ca.gov

They have a California Private School Directory for sale for $17.50 plus tax and $4.95 shipping. This directory is also available at public libraries.

Archdiocese of San Francisco

Office of Catholic Schools

443 Church Street

San Francisco, CA 94114

(415) 565-3660

The Archdiocese of San Francisco Office of Catholic Schools has information about Catholic schools in the San Francisco, Marin, and San Mateo counties.

Archdiocese of Oakland

Office of Catholic Schools

2900 Lakeshore Avenue

Oakland, CA 94610

(510) 893-4711

The Archdiocese of Oakland Office of Catholic Schools has information about Catholic schools in Alameda and Contra Costa counties.

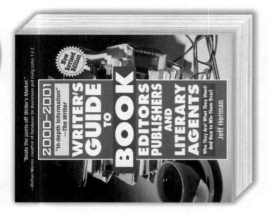

To Order Books

Please send me the following items:

Quantity	Title	Unit Price	Total
	Writer's Guide to Book Editors, Publishers, and Literary Agents, 2000-2001	$	$
	You Can Save the Animals	$	$
		$	$
		$	$
		Subtotal	$
		7.25% Sales Tax (CA only)	$
		7% Sales Tax (PA only)	$
		5% Sales Tax (IN only)	$
		7% G.S.T. Tax (Canada only)	$
		Priority Shipping	$
		Total Order	$

FREE
Ground Freight
in U.S. and Canada

Foreign and all Priority Request orders:
Call Customer Service
for price quote at 916-787-7000

By Telephone: With American Express, MC, or Visa, call 800-632-8676, Monday–Friday, 8:30–4:30. **www.primapublishing.com**

By E-mail: sales@primapub.com

By Mail: Just fill out the information below and send with your remittance to:

Prima Publishing ▪ P.O. Box 1260BK ▪ Rocklin, CA 95677

Name _____

Address _____

City _____ State _____ ZIP _____

American Express/MC/Visa# _____ Exp. _____

Check/money order enclosed for $ _____ Payable to Prima Publishing

Daytime telephone _____

Signature _____